GETTING TO KNOW

JESUS

■

GETTING TO KNOW

JESUS

DAILY ENCOUNTERS WITH THE LORD
FROM HIS BIRTH TO HIS ASCENSION

■

ERIC KAMPMANN

For inquiries about volume orders, please contact:
Beaufort Books
27 West 20th Street, Suite 1102
New York, NY 10011
sales@beaufortbooks.com

Published in the United States by Beaufort Books
www.beaufortbooks.com

Distributed by Midpoint Trade Books
www.midpointtrade.com

ISBN 978-0-82530-790-4

Printed in the United States of America

Interior design by Elyse Strogin and Neuwirth & Associates
Cover Design by Mark Karis

CONTENTS

I fall back on the response of Bishop Ambrose, mentor of Augustine, who was asked on his deathbed whether he feared facing God at judgment. "We have a good Master," Ambrose replied with a smile. I learn to trust God with my doubts and struggles by getting to know Jesus. If that sounds evasive, I suggest it accurately reflects the centrality of Jesus in the New Testament. We start with him as the focal point and let our eyes wander with care into the margins.

By looking at Jesus, I gain insight into how God feels about what goes on down here. Jesus expresses the essence of God in a way that we cannot misconstrue.

—Philip Yancey
Reaching for the Invisible God

FOREWORD

CHUCK DAVIS

I DO NOT REMEMBER how we got started. But there we were, in my son Jordan's bedroom, which he had converted into a basic sound studio. Eric and I would read a passage of the Bible from the wisdom literature of the Hebrew Scriptures (Old Testament). Then we would have a three to five minute dialogue expounding on the text from the larger context of the entire Bible. We would complete ten to fifteen recordings per session staying a couple months ahead of the podcast schedule.

Then, one day, Eric revealed to me something that was so ingrained in my methodology that I never really thought about it. What made my message unique was the emphasis on bringing it back to Jesus—the Centrality of Christ. This led to our second year of podcasts, "Walking in the Footsteps of Jesus."

So what has the process been like for me? Friendship, gratefulness, and renewed commitment.

First, friendship. The recording sessions moved from my son's bedroom to the church basement or my study. We added Scott, a member of our church, as our new recording technician. Our friendship grew. We laughed. We rabbit-trailed. We shared life. We prayed for one another. We grew together as Christ followers around the Word and the life of Jesus.

Second, gratefulness. As Eric would ask me spontaneous and unrehearsed questions on the biblical text, I was amazed at how much of the Word of God was deep inside of me. The Holy Spirit would open files in my mind that had been stored over the past fifty-plus years of being in the text. And it was not just knowledge but heartfelt living of the Word. My gratefulness is rooted in my heritage of being raised in the Word. My parents, my Sunday School teachers, my pastors, my college and seminary professors, and my distant mentors through books, have all instructed me in the Word. And, maybe most importantly, daily reading, study, meditation, and memorization of that Word, almost every day as an adult, has transformed my life. I am sometimes brought to tears in my morning quiet times in appreciation for the life that I have been given—set apart in and unto Jesus and saturated by the Word of God.

Third, renewed commitment. Walking with Eric and knowing his story has reminded me of the power of the Word in itself. Eric's testimony points to the power of God's Word. Without help from all the crutches that I was given, Eric one day picked up a Bible, and through the reading of that Word, was transformed. This is why I daily recommit to the preaching, teaching, and simple witness to the Word of God. Eric is an incarnational reminder to me of the value and outcome of giving my life to this calling and passion.

As the prophet Isaiah declares—"as the rain brings forth a harvest, so the Word of God will not return void." Or as the writer of Hebrews declares—"for the Word of God is living and active . . . able to shape and correct us." Or as Paul reminds, the Word of God is "the sword of the Spirit" and that all "Scripture is God breathed and profitable for transforming us." And especially as Jesus reminded us, "people who build their lives on a solid foundation that will not crumble in life storms, are those who not only hear the Word but do it." Those are all my quick paraphrases of favorite declarations of the value of the written Word when experienced through the lens of a relationship with God through the Living Word, Jesus.

May your journey be as rich as mine has been through your discovery of a vibrant relationship to God the Father, through knowing Jesus, and made alive by the Holy Spirit.

INTRODUCTION

ERIC KAMPMANN

N FEBRUARY 1991, AS I emerged from some very difficult years running my business, I discovered a "lectionary" in the back of a prayer book. I had been reading in the Bible on a pretty consistent basis during the time of my troubles, but finding a daily reading guide was a very exciting revelation for me. I began using the lectionary on a daily basis and I came to love and depend upon it more and more as time went by. In fact, *Getting to Know Jesus* would not exist if that lectionary had not been discovered that day. It became foundational for my growing knowledge and passion for the entire Bible and what it taught me about the human condition that I had not known before.

In 2007, I published a devotional called *Trail Thoughts* that the senior pastor of the church I attended, Chuck Davis, had read and liked. A few years later in 2011, we got together to produce a daily podcast on the wisdom books in the Old Testament as a way to reach members of the church who commute into New York City every day.

The podcasts were short, unrehearsed conversations that focused on a biblical verse of the day. In our response to the daily reading, we would draw attention to the historical, theological, and contemporary importance of what was being revealed through that particular verse. The central focus was the relevance of biblical wisdom literature as it related to our own secular culture. We were trying to show that the Bible is not one of many stories important to our times, but is the central narrative that helps us grapple with the very real mysteries that infuse our everyday lives.

In March 2012, I traveled to Israel with a group of twenty men and women under the leadership of Professor Bryan Widbin. Just before the trip to Israel, Chuck Davis and I began to talk about producing a new series of podcasts to follow up on the series on the wisdom books in the Old Testament.

Professor Widbin teaches Old Testament Studies at Alliance Theological Seminary and he has led trips to Israel for over thirty years. His leadership, knowledge, and passion for Jesus Christ had a profound impact on everyone on this trip; it was his remarkable commitment and authenticity that would lead to the writing of *Getting to Know Jesus*.

It was witnessing Bryan Widbin's passionate devotion to Jesus that opened my eyes to a gaping hole in my own biblical journey. For while I read the Bible daily, I had never gotten to a place where I could declare with Peter, that Jesus was "the Christ, the Son of the living God" (Matthew 16:16). It is a huge step from being an educated secular fence sitter to fully embracing Peter's revelation.

And while I had come very far from the troubles of the late 1980's, I still hesitated in committing fully in the Lordship of Jesus Christ. But through both Chuck Davis and Bryan Widbin, I saw first-hand what genuine faith looks like. It is not loud or boastful, nor does it make unsupportable claims or puffed up pronouncements. The kind of faith I witness through these two men is attractive and assured, open and vulnerable, but bold and powerful at the same time. I saw the Jesus I did not know in the men I did know and I wanted to get more of what both men had in such full measure. Thus was born the podcast series Chuck Davis and I recorded during 2013. (These podcasts will soon be available at *GettingToKnowJesus.com* or through our Getting-ToKnowJesus App available through Amazon and iTunes.)

By the time Chuck and I completed our series on Jesus, I wanted to take our efforts further by producing a devotional that would present the life of Jesus based on accounts in the four Gospels selected for the podcasts. In 2014, I began writing brief commentaries using the recorded discussions between Chuck and myself.

During the two years of recordings and writings, I built on the foundation that seemed to have begun in the late 1980's. And it was in 2012, in the shadow of Masada in the desert of Israel, that I finally made the decision to truly focus on getting to know Jesus by walking in his footsteps as given to us in the four Gospels. Not only did I want to come to know Jesus, but I wanted to do what Christians have been doing for over two thousand years: I wanted to go out into the world to help others come to know him as well.

GETTING TO KNOW

JESUS

AN OVERVIEW OF THE YEAR AHEAD

When I came to you, brothers, I did not come with eloquence or superior wisdom as I proclaimed to you the testimony about God. For I resolved to know nothing while I was with you except Jesus Christ and him crucified. I came to you in weakness and fear, and with much trembling. My message and my preaching were not with wise and persuasive words, but with a demonstration of the Spirit's power, so that your faith might not rest on men's wisdom, but on God's power. 1 CORINTHIANS 2:1–5

■

WHAT DOES IT MEAN to be a follower of Jesus Christ? In his letter to the Philippians, Paul says that he considers "everything a loss compared to the surpassing greatness of knowing Christ Jesus my Lord, for whose sake I have lost all things . . ." (Philippians 3:8). In his early days, Paul was a persecutor of the young church; he stood as a witness as Stephen was stoned to death for his belief in Christ. It was on Paul's journey to Damascus that he was stopped in his tracks and transformed from persecutor to believer. But his conversion was only the beginning of a mission that would reach from Jerusalem to Ephesus, Athens, Rome, and many other countries and cities in the Mediterranean world. Paul's mission, though, came at a cost, because while he had "resolved to know nothing . . . except Jesus Christ and him crucified," the world resisted mightily: "Once I was stoned. Three times I was shipwrecked; a night and a day I was adrift at sea." He goes on to say that on frequent journeys he experienced "danger from rivers, danger from robbers, danger from my own people, danger from Gentiles, danger in the city, danger in the wilderness, danger at sea, danger from false brothers, in toil and hardship, through many a sleepless night, in hunger and thirst, often without food, in cold and exposure" (2 Corinthians 11:25–27). And yet despite all of this, Paul said that the only thing in the whole world that matters is "to know Christ and the power of his resurrection and the fellowship of sharing in his sufferings . . ." (Philippians 3:10).

He is the image of the invisible God, the firstborn over all creation. For by him all things were created: things in heaven and on earth, visible and invisible, whether thrones or powers or rulers or authorities; all things were created by him and for him. He is before all things, and in him all things hold together. COLOSSIANS 1:15–17

■

JESUS IS ALL IN all. He made visible in human form all the attributes of God. He is the "firstborn over all creation." All things, whether visible or invisible, "were created by him and for him." Simply put, in these verses Paul is proclaiming the supremacy of Christ. From prison, John the Baptist asked Jesus, "Are you the one who was to come, or should we expect someone else?" This is a question that followed Jesus all the way to the cross. At a later time, Jesus asked his own followers, "But what about you? Who do you say I am?" (Matthew 16:15)

Many have undertaken to draw up an account of the things that have been fulfilled among us, just as they were handed down to us by those who from the first were eyewitnesses and servants of the word. Therefore, since I myself have carefully investigated everything from the beginning, it seemed good also to me to write an orderly account for you, most excellent Theophilus, so that you may know the certainty of the things you have been taught. LUKE 1:1–4

■

IN THIS PREFACE TO his Gospel, Luke addresses a man named Theophilus (that when translated means "one who loves God"). Theophilus may have been a patron or he may have been a close friend or associate of Luke's, though he does not make an appearance in any of the other books of the New Testament. Whoever he might have been, Luke's mission was "to write an orderly account . . . so that you may know the certainty of the things you have been taught." Luke was writing to those who had not known Jesus during his three years in Galilee and Judea but had since become part of a fast-growing Christian community throughout the Mediterranean world. Luke traveled with Paul and other leaders of the Church, but false teaching was creeping in through messengers who did not know Jesus. Luke understood the importance of being true to what actually happened, though he did not claim to be an impartial observer; like Theophilus, he is "one who loves God." But his love of God created an even greater necessity to be truthful, and so Luke tells Theophilus and all readers that he has investigated everything from the beginning, including those who "were eyewitnesses and servants of the word."

IN THE BEGINNING

In the beginning was the Word, and the Word was with God, and the Word was God. He was with God in the beginning.
JOHN1: 1–2

■

IF LUKE IS THE historian, John is the theologian. He opens his Gospel with a statement that echoes the first words of Genesis: "In the beginning . . ." John is telling the reader that he is not just writing about an important man of his time; he is telling us that we are entering a realm of cosmic significance. He is talking about the God who, through the power of His Word, created the universe and everything in it and was moving again in a new way, not to create the world, but to restore it by sending his Son, Jesus Christ.

IN HIM WAS LIFE

Through him all things were made; without him nothing was
made that has been made. In him was life, and that life was the
light of men. JOHN 1:3–4

■

AS THE SPIRIT OF God hovered over creation, "God said, 'Let there
be light,' and there was light" (Genesis 1:3). Jesus is the light that
gives life to a dying world that has fallen away from the source of
life. God sent this light into our world to give the world access to
true life. While in Macedonia, Paul explained it this way: "God did
this so that men would seek him and perhaps reach out for him and
find him, though he is not far from each one of us. For in him we
live and move and have our being" (Acts 17:27–28).

THE TRUE LIGHT

The true light that gives light to everyone was coming into the world. He was in the world, and though the world was made through him, the world did not recognize him. He came to that which was his own, but his own did not receive him. JOHN 1:9–11

■

IN CONTRAST TO THE light of God, the fallen world is colored in darker shades because sin has entered through the subterfuge of Satan with his bottomless quest to undermine mankind's relationship with God. After Adam and Eve departed from Eden, they entered a world of sin, death, and the consequences that flow from falling into the traps set by the "father of lies" (John 8:44). When Cain, their son, was tempted to attack and kill his brother Abel out of envy, God remained present and warned Cain of the costs of submitting to temptation: "Why are you angry? Why is your face downcast? If you do what is right, will you not be accepted? But if you do not do what is right, sin is crouching at your door, it desires to have you, but you must master it" (Genesis 4:8). Later, we learn that as punishment for his crime against his brother, Cain became "a restless wanderer of the earth" (Genesis 4:14). This remained the underlying condition for men and women until God determined that the time had come to send his Son into the world on a rescue mission that would open the way to a very different kind of story for the lost and weary.

The Word became flesh and made his dwelling among us. We have seen his glory, the glory of the one and only Son, who came from the Father, full of grace and truth. JOHN 1:14

■

IN THE OLD TESTAMENT, God dwelled amongst his people first in a tent and then in a tabernacle or temple: ". . . for the glory of the Lord filled the temple" (2 Kings 8:11). When John says, "The Word . . . made his dwelling among us," he uses a Greek word that also can mean tent or tabernacle. God's presence among his people was first in a tent (Exodus 40:34–35), then in a temple, and now as a person— Jesus Christ—who was an exact representation on earth of the Father.

John testifies concerning him. He cries out, saying, "This was he of whom I said, 'He who comes after me has surpassed me because he was before me.'" From the fullness of his grace we have all received one blessing after another. For the law was given through Moses; grace and truth came through Jesus Christ. JOHN 1:15–17

■

JOHN'S GOSPEL IS ALL about witnesses giving testimony about Jesus. One example is John the Baptist (John the Baptist and the author of the Gospel of John are different men): "There came a man who was sent from God; his name was John. He came as a witness to testify concerning that light, so that through him all men might believe"(John 1:6–7). John confirmed the Scriptural expectation that a prophet would come before the Messiah to make way for him. But others testify as well, including God Himself, the Holy Spirit, the disciples, and "a great cloud of witnesses" down through the ages even to the present moment. We are those witnesses called to testify before our families, friends, communities, and beyond.

No one has ever seen God, but the one and only Son, who is himself God and is in closest relationship with the Father, has made him known. JOHN 1:18

■

TOWARD THE END OF his life, Moses sought to encounter God, but even Moses could not look at God directly for "my [God's] face must not be seen" (Exodus 33:23). God was protecting Moses because being in the presence of the holiness of God would have shattered Moses or any man in his fallen state. Still, God desires to bridge the gap between himself and the creatures he created. It is the graciousness of God that caused him to step down to the human level through the incarnation of Jesus Christ and thus make himself accessible to us in our alienated condition.

LINE OF ABRAHAM AND LINE OF DAVID

This is the genealogy of Jesus the Messiah the son of David, the son of Abraham . . . MATTHEW 1:1

■

WHY DID MATTHEW CHOOSE to begin his Gospel with a genealogy? He states that Jesus' lineage goes back to Abraham: "Thus there were fourteen in all from Abraham to David, fourteen from David to the exile to Babylon, and fourteen from the exile to the Christ" (Matthew 1:17). This is important because God promised David that his son will reign forever (2 Samuel 7:5–16). But there is more: Five named in the genealogy are women, and of the five, three are Gentiles. This is an early indication that no one is excluded from God's story, even if some have lived less-than-exemplary lives or possess questionable credentials. All of this suggests a very big story is unfolding, and at the center of it all is God, who through his Son is moving into the human story.

ZECHARIAH

Once when Zechariah's division was on duty and he was serving as priest before God, he was chosen by lot, according to the custom of the priesthood, to go into the temple of the Lord and burn incense. And when the time for the burning of incense came, all the assembled worshipers were praying outside. LUKE 1:8–10

■

MEET ZECHARIAH. HE WAS a very ordinary man who led a decent life. He was the husband of Elizabeth. They were in their middle years and without children. There seemed to be nothing very special about him or his wife, except that she was the cousin of Mary. Luke tells us that Zechariah had been selected by lot to serve as a priest before God in the temple. This too was an ordinary custom. But what was about to happen was anything but ordinary, because God was about to burst into the mundane world of the ordinary in a surprising and extraordinary way. Zechariah was about to become part of the birth narrative of Jesus Christ.

DO NOT BE AFRAID

Then an angel of the Lord appeared to him, standing at the right side of the altar of incense. When Zechariah saw him, he was startled and was gripped with fear. But the angel said to him: "Do not be afraid, Zechariah; your prayer has been heard. Your wife Elizabeth will bear you a son, and you are to call him John." LUKE 1:11–13

■

SUDDENLY ZECHARIAH WAS STARTLED and shaken with fear. The ordinary features of his existence were shattered and blown away as the supernatural hand of God entered the natural realm. The angel of the Lord gave him a message he could not fully understand: His wife Elizabeth would be with child and he was to call the child John. Zechariah's prayer had been answered, but God had a special role for this child, which we will see as the story of Jesus unfolds.

When his time of service was completed, he returned home. After this his wife Elizabeth became pregnant and for five months remained in seclusion. "The Lord has done this for me," she said. "In these days he has shown his favor and taken away my disgrace among the people." LUKE 1:23–25

∎

WITH ZECHARIAH AND ELIZABETH we see two starkly contrasting responses to God's intervention into their otherwise normal lives. Once his fear of the angel dissipated, Zechariah asked, "How can I be sure of this? I am an old man and my wife is well along in years." He expressed doubt because, naturalistically, the angel's claim made no sense. Zechariah substituted his own reasoning for God's supernatural purpose. With Elizabeth's response to the miracle of her pregnancy, we hear beautiful words of faith: "The Lord has done this for me . . . In these days he has shown his favor and taken away my disgrace among the people." When God's favor came upon Elizabeth, she did not resist it or question it; she lined up with it.

In the sixth month of Elizabeth's pregnancy, God sent the angel Gabriel to Nazareth, a town in Galilee, to a virgin pledged to be married to a man named Joseph, a descendant of David. The virgin's name was Mary. The angel went to her and said, "Greetings, you who are highly favored! The Lord is with you." LUKE 1:26–28

■

THE MARY WE MEET here was anything but a conspicuous figure in history. She was young and not yet wed, and she came from a town that was off the beaten path. From the world's perspective, Mary was very unimportant, and except for the fact that she was pledged to be married, she did not appear to have many promising prospects. But God does not judge through the eyes of the world. For the angel Gabriel told Mary that she is "highly favored." The God of the universe, the God of Abraham, Isaac, and Jacob, had chosen a young virgin to become his instrument in bringing about the salvation of all mankind in a way that defies human reason. To the world, this young woman could not possibly have been so favored by God. But the angel said otherwise.

Mary was greatly troubled at his words and wondered what kind of greeting this might be. But the angel said to her, "Do not be afraid, Mary; you have found favor with God. You will conceive and give birth to a son, and you are to call him Jesus. He will be great and will be called the Son of the Most High. The Lord God will give him the throne of his father David, and he will reign over Jacob's descendants forever; his kingdom will never end." LUKE 1:29–33

■

HOW WAS MARY TO take in what was being told to her? That she was "greatly troubled" must be read as an understatement. First she was told she would give birth to a son, but not just any son—the "Son of the Most High." He would be given "the throne of his father David," and "he will reign over Jacob's descendants and his kingdom will never end." She was told that she would be the instrument of the fulfillment of many prophecies related to the coming of the Messiah. If you are Mary, how can you possibly take this in? How can a young woman of such a lowly station in life be favored in such a profoundly significant way?

"How will this be," Mary asked the angel, "since I am a virgin?" The angel answered, "The Holy Spirit will come on you, and the power of the Most High will overshadow you. So the holy one to be born will be called the Son of God. Even Elizabeth your relative is going to have a child in her old age, and she who was said to be unable to conceive is in her sixth month. For no word from God will ever fail." LUKE 1:34–37

■

"HOW WILL THIS BE?" Mary's question is our question. How is it possible for a virgin to give birth? Almost instinctively we reject the reality of supernatural causation, and so we approach this moment with a heavy dose of skepticism. And we are not alone. Even Thomas Jefferson took scissors to his Bible to eliminate the miracles that gave intellectual discomfort to so many men and women of the Enlightenment. But should we be so swift to judge? If we open up to the reality of miracles existing all around us—starting with the existence of life itself—then the supernaturally initiated events described here by Luke do not seem so improbable.

And Mary said: "My soul glorifies the Lord and my spirit rejoices in God my Savior, for he has been mindful of the humble state of his servant. From now on all generations will call me blessed, for the Mighty One has done great things for me—holy is his name. His mercy extends to those who fear him, from generation to generation. He has performed mighty deeds with his arm; he has scattered those who are proud in their inmost thoughts . . . He has helped his servant Israel, remembering to be merciful to Abraham and his descendants forever, just as he promised our ancestors."
LUKE 1:46–51, 54

■

MARY'S "MAGNIFICAT" IS HER response to what she heard from the angel Gabriel. She spontaneously breathed out praise by acknowledging through her song of worship that every blessing comes from God and she has been blessed by being a steward of those blessings. Her words of praise point to a gracious God: "My soul glorifies the Lord and my spirit rejoices in God my savior, for he has been mindful of the humble state of his servant." Her response is exemplary, a model of humility before the holy purposes of the Lord her God.

Then they made signs to his father, to find out what he would like to name the child. He asked for a writing tablet, and to everyone's astonishment he wrote, "His name is John." LUKE 1:62–63

■

OF THE FOUR GOSPELS, Luke gives the most detailed account of John's birth. In a sense, John's birth parallels the account of Jesus' nativity. There was the visitation of an angel of the Lord, the annunciation, and the promise of a miraculous birth. Furthermore, Elizabeth and Mary were relatives and both women submitted to the will of God. Suddenly Elizabeth and Mary were thrust into God's larger narrative. Neither knew what the outcome would be, but both accepted their mission in humility and faith.

A DREAM

This is how the birth of Jesus Christ came about: His mother Mary was pledged to be married to Joseph, but before they came together, she was found to be with child through the Holy Spirit. Because Joseph her husband was a righteous man and did not want to expose her to public disgrace, he had in mind to divorce her quietly. But after he had considered this, an angel of the Lord appeared to him in a dream and said, "Joseph son of David, do not be afraid to take Mary home as your wife, because what is conceived in her is from the Holy Spirit. She will give birth to a son, and you are to give him the name Jesus, because he will save his people from their sins." MATTHEW 1:18–21

■

WE HAVE FOUR ACCOUNTS of the life of Jesus, but only two of them, Luke's and Matthew's, give us a detailed picture of what happened in Nazareth and Bethlehem. It is Matthew's account that gives the most complete picture of Joseph, who eventually married Mary and served as Jesus' earthly father. When Joseph learned that Mary was with child, he did not humiliate and reject her; rather, he did the opposite by protecting her from harm and disgrace. Matthew also tells us that God intervened through the agency of an angel in a dream, who instructed Joseph on what to do because the child "conceived in her is from the Holy Spirit (who will one day) save his people from their sins." The angel of the Lord gave a very direct declaration of God's purpose both to Joseph then and to us now.

THE VIRGIN WILL BE WITH CHILD

All this took place to fulfill what the Lord had said through the prophet: "The virgin will be with child and will give birth to a son, and they will call him Immanuel" (which means, "God with us"). When Joseph woke up, he did what the angel of the Lord had commanded him and took Mary home as his wife. But he had no union with her until she gave birth to a son. And he gave him the name Jesus. MATTHEW 1:22–25

■

JOSEPH HAD BEEN ON a predictable life path when suddenly he was stopped in his tracks by what was said to him in a dream. Matthew says that when Joseph woke up "he did what the angel of the Lord had commanded him and took Mary home as his wife." Joseph had retired for the night just as he must have done every night, but he woke to a new reality and a new role. He had been chosen, but he had to be willing to accept this role of protector, even if that meant shame or danger. He was obedient to the vision: he stood by Mary in her pregnancy and obeyed the angel's command to name the baby Jesus when the time came for his birth. Joseph's decision to obey was an heroic choice for a man who was not trying to be a hero.

BETHLEHEM

So Joseph also went up from the town of Nazareth in Galilee to Judea, to Bethlehem the town of David, because he belonged to the house and line of David. He went there to register with Mary, who was pledged to be married to him and was expecting a child. While they were there, the time came for the baby to be born, and she gave birth to her firstborn, a son. She wrapped him in cloths and placed him in a manger, because there was no guest room available for them. LUKE 2:4–7

■

LUKE TELLS THE STORY of real people traveling a rough and dusty road from one small town to another in order to obey an edict of the occupying Roman authorities. Through these events, a multidimensional prophecy was fulfilled. For the Messianic King came from the line of David: "The Lord swore an oath to David, a sure oath that he will not revoke: 'One of your own descendants I will place . . . on your throne for ever and ever'" (Psalm 132:11–12). In addition, this king came from David's city Bethlehem: "But you, Bethlehem Ephrathah, though you are small among the clans of Judah, out of you will come for me one who will be ruler over Israel, whose origins are from of old, from ancient times" (Micah 5:2). That long road between Nazareth and Bethlehem was a road known by God long before Mary and Joseph ever began to travel it.

And there were shepherds living out in the fields nearby, keeping watch over their flocks at night. An angel of the Lord appeared to them, and the glory of the Lord shone around them, and they were terrified. But the angel said to them, "Do not be afraid. I bring you good news that will cause great joy for all the people. Today in the town of David a Savior has been born to you; he is the Messiah, the Lord. This will be a sign to you: You will find a baby wrapped in cloths and lying in a manger." LUKE 2:8–12

■

WHEN A PASSAGE FROM the Bible is read and heard many times, often its significance is obscured by its familiarity. This is one of those instances where the mystery and wonder of the moment is laden with distant memories of innumerable Christmas pageants. For here something unexpected happened: The birth of the King of Kings was announced to mere shepherds on a hillside outside of a small town on the perimeter of Jerusalem. Why shepherds? John later announced Jesus as "the Lamb of God who takes away the sins of the world." We are reminded of the Passover sacrifice and the substitutionary sacrifice of the ram that God provided to Abraham in place of his one-and-only son Isaac. By the world's standards the angel of the Lord had it all wrong, but the bigger story is that the baby in the manger in Bethlehem was born to die, not as a hero or martyr, but as a substitutionary sacrifice for each one of us. As John the Baptist said much later, "Look, the Lamb of God, who takes away the sin of the world!" (John 1:29)

THE SHEPHERDS PRAISED GOD

When the angels had left them and gone into heaven, the shepherds said to one another, "Let's go to Bethlehem and see this thing that has happened, which the Lord has told us about." So they hurried off and found Mary and Joseph, and the baby, who was lying in the manger. When they had seen him, they spread the word concerning what had been told them about this child, and all who heard it were amazed at what the shepherds said to them. LUKE 2:15–18

■

THE SHEPHERDS RECEIVED GOOD news from the angel of God, then, in an act of faith, they went to Bethlehem to confirm the truth of what they had been told, and, finally, "they spread the word concerning what has been told them about this child . . ." To receive, to go, and to tell is the Christian mission in a nutshell, and it is given to us at the very beginning of Christ's life on earth. "How beautiful on the mountains are the feet of those who bring good news . . ." (Isaiah 52:7).

HE WAS NAMED JESUS

On the eighth day, when it was time to circumcise the child, he was named Jesus, the name the angel had given him before he was conceived. LUKE 2:21

■

HEBREW TRADITION CALLS FOR the parents of a newborn to use a family name for the child, but this was not the case with either John or Jesus. In both instances an angel of the Lord provided the name. There is a hidden significance in this that has implications far beyond the family of Mary and Joseph. The name *Jesus* shares the same root as the name *Joshua*, which means God's salvation. It was Joshua who played a crucial role in the salvation history of Israel. For it was Joshua who took up the mantle after Moses died and led the desert-bound nation of Israel across the Jordan River into the Promised Land. "Be strong and courageous," God told Joshua, "because you will lead these people to inherit the land I swore to their forefathers to give them" (Joshua 1:6). As with Joshua, the infant Jesus came to fulfill God's promise to open the way to salvation, not just for Israel, but for every man and woman of every tribe and nation.

SIMEON

Now there was a man in Jerusalem called Simeon, who was righteous and devout. He was waiting for the consolation of Israel, and the Holy Spirit was on him. It had been revealed to him by the Holy Spirit that he would not die before he had seen the Lord's Messiah. Moved by the Spirit, he went into the temple courts. When the parents brought in the child Jesus to do for him what the custom of the Law required, Simeon took him in his arms and praised God, saying, "Sovereign Lord, as you have promised, you may now dismiss your servant in peace. For my eyes have seen your salvation, which you have prepared in the sight of all nations: a light for revelation to the Gentiles, and the glory of your people Israel." LUKE 2:25–32

■

SIMEON HAD BEEN WAITING for a sign. He had received a promise from God, and now the moment had arrived, but how did he know? Simeon had not charted the alignment of the stars, nor did he depend on reason or mere scholarship. No, he had been blessed with a revelation from God, and Luke makes it clear where Simeon's knowledge came from. Simeon's recognition that the Christ child was the promised Messiah came from the Holy Spirit. Luke tells us that the "Holy Spirit was on him." He uses the words "Holy Spirit" or "Spirit" three times to emphasize that Simeon was seeing the truth through God's eyes. Simeon was so sure of this truth that he praised God by proclaiming the promise fulfilled. Simeon's waiting had ended and his earthly life was complete.

ANNA

There was also a prophet, Anna, the daughter of Penuel, of the tribe of Asher. She was very old; she had lived with her husband seven years after her marriage, and then was a widow until she was eighty-four. She never left the temple but worshiped night and day, fasting and praying. Coming up to them at that very moment, she gave thanks to God and spoke about the child to all who were looking forward to the redemption of Jerusalem. When Joseph and Mary had done everything required by the Law of the Lord, they returned to Galilee to their own town of Nazareth. LUKE 2:36–39

■

WHAT MAKES JESUS' STORY so unique? In most narratives, a king would be surrounded by the rich and powerful, he would be feted by poets and songwriters, and he would inhabit palaces and fortresses apart from the teeming populace. But not here. Luke introduces us to many who are unknown, unimportant, and seemingly powerless in the eyes of the high and mighty. Luke presents us with Elizabeth and Mary, Simeon and Anna, and others who by worldly standards should be marginalized. It is a seemingly upside-down world, but as we will soon learn, Jesus came into the world for just this reason: In the eyes of God, the world was and is upside down. Jesus came to change all of that.

THE VISIT OF THE MAGI

After Jesus was born in Bethlehem in Judea, during the time of
King Herod, Magi from the east came to Jerusalem and asked,
"Where is the one who has been born king of the Jews? We saw his
star when it rose and have come to worship him." MATTHEW 2:1–2

■

THE MAGI, WISE MEN from Persia and regions in the east, discerned
an alignment in the stars in the heavens that told of an event so
monumental that they risked a long and dangerous journey to come
to Jerusalem to find and worship the child born to be king of the
Jews. Here we have another sign that the supernatural hand of God
is at work in the natural world. Ironically, the Magi first went to the
court of Herod the Great, an utterly ruthless political figure appointed by the Romans to oversee the Jewish territories. The wise
men were treated well and they presented the king with the "good
news" that an heir to the throne of David had been born whom they
had come to find and worship.

THE MESSIAH IS IN BETHLEHEM

When King Herod heard this he was disturbed, and all Jerusalem with him. When he had called together all the people's chief priests and teachers of the law, he asked them where the Messiah was to be born. "In Bethlehem in Judea," they replied, "for this is what the prophet has written, 'But you, Bethlehem, in the land of Judah are by no means least among the rulers of Judah; for out of you will come a ruler who will shepherd my people Israel.'" MAT-THEW 2:3–6

■

HEROD HAD SPENT HIS entire life building up his own political power, and he was not going to take any perceived threat as good news. When the Magi told him of another king who would become king of the Jews, he was troubled. Worse, the chief priests and teachers of the law confirmed that the prophet Micah had written that the Messiah would come from David's city of Bethlehem. Furthermore, Herod's close advisors told him that this king would be no ordinary ruler because his "origins are from of old, from ancient times" (Micah 5:2). Herod was deeply disturbed by this, but he dissembled and said nothing that would tip off the Magi that he was hatching other plans for this newborn "king of the Jews."

Then Herod called the Magi secretly and found out from them the exact time the star had appeared. He sent them to Bethlehem and said, "Go and search carefully for the child. As soon as you find him, report to me, so that I too may go and worship him." **MATTHEW 2:7–8**

■

MARY AND THE SHEPHERDS and Simeon and Anna all recognized the hand of God at work in the birth of Jesus. The Magi came to Jerusalem to find and worship the one true king of the Jews. But a subplot developed with Herod's reaction to the news. Herod was disturbed because he sensed a threat; an enemy had appeared on the scene and Herod must act or risk losing everything. He told the Magi to search Bethlehem to find the child so that he too could worship him. But Herod had only malice in his heart; his malevolent paranoia manifested a desire to kill and destroy, not worship and praise. Herod was the first in a long line of enemies of Christ who represented the powers of the kingdoms of this world. Jesus was a threat to these enemies even as a little child.

After they had heard the king, they went on their way, and the star they had seen when it rose went ahead of them until it stopped over the place where the child was. When they saw the star, they were overjoyed. On coming to the house, they saw the child with his mother Mary, and they bowed down and worshiped him. Then they opened their treasures and presented him with gifts of gold, frankincense and myrrh. And having been warned in a dream not to go back to Herod, they returned to their country by another route. MATTHEW 2:9–12

■

AFTER PRESENTING GIFTS TO the Christ child, the Magi heeded a warning from a dream and did not return to Jerusalem as Herod commanded. But were they ever in Bethlehem? We learn from Luke that after consecrating Jesus in the temple, Joseph and Mary returned with their child to Nazareth in Galilee and not to Bethlehem. Matthew never says that the Magi followed the star to Jesus' place of birth; he only says "the star they had seen when it rose went ahead of them until it stopped over the place where the child was." Because we have merged the two Christmas stories into one, we assume that, like the shepherds in the fields, the Magi went to the place where the child was born. If we read the two accounts carefully, it is probable that the Magi arrived long after the birth, when Joseph and Mary were in a house in Nazareth. Because they did not return to Herod, he continued to believe the child was still in Bethlehem. This misconception would compound the tragedy soon to come.

ESCAPE TO EGYPT

When they had gone, an angel of the Lord appeared to Joseph in a dream. "Get up," he said, "take the child and his mother and escape to Egypt. Stay there until I tell you, for Herod is going to search for the child to kill him." So he got up, took the child and his mother during the night and left for Egypt, where he stayed until the death of Herod. And so was fulfilled what the Lord had said through the prophet: "Out of Egypt I called my son." MAT-THEW 2:13–15

■

MATTHEW WAS WRITING TO Hebrew followers of Jesus, so the idea of escaping to Egypt would have been seen as strange and ironic. Every Jew knew the story of Moses and the escape from Egypt through the Red Sea and the desert to freedom in a promised land. But Joseph and Mary were told by an angel of the Lord to escape back into the land of bondage. How could this be? First, Matthew tells his readers that this escape from danger into Egypt was to fulfill a prophecy of Scripture: "Out of Egypt I called my son" (Hosea 11:1). But this also indicates that the Promised Land had lost its way, symbolized by the complete corruption of Herod, who ruled over Israel as a surrogate for the Roman occupiers. Herod desired to kill the Christ child. He may have wielded power over the people of God, but he had completely lost his way and had become an enemy of God.

WEEPING AND GREAT MOURNING

When Herod realized that he had been outwitted by the Magi, he was furious, and he gave orders to kill all the boys in Bethlehem and its vicinity who were two years old and under, in accordance with the time he had learned from the Magi. Then what was said through the prophet Jeremiah was fulfilled: "A voice is heard in Ramah, weeping and great mourning, Rachel weeping for her children and refusing to be comforted because they are no more."
MATTHEW 2:16–18

■

WHEN WE LOOK BACK at the unthinkable mayhem of the twentieth century, we are tempted to consider the devilish works of Hitler, Mao, and Stalin to be aberrations on the road of human progress. But aren't these modern tyrants merely political descendants of Herod, who in his corrupt rage ordered the murder of children? The truth is that a godless ruler is able to enforce terrible suffering because he has the power to do whatever he wants. He is capable of anything, including "wickedness, envy, greed, and depravity . . . murder, strife, deceit and malice" (Romans 1:29). The little children of Bethlehem were defenseless against such a man as this.

CHILDHOOD

And the child grew and became strong; he was filled with wisdom,
and the grace of God was upon him. LUKE 2:40

■

THE GOSPELS OF LUKE and Matthew give us a detailed picture of
the birth and early life of Jesus, but less is known of the period
between his return from Egypt and his early ministry. Luke does
tell us this: Jesus "grew and became strong; he was filled with wisdom and the grace of God was upon him." Unlike in his earliest
days, the dangers had dissipated and he participated in the usual
activities of normal family life. We know he lived in the family of
Joseph and Mary in Nazareth, developing skills as either a carpenter
or stonemason. His time in Nazareth was a prelude to the three
years of ministry that still lay ahead.

MY FATHER'S HOUSE

Every year his parents went to Jerusalem for the Feast of the Pass-over. When he was twelve years old, they went up to the Feast, according to the custom. After the Feast was over, while his parents were returning home, the boy Jesus stayed behind in Jerusalem, but they were unaware of it. Thinking he was in their company, they traveled on for a day. Then they began looking for him among their relatives and friends. When they did not find him, they went back to Jerusalem to look for him. After three days they found him in the temple courts, sitting among the teachers, listening to them and asking them questions. Everyone who heard him was amazed at his understanding and his answers. When his parents saw him, they were astonished. His mother said to him, "Son, why have you treated us like this? Your father and I have been anxiously searching for you." "Why were you searching for me?" he asked. "Didn't you know I had to be in my Father's house?" But they did not understand what he was saying to them. Then he went down to Nazareth with them and was obedient to them. But his mother treasured all these things in her heart. LUKE 2:41–51

■

THE STORY OF A precocious twelve-year-old boy going up to Jerusalem and impressing all the teachers in the temple court foreshadows a very different reaction to his later public ministry. A twelve-year-old boy is no threat to the established priesthood, but it is something else altogether when a thirty-year-old man comes riding into Jerusalem on a donkey with crowds of people shouting: "Hosanna to the son of David! Blessed is he who comes in the name of the Lord!"(Matthew 21:9) Even at twelve, though, Jesus was not confused about his genuine identity: "Didn't you know I had to be in my Father's house?"

REPENT, FOR THE KINGDOM
OF HEAVEN IS NEAR

In those days John the Baptist came, preaching in the Desert of Judea and saying, "Repent, for the kingdom of heaven is near." This is he who was spoken of through the prophet Isaiah: "A voice of one calling in the desert, 'Prepare the way for the Lord, make straight paths for him.'" John's clothes were made of camel's hair, and he had a leather belt around his waist. His food was locusts and wild honey. MATTHEW 3:1–4

■

JOHN REENTERS THE STORY dressed in clothes made of camel's hair and with a leather belt around his waist, saying, "Prepare the way for the Lord, make straight paths for him." John was in a desert region away from Jerusalem, the center of political and religious power. He had taken up the role of the great prophets of Israel by warning the people to repent. One meaning of the word *Torah* is *path* or *God's way*. The people had wandered away from God's right path, or, in Isaiah's words, "We all, like sheep, have gone astray, each of us has turned to his own way" (Isaiah 53:6). The people yearned for liberation from the Roman occupiers, but John was speaking about a different kind of liberation that would lead to the Way. The moment of its arrival was imminent.

YOU BROOD OF VIPERS!

John said to the crowds coming out to be baptized by him, "You brood of vipers! Who warned you to flee from the coming wrath? Produce fruit in keeping with repentance. And do not begin to say to yourselves, 'We have Abraham as our father.' For I tell you that out of these stones God can raise up children for Abraham. The ax is already at the root of the trees, and every tree that does not produce good fruit will be cut down and thrown into the fire."
LUKE 3:7–9

■

NEVER UNDERESTIMATE THE HUMAN propensity to drift. We may begin well, but soon enough our attention is grabbed by a diversion and we wander inadvertently off the good path. We can become so transfixed by any kind of shiny bauble that we do not notice that we have become blind and lost. This was the condition of the people of Israel; they had drifted from their first love and had become no better than "a brood of vipers." John was a prophet in the great tradition of Isaiah, Jeremiah, and Elijah who, himself, was called "a troubler of Israel" by Ahab, a truly wicked king (2 Kings 18:17). John was also a troubler because he was dispensing tough love by preaching the truth that the people and their leaders had abandoned the God who favored them: "Who warned you to flee from the coming wrath? Produce fruit in keeping with repentance."

IS JOHN THE CHRIST?

The people were waiting expectantly and were all wondering in their hearts if John might possibly be the Christ. John answered them all, "I baptize you with water. But one more powerful than I will come, the thongs of whose sandals I am not worthy to untie. He will baptize you with the Holy Spirit and with fire. His winnowing fork is in his hand to clear his threshing floor and to gather the wheat into his barn, but he will burn up the chaff with unquenchable fire." And with many other words John exhorted the people and preached the good news to them. LUKE 3:15–18

■

JOHN TOLD THE PRIESTS and Levites of Jerusalem that he baptizes with water but one would appear who would baptize with the Holy Spirit. He further testified that this man "is the Son of God." John testified that God is moving in the world and something new and unexpected is about to happen. In the Semitic world, water immersion was thought of as an outward symbol of being made pure before God. But water baptism is only a shadow of what is to come, for the Holy Spirit is not a symbol but is God himself made available through the sacrificial death of his one and only Son, Jesus Christ.

JOHN BAPTIZED JESUS

Then Jesus came from Galilee to the Jordan to be baptized by John. But John tried to deter him, saying, "I need to be baptized by you, and do you come to me?" Jesus replied, "Let it be so now; it is proper for us to do this to fulfill all righteousness." Then John consented. As soon as Jesus was baptized, he went up out of the water. At that moment heaven was opened, and he saw the Spirit of God descending like a dove and lighting on him. And a voice from heaven said, "This is my Son, whom I love; with him I am well pleased." MATTHEW 3:13–17

■

ONCE AGAIN WE ENCOUNTER a surprise: Why would Jesus, the Son of God, require baptism from John? John said, "I need to be baptized by you . . ." but Jesus replied that he himself must be baptized "to fulfill all righteousness." This is the pivotal moment between preparation and action. Jesus fulfilled all righteousness by accepting the role the Father designated for him: "Who, being in very nature God, did not consider equality with God something to be grasped, but made himself nothing, taking on the very nature of a servant, being made in human likeness" (Philippians 2: 6–7). Jesus put his God nature on the shelf and put on his man nature. He was obedient to God's purpose for him. This is why the voice from heaven said, "This is my Son, whom I love; with him I am well pleased."

JOHN'S TESTIMONY

Then John gave this testimony: "I saw the Spirit come down from heaven as a dove and remain on him. I would not have known him, except that the one who sent me to baptize with water told me, 'The man on whom you see the Spirit come down and remain is he who will baptize with the Holy Spirit.' I have seen and I testify that this is the Son of God." The next day John was there again with two of his disciples. JOHN 1:32–35

■

THE MYSTERY BEHIND THE explosive growth of the church in the first century can be understood partially through the power of testimony and witness. John said, "I have seen and I testify this is the Son of God." John himself had a large following. He was known to be a truth teller, and people from Jerusalem pursued him and were baptized by him because many considered him to be a prophet of God. So when he testified about Jesus, people began to notice. The Gospel says that John the Baptist was sent from God to testify as a witness about Jesus so that "through him all men might believe." After John's influence decreased and Jesus' ministry grew, the testimony of witnesses increased as well. We have the testimony of God's Word through the prophets. We have Jesus' testimony about himself, we have the testimony of the early disciples, and we have the testimony of the innumerable people who received the testimony of all these witnesses and began to testify themselves about Jesus.

Jesus, full of the Holy Spirit, returned from the Jordan and was led by the Spirit in the desert, where for forty days he was tempted by the devil. He ate nothing during those days, and at the end of them he was hungry. The devil said to him, "If you are the Son of God, tell this stone to become bread." Jesus answered, "It is written: 'Man does not live on bread alone.'" LUKE 4:1–4

■

JESUS WAS LED INTO the wilderness, and he ate nothing for forty days. His hunger must have been all consuming and then, out of nowhere, he received an offer of relief. Produce a miracle, said the tempter, and I may recognize you for who you are. But by implication Satan is also saying if you accede to my offer, you will forever bow down to me. This challenge to Jesus as Lord will be repeated time and again during his three-year ministry. Here the devil was actually saying: Use your power to satisfy your bodily craving. This, of course, is a complete contradiction of God's purpose. Jesus replied by quoting from Deuteronomy, which simply declares that man, as God created him, is more than an accumulation of appetites. While not denying the necessity of food, Jesus declares that man has a higher purpose to his existence: "Man does not live on bread alone, but on every word that comes from the mouth of the Lord" (Deuteronomy 8:3).

The devil led him up to a high place and showed him in an instant all the kingdoms of the world. And he said to him, "I will give you all their authority and splendor, for it has been given to me, and I can give it to anyone I want to. So if you worship me, it will all be yours." Jesus answered, "It is written: 'Worship the Lord your God and serve him only.'" LUKE 4:5–8

■

IF THE FIRST TEMPTATION was one of provision, the second was one of power. Satan declared that all the kingdoms of the world had been given to him. But who gave him that power? Certainly God did not give over all of this to Satan. If we go back to the Genesis story, it says that God blessed the man and the woman and gave them rule over the earth and "everything that has the breath of life in it . . ." But once the fall took place, mankind ceded authority to Satan. Jesus came to defeat Satan and restore the rightful authority to those who through the power of the Holy Spirit acknowledge God and worship him and him only.

The devil led him to Jerusalem and had him stand on the highest point of the temple. "If you are the Son of God," he said, "throw yourself down from here. For it is written: 'He will command his angels concerning you to guard you carefully; they will lift you up in their hands, so that you will not strike your foot against a stone.'" Jesus answered, "It says: 'Do not put the Lord your God to the test.'" LUKE 4:9–12

■

IN THE LAST OF the three temptations, Satan's strategy to confuse and undermine Jesus has a familiar ring to it. In the Garden of Eden he created confusion by raising doubt: "Did God really say, 'you must not eat from any tree in the garden'?" God, of course, was specific about this one prohibition, but the question did its job, and soon enough both Adam and Eve chose to do the one thing God warned them not to do. Ever adaptive, Satan attempted to subvert Christ's mission through a distorted use of Scripture. His weapon was to instill doubt: If you are the Son of God, prove it to me by testing the scriptural claim that God will protect you. But the psalm does not say what Satan implies. It says, "If you make the most high your dwelling . . . then no harm will befall you, no disaster will come near your tent" (Psalm 91:9–10). Unlike Adam and Eve, Jesus was not deceived, and he simply said, "Do not put the Lord your God to the test."

HE WILL WAIT FOR AN OPPORTUNE TIME

When the devil had finished all this tempting, he left him until an opportune time. LUKE 4:13

■

JESUS SUCCESSFULLY RESISTED THE third temptation, but this was but one battle in a much larger war. Jesus knew this and so should we. When Luke says that Satan "left him until an opportune time," Luke merely means that Satan had retreated and will wait for another moment to subvert God's plan. Remember, the events in Eden were but a skirmish in the epic battle between the fallen angel Satan and God Himself. This battle preceded the conflicts underlining the biblical narrative (Revelation 12:7–9). And so, even though he failed here, Satan did not give up and he continued to attack throughout Jesus' three-year ministry.

JESUS CALLED PETER

Andrew, Simon Peter's brother, was one of the two who heard what John had said and who had followed Jesus. The first thing Andrew did was to find his brother Simon and tell him, "We have found the Messiah" (that is, the Christ). And he brought him to Jesus. Jesus looked at him and said, "You are Simon son of John. You will be called Cephas" (which, when translated, is Peter). JOHN 1:40–42

■

THE SETTING IS THE region of Galilee. This is where Jesus became known for his extraordinary power to heal, and it is where he met Andrew. Eventually Andrew became a disciple, but here his role was to introduce his brother Peter to Jesus in an extraordinary way: "We have found the Messiah." We do not know much more about Andrew, but we do know that at this moment he showed great insight by correctly identifying Jesus. In a sense, he is a model for all Christians who follow Jesus. We, likewise, should take on this role as conduit: Every Peter will learn of Jesus through a witness. Every Peter will have his Andrew.

COME AND SEE

Philip, like Andrew and Peter, was from the town of Beth-saida. Philip found Nathanael and told him, "We have found the one Moses wrote about in the Law, and about whom the prophets also wrote—Jesus of Nazareth, the son of Joseph." "Nazareth! Can anything good come from there?" Nathanael asked. "Come and see," said Philip. JOHN 1:44–46

■

WHEREAS ANDREW INTRODUCED JESUS to Peter with the excla-mation, "We have found the Messiah," Nathanael reacted with skepticism bordering on intellectual contempt. Nathanael was a learned man, and he knew that the prophet Micah had identified Bethlehem, the city of David, as the place of origin of the Messiah (Micah 5:2). He dismissed Nazareth with, "Can anything good come from there?" Nathanael's initial response was to reject before he could actually see for himself. His mind had been clouded with layer upon layer of preconceptions as to what the Messiah would be like. But Philip persisted, and Nathanael was about to encounter the unexpected in a way he could never have anticipated.

A TRUE ISRAELITE

When Jesus saw Nathanael approaching, he said of him, "Here is a true Israelite, in whom there is nothing false." "How do you know me?" Nathanael asked. Jesus answered, "I saw you while you were still under the fig tree before Philip called you." Then Nathanael declared, "Rabbi, you are the Son of God; you are the King of Israel." JOHN 1:47–49

■

NATHANAEL, THE SCHOLAR AND intellectual, who had come to know things through study, suddenly, in the presence of Jesus, experienced a knowledge that flows through revelation. Apparently, Jesus revealed something that only Nathanael could know. Perhaps he was praying under the fig tree for the salvation of Israel. We will never know for sure. But in response to Jesus, Nathanael blurted out, "Rabbi, you are the Son of God; you are the King of Israel." Simeon and Anna were waiting in great expectation for the Christ child and knew him when they saw him, but Nathanael could not see the truth until God intervened to allow for clear vision. In this way, Nathanael foreshadows the conversion of Saul, who was blinded by his hatred of Christ. It was only when he accepted Christ in Damascus that "something like scales fell from (his) eyes and he could see again" (Acts 9:18).

A WEDDING IN CANA

On the third day a wedding took place at Cana in Galilee. Jesus' mother was there, and Jesus and his disciples had also been invited to the wedding. When the wine was gone, Jesus' mother said to him, "They have no more wine." "Dear woman, why do you involve me?" Jesus replied. "My time has not yet come." His mother said to the servants, "Do whatever he tells you." Nearby stood six stone water jars, the kind used by the Jews for ceremonial washing, each holding from twenty to thirty gallons. Jesus said to the servants, "Fill the jars with water," so they filled them to the brim.
JOHN 2:1–7

■

JESUS NEEDED TO KEEP God's greater purpose in view as he engaged in the events of everyday life. And so when his mother Mary turned to him to intervene to prevent an embarrassing problem from ruining an otherwise festive wedding party, he resisted, saying his time had not yet come. What did he mean? Clearly, it was not his intention to become a magician, nor did he wish to prematurely bring notice to himself. Later on, he would admonish those whom he had healed not to tell anyone. Nor did he want to fall into Satan's temptation of "proving" he is the Son of God. The stage had not yet been set for Jesus to explode onto the scene. He is both the Son of Man and the Son of God, but it was Jesus the man who needed to remain obedient to the Father's will, even if that meant avoiding public displays until his time had truly come.

Then he told them, "Now draw some out and take it to the master of the banquet." They did so, and the master of the banquet tasted the water that had been turned into wine. He did not realize where it had come from, though the servants who had drawn the water knew. Then he called the bridegroom aside and said, "Everyone brings out the choice wine first and then the cheaper wine after the guests have had too much to drink; but you have saved the best till now." This, the first of his miraculous signs, Jesus performed at Cana in Galilee. He thus revealed his glory, and his disciples put their faith in him. JOHN 2:8–11

■

IMAGINE A WEDDING CELEBRATION where the food and wine vanish. It seems inconceivable because weddings are about love, joy, and bounty. When the wine suddenly ran out in the middle of the feast, a crisis quickly developed, and Jesus' mother turned to her son for help. Though this moment was not the right time for him, Jesus was obedient and quickly performed his first miracle of turning water into wine. Most of the people attending the wedding feast did not realize what had happened, but the disciples knew, because John's Gospel says that after Jesus had revealed his glory, "his disciples put their faith in him." In a sense Jesus could not refuse his mother's intervention because he is the Son of an extravagant and bountiful God.

When it was almost time for the Jewish Passover, Jesus went up to Jerusalem. In the temple courts he found men selling cattle, sheep, and doves, and others sitting at tables exchanging money. So he made a whip out of cords, and drove all from the temple area, both sheep and cattle; he scattered the coins of the money changers and overturned their tables. To those who sold doves he said, "Get these out of here! How dare you turn my Father's house into a market!" His disciples remembered that it is written: "Zeal for your house will consume me." JOHN 2:13–17

■

WE MOVE FROM CANA in Galilee to the very seat of religious and political power: Jerusalem. We recall that Jesus had been there another time, when he was about twelve years old and the priests and leaders of the Temple marveled at his knowledge and wisdom. Now he had returned to find that the Holy Temple of God had become a chaotic marketplace where buying and selling was the primary activity, crowding out the experience of being in the presence of a holy and forgiving God. And so we see a very different Jesus, one whose righteous anger recalls the prophecies of Isaiah: "Jerusalem staggers, Judah is falling; their words and deeds are against the Lord, defying his glorious presence" (Isaiah 3:8).

A NEW TEMPLE

Then the Jews demanded of him, "What miraculous sign can you show us to prove your authority to do all this?" Jesus answered them, "Destroy this temple, and I will raise it again in three days." The Jews replied, "It has taken forty-six years to build this temple, and you are going to raise it in three days?" But the temple he had spoken of was his body. After he was raised from the dead, his disciples recalled what he had said. Then they believed the Scripture and the words that Jesus had spoken. JOHN 2:18–22

■

LET US PAUSE TO reflect on how Jesus uses language in this passage. He says, "Destroy this temple, and I will raise it again in three days." The people listening would have heard this claim as bravado. If they interpreted his words literally, they would have missed his meaning. John interjects that Jesus was not really talking about the temple; he was speaking figuratively about his body: Kill me and I will rise in three days. Jesus was not making an exaggerated statement. He was actually prophesying that he would be crucified and then on the third day be raised from the dead.

Now while he was in Jerusalem at the Passover Feast, many people saw the miraculous signs he was doing and believed in his name. But Jesus would not entrust himself to them, for he knew all men. He did not need man's testimony about man, for he knew what was in a man. JOHN 2:23–25

■

JOHN SAYS THAT JESUS performed many miraculous signs while in Jerusalem, and they "believed in his name." But Jesus was not deceived. Jesus was not trying to win a popularity contest, nor was he trying to sway the crowd with political rhetoric. He came "to save the people from their sins" (Matthew 1:21). He did not entrust himself to the people because he knew what had become of the hearts of men. Jesus knew the nature of the world he had entered. It was a world of men and women who had fallen away from God: "The Lord looks down from heaven on the sons of men to see if there are any who understand, any who seek God. All have turned aside, they have together become corrupt; there is no one who does good, not even one" (Psalm 14:2–3).

NICODEMUS

Now there was a man of the Pharisees named Nicodemus, a member of the Jewish ruling council. He came to Jesus at night and said, "Rabbi, we know you are a teacher who has come from God. For no one could perform the miraculous signs you are doing if God were not with him." In reply Jesus declared, "I tell you the truth, no one can see the kingdom of God unless he is born again." "How can a man be born when he is old?" Nicodemus asked. "Surely he cannot enter a second time into his mother's womb to be born!" Jesus answered, "I tell you the truth, no one can enter the kingdom of God unless he is born of water and the Spirit. Flesh gives birth to flesh, but the Spirit gives birth to spirit. You should not be surprised at my saying, 'You must be born again.' The wind blows wherever it pleases. You hear its sound, but you cannot tell where it comes from or where it is going. So it is with everyone born of the Spirit." JOHN 3:1–8

■

NICODEMUS WAS A PHARISEE, a member of the ruling religious class. He came to Jesus at night because Jesus was considered an outsider, much like John the Baptist. Nicodemus was worried that his peers would consider such a visit unseemly, even dangerous. But he went anyway, bringing along all the ruling-class assumptions that pass for theological truth. It is important to note that Jesus and Nicodemus seemed to be talking at cross-purposes: Nicodemus used literal, commonsense language, whereas Jesus answered in the language of the Holy Spirit. "How can a man be born when he is old?" asked Nicodemus. Jesus replied that he is talking about a different kind of birth: "Flesh gives birth to flesh, but the Spirit gives birth to spirit." Jesus was declaring to Nicodemus (and to us) that if our philosophy does not consider the truth of the presence of the Holy Spirit of God, then it is nothing more than an intellectual construction of men; it does not come from God.

HE GAVE HIS OWN SON FOR US

For God so loved the world that he gave his one and only Son, that whoever believes in him shall not perish but have eternal life. For God did not send his Son into the world to condemn the world, but to save the world through him. Whoever believes in him is not condemned, but whoever does not believe stands condemned already because he has not believed in the name of God's one and only Son. JOHN 3:16–18

■

IF WE EVER NEEDED an explanation for why Jesus, the Son of God, came to walk upon the earth, here it is. God sent his one-and-only Son into the world to save us. Whether we admit it or not, all men and women are in a sinful state and stand condemned before God. It is the Son, the one without sin, who stands in our place as a sufficient sacrifice for our accumulated guilt. Many will not acknowledge the necessity of the cross because they cannot see why it is needed. However, the whole weight of the biblical narrative, from Adam to Jesus, rests on the reality of the power of sin to separate us from the God who loves us. David, in his confessional psalm, explains how deep and intractable the problem really is: "Surely I was sinful at birth, sinful from the time my mother conceived me" (Psalm 51:5).

This is the verdict: Light has come into the world, but men loved darkness instead of light because their deeds were evil. Everyone who does evil hates the light, and will not come into the light for fear that his deeds will be exposed. But whoever lives by the truth comes into the light, so that it may be seen plainly that what he has done has been done through God. JOHN 3: 19–21

■

JESUS SAYS, "THIS IS the verdict," and then he unfolds in summary form the entire history of man flailing through the darkness without the light of God. He says that men loved darkness because they preferred the evil they knew to the God they had abandoned. It is the weight of guilt and shame that drives us further into the darkness. We will do anything not to be found out. Jesus says, "Everyone who does evil hates the light, and will not come into the light for fear that his deeds will be exposed." It is this fear of exposure that separates us from the light of the God who loves us. And so, rather than accept God's amazing grace, we slink away into the shadows in the company of fellow sufferers, rejecting the invitation open to all.

HE MUST BECOME GREATER;
I MUST BECOME LESS

An argument developed between some of John's disciples and a certain Jew over the matter of ceremonial washing. They came to John and said to him, "Rabbi, that man who was with you on the other side of the Jordan—the one you testified about—well, he is baptizing, and everyone is going to him." To this John replied, "A man can receive only what is given him from heaven. You yourselves can testify that I said, 'I am not the Christ but am sent ahead of him.' The bride belongs to the bridegroom. The friend who attends the bridegroom waits and listens for him, and is full of joy when he hears the bridegroom's voice. That joy is mine, and it is now complete. He must become greater; I must become less."
JOHN 3:25–30

■

DO WE TAKE JOHN the Baptist seriously when he says of Christ: "He must become greater; I must become less"? After all, John was something of a celebrity with a large following of people from all over Israel. Who willingly gives up fortune or fame? Most of us spend our productive years accumulating and achieving, but John simply says, "I am not the Christ but am sent ahead of him." He understood his role and honored it: "A man can receive only what is given him from heaven." His disciples tempted him by warning that his followers were going over to someone else. But John did not take the bait. He knew that his moment was fleeting and soon the crowds would be gone, but John had fulfilled his mission. He had been a good steward, and so he could say, "That joy is mine, and it is now complete."

GOD IS TRUTHFUL

The one who comes from above is above all; the one who is from the earth belongs to the earth, and speaks as one from the earth. The one who comes from heaven is above all. He testifies to what he has seen and heard, but no one accepts his testimony. The man who has accepted it has certified that God is truthful. For the one whom God has sent speaks the words of God, for God gives the Spirit without limit. The Father loves the Son and has placed everything in his hands. JOHN 3:31–35

■

JOHN THE BAPTIST'S MINISTRY may have been diminishing, but just as he was departing center stage, he left us with this powerful testimony about Jesus. He says that Jesus "comes from heaven (and) is above all," that he has come from heaven to earth to testify "to what he has seen and heard," that he "speaks the words of God," that God "gives the Spirit without limit," and that God the Father "loves the Son and has placed everything in his hands." John is making an audacious claim: The Messiah, the true King of Israel, had finally come.

GALILEE

The Pharisees heard that Jesus was gaining and baptizing more disciples than John, although in fact it was not Jesus who baptized, but his disciples. When the Lord learned of this, he left Judea and went back once more to Galilee. JOHN 4:1–3

■

WHY DID JESUS LEAVE Judea and return to Galilee? This passage does not provide an explicit reason. We do know that the Pharisees were a crucial part of the political structure beholden to the occupying Roman masters. To them, John was a troublemaker who needed to be watched and controlled; they feared that he would appeal to the people's desire for liberation from the Roman yoke. The Pharisees could not tolerate perceived threats to their power base and would move for almost any reason to quash rebellion. So when Jesus heard that the Pharisees believed he was directly associated with John the Baptist, he left to return to Galilee to teach, preach, and heal during the early days of his ministry. Jesus knew that "his time had not yet come" (John 2:4).

For Herod himself had given orders to have John arrested, and he had him bound and put in prison. He did this because of Herodias, his brother Philip's wife, whom he had married. For John had been saying to Herod, "It is not lawful for you to have your brother's wife." So Herodias nursed a grudge against John and wanted to kill him. But she was not able to, because Herod feared John and protected him, knowing him to be a righteous and holy man. When Herod heard John, he was greatly puzzled; yet he liked to listen to him. **MARK 6:17–20**

■

AS JESUS' MINISTRY BEGAN to expand, John's role had to "become less." But John did not retire. He continued to be a thorn in the side of the political, social, and financial elite in Jerusalem. He did not mince words: "You brood of vipers! Who warned you to flee from the coming wrath? Produce fruit in keeping with repentance . . . Every tree that does not bear good fruit will be cut down and thrown into the fire" (Luke 3:7, 9). John even targeted Herod, who had married his own brother's wife. She in turn proceeded to use her power and influence to force the king to act against John. Yet Herod did not immediately execute him, for even in the depths of his own venial corruption, Herod could still discern that John was a holy man. Defying his wife's pressure to kill John, Herod protected his prisoner and even "liked to listen to him." Herodias had to wait for an opportune time to exact her revenge.

THE SAMARITAN WOMAN

Now he had to go through Samaria. So he came to a town in Samaria called Sychar, near the plot of ground Jacob had given to his son Joseph. Jacob's well was there, and Jesus, tired as he was from the journey, sat down by the well. It was about the sixth hour. When a Samaritan woman came to draw water, Jesus said to her, "Will you give me a drink?" (His disciples had gone into the town to buy food.) The Samaritan woman said to him, "You are a Jew and I am a Samaritan woman. How can you ask me for a drink?" (For Jews do not associate with Samaritans.) JOHN 4:4–9

■

WHEN JESUS LEFT JUDEA to return to Galilee, he decided to travel through Samaria. This was unusual, because Jewish travellers would go out of their way to avoid Samaria and the Samaritans who lived there. Jesus stopped at Jacob's well in the town of Sychar. When a woman came to fetch water from the well, Jesus asked her to give him a drink, and what followed was no ordinary conversation. Even though she was a Samaritan and a woman of questionable reputation, Jesus went out of his way to cross social and conventional barriers to bring revelation to her and to her town. This encounter provides an early picture of Jesus reaching beyond the boundaries of a single nation. Jesus may have come to the Jews first, but his mission is to save all men and women, Gentiles and Jews alike.

Jesus went into Galilee, proclaiming the good news of God. "The time has come," he said. "The kingdom of God is near. Repent and believe the good news!" **MARK 1:14B–15**

■

WE PRAY "YOUR KINGDOM come" as part of our recitation of The Lord's Prayer, but what did Jesus mean by this? Certainly, as he began his ministry in the region of Galilee, the people would have understood this declaration in historical and political terms. They yearned for the end of Roman rule and the restoration of the glorious kingdoms of David and Solomon. But their interpretations missed the mark. Jesus was not identifying himself as a political liberator or revolutionary. He was referring to the kingdom of the Lord's Prayer—God's kingdom—that far surpasses anything men could invent or build. Jesus was announcing the restoration of the real thing and he was telling the people that his mission comes from God Himself.

THE NEWS SPREAD IN GALILEE

Jesus returned to Galilee in the power of the Spirit, and news about him spread through the whole countryside. He was teaching in their synagogues, and everyone praised him. LUKE 4:14–15

■

NO ONE SEEMED TO expect the Messiah to come out of Nazareth in Galilee. Recall that when Philip discovered Jesus and went to tell Nathanael, Nathanael expressed the contempt felt by the educated classes toward the people in the regions surrounding the Sea of Galilee: "Nazareth! Can anything good come from there?" (John 1:46) Nathanael changed his mind when he met Jesus, and he was not the only person who experienced the grace and power of the presence of Jesus. Throughout the region, people were being miraculously healed and the news was spreading quickly. But far away in Jerusalem, only the faintest echoes were being heard about the ministry of Jesus. The region was too insignificant, and so the ruling class remained temporarily isolated from what became a gathering storm. Ironically, when the religious leaders realized that many people were following Jesus and even proclaiming him as Messiah, they countered by using Scripture to show that "a prophet does not come out of Galilee" (John 7:52). Isaiah, however, had prophesized that one would (Isaiah 9:1).

PETER'S MOTHER-IN-LAW

When Jesus came into Peter's house, he saw Peter's mother-in-law lying in bed with a fever. He touched her hand and the fever left her, and she got up and began to wait on him. When evening came, many who were demon possessed were brought to him, and he drove out the spirits with a word and healed all the sick. This was to fulfill what was spoken through the prophet Isaiah: "He took up our infirmities and bore our diseases." MATTHEW 8:14–17

■

WE KNOW THAT PETER had a brother, Andrew, but there is no mention of his wife or children, or if he even had children. Instead, we know that Peter was a fisherman on the Sea of Galilee near Capernaum. It would be one thing if Peter were a young unmarried man with no attachments when Jesus called him to leave everything and follow him. But Peter was attached; he had a business and family, and yet despite these relationships, he put everything aside and began to follow Jesus. This was a profoundly significant decision, and Peter made it almost instantaneously. Leaving his family, friends, and work behind was a costly decision with great uncertainty attached to it. Jesus knows there is a cost to following him and he does not want us to believe otherwise. Here is what he says to his disciples: "Still another said, 'I will follow you, Lord; but first let me go back and say goodbye to my family.' Jesus replied, 'No one who puts his hand to the plow and looks back is fit for service in the kingdom of God'" (Luke 9:61–62).

THE SECOND MIRACULOUS SIGN

The (Royal Officer) took Jesus at his word and departed. While he was still on the way, his servants met him with the news that his boy was living. When he inquired as to the time when his son got better, they said to him, "The fever left him yesterday at the seventh hour." Then the father realized that this was the exact time at which Jesus had said to him, "Your son will live." So he and his entire household believed. This was the second miraculous sign that Jesus performed, having come from Judea to Galilee. JOHN 4:50B–54

■

WHEN WE MEET A person for the first time, we quickly begin to ascertain exactly where they fit into our categories of acceptability. Where do they live? Where did they go to college? What do they do for a living? This tendency to identify someone through certain religious and socio-economic categories is as prevalent today as it was in Jesus' time. But Jesus is a barrier breaker: Artificial boundaries do not constrict him. And so the Royal Official, who may have been a Gentile, came to Jesus in distress to ask him to save his dying son. Jesus asked him no questions, he just said, "You may go. Your son will live." Jew or Gentile, royal or commoner, Jesus responds to the human crisis, not to the identity of the suffering father. Jesus crossed boundaries all the way to the cross itself and continues to do so right up to this very moment.

I AM A SINFUL MAN!

When he had finished speaking, he said to Simon, "Put out into deep water, and let down the nets for a catch." Simon answered, "Master, we've worked hard all night and haven't caught anything. But because you say so, I will let down the nets." When they had done so, they caught such a large number of fish that their nets began to break. So they signaled their partners in the other boat to come and help them, and they came and filled both boats so full that they began to sink. When Simon Peter saw this, he fell at Jesus' knees and said, "Go away from me, Lord; I am a sinful man!" LUKE 5:4–8

■

WHEN PETER SAID, "GO away from me, Lord; I am a sinful man!" he acknowledged the chasm that exists between the holiness that is God and the sinfulness that is in all men and women. This is exactly what happened when Isaiah experienced a vision of God: "'Woe to me!' I cried. 'I am ruined! For I am a man of unclean lips, and I live among a people of unclean lips, and my eyes have seen the King, the Lord Almighty'" (Isaiah 6:5). Jesus did not abandon Peter; he enlisted him. Peter's exclamation was based on his realization that God is God and he is not. It was on the shore of the Sea of Galilee that Peter began the long journey of aligning himself with God's vision for his life. It was Jesus who made possible this first step for Peter.

HAVE YOU COME TO DESTROY US?

They went to Capernaum, and when the Sabbath came, Jesus went into the synagogue and began to teach. The people were amazed at his teaching, because he taught them as one who had authority, not as the teachers of the law. Just then a man in their synagogue who was possessed by an evil spirit cried out, "What do you want with us, Jesus of Nazareth? Have you come to destroy us? I know who you are—the Holy One of God!" "Be quiet!" said Jesus sternly. "Come out of him!" The evil spirit shook the man violently and came out of him with a shriek. The people were all so amazed that they asked each other, "What is this? A new teaching—and with authority! He even gives orders to evil spirits and they obey him."
MARK 1:21–27

■

CAPERNAUM RESTED ON THE northern shore of the Sea of Galilee, not far from where the Jordan River flows down from the highlands. It was not a huge town in Jesus' day, but it was active, filled with common people earning a living off the natural resources abounding there. It was in this place that Jesus chose to demonstrate the power of his authority over nature, sickness, and even demonic spirits. The people who witnessed his miracles were astonished and perplexed: "What is this? A new teaching—and with authority! He even gives orders to evil spirits and they obey him." Who, indeed?

EVERYONE IS LOOKING FOR YOU!

Very early in the morning, while it was still dark, Jesus got up, left the house and went off to a solitary place, where he prayed. Simon and his companions went to look for him, and when they found him, they exclaimed, "Everyone is looking for you!" Jesus replied, "Let us go somewhere else—to the nearby villages—so I can preach there also. That is why I have come." So he traveled throughout Galilee, preaching in their synagogues and driving out demons. MARK 1:35–39

■

WHY DID JESUS RISE early to go to a solitary place to pray to the Father? The answer is that he had the same human needs that all people have. Jesus was on a mission: He had been traveling from town to town, preaching, teaching, and healing, and crowds gathered to follow him. His disciples said, "Everyone is looking for you!" Jesus needed to pause, he needed to reflect, and most of all, he needed to renew his energy and direction by seeking guidance from the Father. We should take heed, as we need to pause in the swirl of everyday endeavors. We need to pray for our daily bread so that we can continue to fight the good fight. We need to pray to resist temptation, to forgive and be forgiven, and to accept the authority given to us through the Holy Spirit to play the role God has gifted us in restoring God's kingdom here on earth.

I AM WILLING

A man with leprosy came to him and begged him on his knees, "If you are willing, you can make me clean." Filled with compassion, Jesus reached out his hand and touched the man. "I am willing," he said. "Be clean!" Immediately the leprosy left him and he was cured. Jesus sent him away at once with a strong warning: "See that you don't tell this to anyone. But go, show yourself to the priest and offer the sacrifices that Moses commanded for your cleansing, as a testimony to them." Instead he went out and began to talk freely, spreading the news. As a result, Jesus could no longer enter a town openly but stayed outside in lonely places. Yet the people still came to him from everywhere. MARK 1:40–45

■

A PERSON AFFLICTED WITH leprosy experiences an outward corruption of the skin. This disease can infect others, condemning lepers to a life exiled from the community of the healthy. As seen here, lepers also represent a visible sign of another kind of disease. Though often unseen, sin is just as lethal as physical disease and shares many of the same characteristics. Jesus did not shun the man with leprosy but felt compassion and touched him. The leper was healed, and he was sent to the priests to give thanks to God. And so it is for sinners. Jesus says elsewhere, "It is not the healthy who need a doctor, but the sick. I have not come to call the righteous, but sinners" (Mark 2:17).

THE PARALYTIC

Some men brought to him a paralytic, lying on a mat. When Jesus saw their faith, he said to the paralytic, "Take heart, son; your sins are forgiven." At this, some of the teachers of the law said to themselves, "This fellow is blaspheming!" Knowing their thoughts, Jesus said, "Why do you entertain evil thoughts in your hearts? Which is easier: to say, 'Your sins are forgiven,' or to say, 'Get up and walk'? But so that you may know that the Son of Man has authority on earth to forgive sins . . ." Then he said to the paralytic, "Get up, take your mat and go home." And the man got up and went home. When the crowd saw this, they were filled with awe; and they praised God, who had given such authority to men.
MATTHEW 9:2–8

■

THE PARALYTIC WAS BROUGHT to Jesus because news had spread throughout the vicinity that Jesus demonstrated an ability to heal the sick. But when he linked sin to the man's physical condition, the "teachers of the law" objected. No man can forgive sins; any man who claims this power is a blasphemer and can be condemned to death for appropriating a power only God can exercise. Jesus did not back off, though. He directly challenged the religious leaders who were questioning him: "Which is easier, to say, 'Your sins are forgiven' or to say, 'Get up and walk'?" Jesus was showing everyone present exactly who he is: As he says in another instance, "With man this is impossible, but not with God; all things are possible with God" (Mark 10:27).

FOLLOW ME

After this, Jesus went out and saw a tax collector by the name of Levi sitting at his tax booth. "Follow me," Jesus said to him, and Levi got up, left everything and followed him. LUKE 5:27–28

■

IT WOULD NOT BE difficult to gloss over this short passage. After all, it describes an event but does not explain it. Levi was a tax collector, a position that was feared and hated by the Jewish people. Not only did tax collectors have the power to take property, but they also worked for the Roman occupiers. So it defied common sense that Levi would drop everything and follow Jesus. This not only puzzles us, it must have puzzled Levi and all the people who knew him. At the same time, though, Jesus tended to call people who seemed miscast as followers and disciples. Jesus continually sought out the unlikeliest of people for his own purposes. We must remember that Jesus chose followers in conformity to the Father's will; what might look like a mistake to us was exactly in line with God's greater purpose.

While Jesus was having dinner at Levi's house, many tax collectors and "sinners" were eating with him and his disciples, for there were many who followed him. When the teachers of the law who were Pharisees saw him eating with the "sinners" and tax collectors, they asked his disciples: "Why does he eat with tax collectors and 'sinners'?" On hearing this, Jesus said to them, "It is not the healthy who need a doctor, but the sick. I have not come to call the righteous, but sinners." MARK 2:15–17

■

JESUS ENTERED A "SINNER'S" house where many disrespectable people were congregating, but in the corner were some who wore their respectability as a garment. Their claim of righteousness masked a haughty self-righteousness that was devoid of mercy and love. The "teachers of the law" had exempted themselves from judgment; they were deluded, of course. No matter what height of social and economic achievement these Pharisees had attained, Jesus implied that they were no different from the tax collectors and "sinners" who had come to Levi's house. There were no genuinely righteous men or women there, only sinners. Jesus has come for all because all are sinners, even those who claim to be righteous.

THE INVALID

Sometime later, Jesus went up to Jerusalem for a feast of the Jews. Now there is in Jerusalem near the Sheep Gate a pool, which in Aramaic is called Bethesda and which is surrounded by five covered colonnades. Here a great number of disabled people used to lay—the blind, the lame, and the paralyzed. One who was there had been an invalid for thirty-eight years. When Jesus saw him lying there and learned that he had been in this condition for a long time, he asked him, "Do you want to get well?" JOHN 5:1–6

■

JESUS ASKED THE INVALID: "Do you want to get well?" We might reply: "What kind of question is that? Of course he wants to get well, who wouldn't?" We might recall, though, that earlier in Galilee, Jesus linked the paralytic's physical disability to a spiritual disability when he proclaimed the sick man's sin forgiven. Jesus cannot cure a man or woman who prefers to cling to his or her sickness. We need to possess the desire to recover, just as we must want to overcome the powerful impulse to sin. Paul describes this battle being waged in the human heart this way: "For what I want to do I do not do, but what I hate I do . . . What I do is not the good I want to do; no, the evil I do not want to do—this I keep on doing" (Romans 7:15,19). To begin the journey to genuine recovery, we must want to get well by acknowledging the presence of contrary desires and impulses embedded deep within our own hearts.

"Sir," the invalid replied, "I have no one to help me into the pool when the water is stirred. While I am trying to get in, someone else goes down ahead of me." Then Jesus said to him, "Get up! Pick up your mat and walk." At once the man was cured; he picked up his mat and walked. The day on which this took place was a Sabbath, and so the Jews said to the man who had been healed, "It is the Sabbath; the law forbids you to carry your mat."
JOHN 5:7–10

■

THE INVALID AT THE pool called Bethesda spent thirty-eight fruitless years trying to get to the healing waters. Jesus asked the right question: Do you really want to become well? But he received an excuse from the invalid rather than an affirmative answer. At this point Jesus acted, healing the man instantly and saying, "Get up! Pick up your mat and walk." Jesus cut through the pretense with an astonishing miracle. But not everyone was pleased; some in authority pointed out that the invalid was not keeping the Sabbath because he was carrying his mat. They disregarded the miracle to enforce a religious law. In a similar situation, as reported by Luke, Jesus had this reaction to the religious taskmasters: "I ask you, which is lawful on the Sabbath: to do good or to do evil, to save life or destroy it?" (Luke 6:9)

PERSECUTION

But he replied, "The man who made me well said to me, 'Pick up your mat and walk.'" So they asked him, "Who is this fellow who told you to pick it up and walk?" The man who was healed had no idea who it was, for Jesus had slipped away into the crowd that was there. Later Jesus found him at the temple and said to him, "See, you are well again. Stop sinning or something worse may happen to you." The man went away and told the Jews that it was Jesus who had made him well. So, because Jesus was doing these things on the Sabbath, the Jews persecuted him. JOHN 5:11–16

■

WE MUST BE CAUTIOUS about literally connecting all disease to sin. In another place Jesus was asked why a certain man was born blind: "'Rabbi, who sinned, this man or his parents, that he was born blind?' 'Neither this man nor his parents sinned,' said Jesus, 'but this happened so that the work of God might be displayed in his life. As long as it is day, we must do the work of him who sent me . . . While I am in the world, I am the light of the world'" (John 9:2–5). The man's condition might have grown out of his own sinful nature, but Jesus was unwilling to ascribe specific causation behind the condition of the blindness of the man. He makes another point altogether: God's purpose is at work in all things, including the man's blindness.

Jesus said to them, "My Father is always at his work to this very day, and I, too, am working." For this reason the Jews tried all the harder to kill him; not only was he breaking the Sabbath, but he was even calling God his own Father, making himself equal with God. Jesus gave them this answer: "I tell you the truth, the Son can do nothing by himself; he can do only what he sees his Father doing, because whatever the Father does the Son also does. For the Father loves the Son and shows him all he does. Yes, to your amazement he will show him even greater things than these. For just as the Father raises the dead and gives them life, even so the Son gives life to whom he is pleased to give it. Moreover, the Father judges no one, but has entrusted all judgment to the Son, that all may honor the Son just as they honor the Father. He who does not honor the Son does not honor the Father, who sent him."

JOHN 5:17–23

∎

JESUS ANSWERED HIS ADVERSARIES by making an extraordinary claim about his unique relationship to the Father: "the Son can do nothing by himself; he can do only what he sees his Father doing, because whatever the Father does the Son also does . . ." Everything Jesus does and says comes from the Father. There is no division and no misunderstanding. Just as Jesus is to the Father, so are his disciples and followers to him. We have the same connection through the power of the Holy Spirit who dwells in our hearts. And just as Jesus speaks the language of the Spirit of God, so we, who follow Christ, must learn to understand that same language as we move through our daily lives.

FROM DEATH TO LIFE

I tell you the truth, whoever hears my word and believes him who sent me has eternal life and will not be condemned; he has crossed over from death to life. I tell you the truth, a time is coming and has now come when the dead will hear the voice of the Son of God and those who hear will live. For as the Father has life in himself, so he has granted the Son to have life in himself. And he has given him authority to judge because he is the Son of Man. Do not be amazed at this, for a time is coming when all who are in their graves will hear his voice and come out—those who have done good will rise to live, and those who have done evil will rise to be condemned. By myself I can do nothing; I judge only as I hear, and my judgment is just, for I seek not to please myself but him who sent me. If I testify about myself, my testimony is not valid. There is another who testifies in my favor, and I know that his testimony about me is valid. JOHN 5:24–32

■

MANY ARE OFFENDED BY Jesus' proclamation that "whoever hears my word and believes him who sent me has eternal life and will not be condemned; he has crossed over from death to life." This offends because it forces a choice: By rejecting God (and the one he sent), we are making a decision that will surely have eternal consequences. Jesus is talking about a time in the indeterminate future when "all who are in their graves will hear his voice and come out—those who have done good will rise to live, and those who have done evil will rise to be condemned." Jesus came down from heaven to bring about a good outcome for all who put their trust in him, for he wishes no one to die a "second death" (Revelation 21:6–8).

You have sent to John and he has testified to the truth. Not that I accept human testimony; but I mention it that you may be saved. John was a lamp that burned and gave light, and you chose for a time to enjoy his light. JOHN 5:33–35

■

JESUS SAID THAT JOHN the Baptist "testified to the truth . . . that you may be saved." Jesus knew the trajectory of John's life, from his ministry in the wilderness to his arrest and execution. But it was John's testimony to the truth that exceeded everything else in importance. For in the end John testified to Jesus' true identity and he proclaimed to all who would listen why they needed to believe in the truth of his revelation that Jesus is the Christ. "The Father loves the Son and has placed everything in his hands. Whoever believes in the Son has eternal life, but whoever rejects the Son will not see life, for God's wrath remains on him" (John 3:35–36).

I have testimony weightier than that of John. For the very work that the Father has given me to finish, and which I am doing, testifies that the Father has sent me. And the Father who sent me has himself testified concerning me. You have never heard his voice nor seen his form, nor does his word dwell in you, for you do not believe the one he sent. You diligently study the Scriptures because you think that by them you possess eternal life. These are the Scriptures that testify about me, yet you refuse to come to me to have life. JOHN 5:36–40

■

THIS EPISODE BEGAN WITH Jesus healing the invalid at the pool called Bethesda. The Jewish leaders objected on the pretense that the miraculous healing led to the breaking of the Sabbath and even to blasphemy. The opposition of the religious rulers grew out of the need to protect their tenuous power base by enforcing all kinds of religious rules. Jesus offended them because the Scripture they misused as a weapon of attack was the very same Scripture that testified about Jesus himself. The truth is that these religious leaders were devoid of the Holy Spirit, employing only their intellect to serve their corrupt purposes. Paul drew the same distinction for the Corinthians: "My message and my preaching were not with wise and persuasive words, but with a demonstrations of the Spirit's power, so that your faith might not rest on men's wisdom, but on God's power" (1 Corinthians 2:4–5).

I do not accept praise from men, but I know you. I know that you do not have the love of God in your hearts. I have come in my Father's name, and you do not accept me; but if someone else comes in his own name, you will accept him. How can you believe if you accept praise from one another, yet make no effort to obtain the praise that comes from the only God? But do not think I will accuse you before the Father. Your accuser is Moses, on whom your hopes are set. If you believed Moses, you would believe me, for he wrote about me. But since you do not believe what he wrote, how are you going to believe what I say? JOHN 5:41–47

■

IF WE ARE SURPRISED that Jesus experienced opposition from the religious leaders in Jerusalem, we shouldn't be. C. S. Lewis called our world "enemy-occupied territory." He meant that the world has been turned upside down; a pretender has taken over, and the rightful King has returned to bring about the restoration of the kingdom of God and put to flight the rulers, authorities, and powers of this dark world (Ephesians 6:12). From the time of his birth in a stable to the slaughter of the innocents to the opposition in Jerusalem, a war was waged against Jesus, and the battle only intensified as he headed toward Gethsemane and Golgotha.

One Sabbath Jesus was going through the grain fields, and his disciples began to pick some heads of grain, rub them in their hands and eat the kernels. Some of the Pharisees asked, "Why are you doing what is unlawful on the Sabbath?" Jesus answered them, "Have you never read what David did when he and his companions were hungry? He entered the house of God, and taking the consecrated bread, he ate what is lawful only for priests to eat. And he also gave some to his companions." Then Jesus said to them, "The Son of Man is Lord of the Sabbath." LUKE 6:1–5

■

JESUS HAD A DECISION to make. His followers were hungry, and so they began to eat kernels of grain as they passed through a field. It appears that some Pharisees were following as well, because they claimed that Jesus and his disciples were breaking the law by "harvesting" the grain on the Sabbath. To the Pharisees, it was better to starve than to break the Sabbath. But Jesus countered with an illustration from Scripture where David and his companions ate consecrated bread to stave off hunger. Then he followed with his interpretation that addressed the objections of the rules-obsessed critics. To paraphrase, Jesus said that God, in his wisdom, created the Sabbath for our rest so that we would lay aside time to be with him. The Sabbath was not created to separate us from God, but to draw us closer to him. Man-made religiosity with its endless rules and regulations can kill our relationship with the God who loves us. Jesus came to breathe life back into that relationship.

Another time he went into the synagogue, and a man with a shriveled hand was there. Some of them were looking for a reason to accuse Jesus, so they watched him closely to see if he would heal him on the Sabbath. Jesus said to the man with the shriveled hand, "Stand up in front of everyone." Then Jesus asked them, "Which is lawful on the Sabbath: to do good or to do evil, to save life or to kill?" But they remained silent. He looked around at them in anger and, deeply distressed at their stubborn hearts, said to the man, "Stretch out your hand." He stretched it out, and his hand was completely restored. Then the Pharisees went out and began to plot with the Herodians how they might kill Jesus. MARK 3:1–6

■

SOME IN THE CROWD questioned Jesus' authority to heal the injured man's hand on the Sabbath, but he quickly turned the table on them by asking a straightforward question: "Which is lawful on the Sabbath: to do good or to do evil, to save life or to kill?" The religious leaders had replaced principle with rules that did not promote goodness and justice. If a rule prohibits us from saving a life, then the rule prevents us from understanding God's principle behind the rule. Rules detached from God's principle of light, life, and love will not save life, nor will such rules bring about justice. Notice that Jesus' anger arose from the fact that his detractors had "stubborn hearts." Their blind adherence to man-made rules had turned them into enemies of God. This is why they decided to conspire with the Herodians to kill Jesus.

CHOOSING HIS DISCIPLES

One of those days Jesus went out to a mountainside to pray, and spent the night praying to God. When morning came, he called his disciples to him and chose twelve of them, whom he also designated apostles: Simon (whom he named Peter), his brother Andrew, James, John, Philip, Bartholomew, Matthew, Thomas, James son of Alphaeus, Simon who was called the Zealot, Judas son of James, and Judas Iscariot, who became a traitor. LUKE 6:12–16

■

JESUS NEEDED TO DECIDE who would be appointed his closest followers. It is worth noting that he did not express anxiety, nor did he seek counsel from those flocking around him. Instead, he put all the concerns and needs of everyday life aside, went to a mountainside, and spent the night praying to his Father. Remember, Jesus said he can do nothing by himself; "he can do only what he sees his Father doing, because whatever the Father does the Son also does" (John 5:19). It was through prayer that Jesus sought guidance to pursue his Father's will completely because he knew he could do nothing himself outside of the Father's will.

Aware of this, Jesus withdrew from that place. Many followed him, and he healed all their sick, warning them not to tell who he was. This was to fulfill what was spoken through the prophet Isaiah: "Here is my servant whom I have chosen, the one I love, in whom I delight; I will put my Spirit on him, and he will proclaim justice to the nations. He will not quarrel or cry out; no one will hear his voice in the streets. A bruised reed he will not break, and a smoldering wick he will not snuff out, till he leads justice to victory. In his name the nations will put their hope." **MATTHEW 12:15B–21**

■

IN TELLING HIS STORY of Jesus, Matthew references Hebrew Scripture as a way of confirming to the Jewish people that Jesus is the fulfillment of everything they had been looking and longing for over many centuries. But Jesus is not a warrior like King David, who came to finally liberate the people from the bondage of Roman occupation. Instead, Jesus traveled around healing many of their diseases while at the same time warning the people "not to tell who he was." Matthew simply reminds his readers that Isaiah prophesized that the Messiah would not necessarily be a king in the usual stereotype: "He will not quarrel or cry out; no one will hear his voice in the streets . . ." (Isaiah 42:2).

Jesus went throughout Galilee, teaching in their synagogues, preaching the good news of the kingdom, and healing every disease and sickness among the people. News about him spread all over Syria, and people brought to him all who were ill with various diseases, those suffering severe pain, the demon possessed, those having seizures, and the paralyzed, and he healed them. MATTHEW 4:23–24

■

WE COME TO AN important pause in Matthew's narrative. Jesus had been actively healing the sick, casting out demons, and teaching, but now we are going to sit on a grassy hillside overlooking the wind-swept Sea of Galilee to listen to Jesus as he opens up a radical understanding of what it truly means to serve the living God.

THE POOR IN SPIRIT

Blessed are the poor in spirit, for theirs is the kingdom of heaven.
MATTHEW 5:3

∎

JESUS BEGINS THE BEATITUDES with a statement that throws into question the direction of our striving hearts. Many of us build our lives stone by stone, thinking that our economic well-being will relieve our thirst for something more than the riches and real estate we may acquire through a lifetime of effort. But wealth by itself cannot quench our thirst or satisfy our longing hearts. The poor are blessed because they are less prone to be blinded by the smokescreen of riches that obscures God's authentic role in this world. The poor are not blessed because they are better. God calls all men and women into relationship with himself. It is just harder for the rich to put their trust in God because they may have decided to trust in the power and position that wealth can bring. "A man who has riches without understanding is like the beasts that perish" (Psalm 49:20).

THOSE WHO MOURN

Blessed are those who mourn, for they will be comforted.
MATTHEW 5:4

■

WHEN WE EXPERIENCE THE loss a friend or a family member, we cry out from the bottom of our hearts because we know something irreversible has taken place. We mourn, but Jesus tells us that God comes beside us to mourn with us and to comfort us. We are blessed at these moments because in the midst of our profound aloneness we experience the presence of God. And when we experience his presence, we realize that when we invite God into our lives, we are not alone and will never be alone. "I will never leave you nor forsake you" (Joshua 1:5).

Blessed are the meek, for they will inherit the earth. **MATTHEW 5:5**

■

AGAIN, JESUS TAKES A counterintuitive tack when stating who will inherit the earth. In his novel *Bonfire of the Vanities*, Tom Wolfe's anti-hero, Sherman McCoy, is the "Master of the Universe," a "god" of Wall Street who exudes antipathy for the nameless swarm of humanity that surrounds him in the city of New York. Sherman is a type that can be found in all the major financial centers in the world. He is trapped in a limousine reality and would have no understanding of what Jesus is telling him and us. When Jesus points to meekness, he is emphasizing humbleness of character. The meek are meek not out of a reservoir of weakness, but through the experience of knowing God and knowing that he is God and we are not:

> O Lord, you have searched me and you know me.
> You know when I sit and when I rise;
> You perceive my thoughts from afar.
> You discern my going out and my lying down;
> You are familiar with all my ways.
> Before a word is on my tongue
> You know it completely, O Lord.
>
> (Psalm 139:1–4)

Blessed are those who hunger and thirst for righteousness, for they
will be filled. MATTHEW 5:6

■

IF WE HUNGER AND thirst for something, we will not stop until
we get it. What is your desert thirst? What do you hunger for above
everything else? Jesus is using physical appetites common to all men
and women to point to the one thing that will actually satisfy. Solomon asked God for the wisdom of "a discerning heart to govern
your people and to distinguish right from wrong" (1 Kings 3:9). By
asking for wisdom he was asking God to bless him with the righteousness that can only come from God. Jesus came down to earth
to make that righteousness available to all: "Be reconciled to God.
God made him who had no sin to be sin for us, so that in him we
might become the righteousness of God" (2 Corinthians 5:20–21).

THE MERCIFUL

Blessed are the merciful, for they will be shown mercy. MATTHEW 5:7

■

AS GOD HAS SHOWN mercy to us, so we should show the same measure of mercy to others. In the Parable of the Unmerciful Servant, Jesus tells of a servant who cannot repay his master a large amount of money. The servant begs for mercy and it is granted. But soon enough, the servant demands repayment of monies owed him, and instead of showing the same kindness when the debtor cannot pay, he has the debtor thrown into prison. When the master is told of this, he asks the forgiven servant, "Shouldn't you have had the same mercy on your fellow servant just as I had for you?" (Matthew 18:23–35) Think of the master in the parable as God, and think of the wicked servant as each one of us. We have received God's mercy; in fact, we receive it everyday and we can never pay it back. But we can show it to others every time we have the opportunity. We can represent God in the world by forgiving just as we have been forgiven.

THE PURE IN HEART

Blessed are the pure in heart, for they will see God. MATTHEW 5:8

■

IF WE HAVE THE means, we wash away the grit and grime that naturally accumulates during our daily engagement with the world. If we don't go through the daily rituals of bathing, we begin to feel out of sorts. But outer cleanliness does not necessarily equate with inner cleanliness. Jesus compares the Pharisees to "whitewashed tombs, which look beautiful on the outside but on the inside are full of dead men's bones and everything unclean" (Matthew 23:27–28). The unclean and diseased heart infects the whole person from the inside out, making it less and less possible to "see God." Jesus is the ultimate heart surgeon who repairs and restores, beginning with the heart and working out from there.

Blessed are the peacemakers, for they will be called sons of God.
MATTHEW 5:9

■

WE HEAR PEOPLE SPEAK of peace all the time, but how can there
be peace when, in the deeper recesses of the heart, we are often at
war with God? It might be said that human history began with the
rebellion in the Garden of Eden. One thoughtless act of defiance led
directly to all the enmity, pain, suffering, murder, and mayhem that
characterize so much of the historical narrative. Peacemaking, as
opposed to peacekeeping, can only take root if we first make peace
with God through Christ. Then genuine peacemaking can begin,
one person at a time.

THE PERSECUTED

Blessed are those who are persecuted because of righteousness, for theirs is the kingdom of heaven. MATTHEW 5:10

■

FROM OUR EARLIEST DAYS, we expect to be rewarded for good behavior. When the opposite occurs, we feel the pain of injustice to our very core. This correlation of good behavior and reward is so pervasive that we often expect that our life will get better if we follow Jesus. But the weight of the narrative thus far suggests the opposite is just as true. Jesus' life was threatened by Herod's troops when he was a young child, he was persecuted and reviled by the religious elite for performing miracles on the Sabbath, and he was even rejected in his hometown of Nazareth. Jesus experienced persecution, his disciples experienced persecution, and the church has experienced persecution down through the ages and even to the present time.

GREAT IS YOUR REWARD IN HEAVEN

Blessed are you when people insult you, persecute you and falsely say all kinds of evil against you because of me. Rejoice and be glad, because great is your reward in heaven, for in the same way they persecuted the prophets who were before you. MATTHEW 5:11–12

■

JESUS WARNS HIS FOLLOWERS that they will experience persecution and "all kinds of evil," but he is not just referring to one period of time two thousand years ago. Jesus is referring to every period until he returns. One contemporary example is the life and martyrdom of Dietrich Bonhoeffer. He was a voice crying out in the wilderness of Nazi Germany, warning of the coming darkness as the totalitarian plague reached even into the church itself. Bonhoeffer was reviled, lied about, and persecuted because he would not abandon Jesus in order to accommodate the Nazi masters. Even when he found a safe haven in England and the United States, he did not rest until he could return to Germany to live out his faith, even to the point of death. But surely "great is (his) reward in heaven."

THE SALT OF THE EARTH

You are the salt of the earth. But if the salt loses its saltiness, how can it be made salty again? It is no longer good for anything, except to be thrown out and trampled by men. MATTHEW 5:13

■

JESUS SAYS TO PRAY that God's kingdom will come. We have been enrolled as foot soldiers in bringing about the restoration of God's kingdom, which is not yet, but will be. Jesus says we are a different kind of soldier. We are like the salt of the earth; as missionaries of the Word, we are here to reach out to a resistant world with the truth of Jesus Christ as Lord and Savior, but in an appealing and winning way. When you become salt of the earth, you take on the characteristic properties of salt: You provide flavor while preserving perishables from corruption. "Let your conversation be always full of grace, seasoned with salt, so that you may know how to answer everyone" (Colossians 4:6).

You are the light of the world. A city on a hill cannot be hidden. Neither do people light a lamp and put it under a bowl. Instead they put it on its stand, and it gives light to everyone in the house. In the same way, let your light shine before men, that they may see your good deeds and praise your Father in heaven. MATTHEW 5:14–16

■

WHEN JESUS SAYS, "YOU are the light of the world," he is commissioning his followers to go out into the world to reflect the light that comes from "your Father in heaven." In the beginning, God said, "'Let there be light,' and there was light (and) God saw that it was good" (Genesis 1:3). With the fatal choice of Adam and Eve in the Garden of Eden, that light was enshrouded but not extinguished. Jesus came to bring light back into a darkened world. The goodness of the light of God is passed through Jesus to his followers, who are to reflect that light much as the moon reflects the light of the sun. By being disciples of Jesus Christ, we are called to pass on the goodness of the Creator of that light just as Jesus passed it on to his own apostles and disciples through the gift of the Holy Spirit.

Do not think that I have come to abolish the Law or the Prophets;
I have not come to abolish them but to fulfill them. I tell you the
truth, until heaven and earth disappear, not the smallest letter, not
the least stroke of a pen, will by any means disappear from the Law
until everything is accomplished. MATTHEW 5:17–18

■

ON SEVERAL OCCASIONS RELIGIOUS rulers accused Jesus of breaking the law, but Jesus countered by reframing our understanding of
God's purpose behind his giving us the law in the first place. Jesus
is saying the law, with all its nuances and complexities, cannot be
an end in itself. Through time and tradition, the law had become
an instrument for enforcing compliance while sustaining a political
power base for an elite few. But God never intended the law to be a
rulebook. It was meant to reflect principles of life that go deeper
than a catalog of rules that need to be checked off in order to get by.
By digging down to the underlying principles, Jesus opens up for us
an understanding that includes God's purpose behind the whole-
ness, fullness, and congruency that truly shapes everything we
experience.

TEACHING AND PRACTICING
THESE COMMANDMENTS

Anyone who breaks one of the least of these commandments and teaches others to do the same will be called least in the kingdom of heaven, but whoever practices and teaches these commands will be called great in the kingdom of heaven. For I tell you that unless your righteousness surpasses that of the Pharisees and the teachers of the law, you will certainly not enter the kingdom of heaven. MATTHEW 5:19–20

■

UNLESS WE RECOGNIZE THAT Jesus is using hyperbole, we will misread the point he is making in this teaching. He is setting up two impossibilities. First, if we break "one of the least of these commandments . . . (we) will be called least in the kingdom of heaven . . ." And then he goes further: ". . . unless your righteousness surpasses that of the Pharisees and the teachers of the law, you will certainly not enter the kingdom of heaven." Why does he do this? At the time, Jesus was teaching people who had conflated God's law with God Himself. God gave us the law as a signpost to point us in his direction and to help us stay on the good and right path. The path may vary from person to person, but it is always leading us back into relationship with God the Father through the guiding Spirit of his Son, Jesus Christ.

BE RECONCILED FIRST

You have heard that it was said to the people long ago, "Do not murder, and anyone who murders will be subject to judgment." But I tell you that anyone who is angry with his brother will be subject to judgment. Again, anyone who says to his brother, "Raca," is answerable to the Sanhedrin. But anyone who says, "You fool!" will be in danger of the fire of hell. Therefore, if you are offering your gift at the altar and there remember that your brother has something against you, leave your gift there in front of the altar. First go and be reconciled to your brother; then come and offer your gift. MATTHEW 5:21–24

■

JUST AS A DEADLY avalanche can begin with something as insignificant as a small stone, so murder can grow out of something trivial, such as calling someone a derogatory name. David's crime began when he saw a beautiful married woman bathing and ended with the premeditated murder of her husband Uriah. Envy drove Cain to lure his brother Abel to an isolated field and strike him dead. Jesus is speaking to the consequences that trailed Adam and Eve after they were exiled from the Garden of Eden. God's law against murder and adultery and other crimes, by itself, cannot stop men and women from initiating actions that sweep them up in destructive consequences. Envy, hatred, and lust cannot be weighed, but what issues forth from a malevolent heart can be heavy indeed: "He who is pregnant with evil and conceives trouble gives birth to disillusionment . . . The trouble he causes recoils on himself; his violence comes down on his own head" (Psalm 7:14, 16)

SETTLE MATTERS QUICKLY WITH
YOUR ADVERSARY

Settle matters quickly with your adversary who is taking you to court. Do it while you are still with him on the way, or he may hand you over to the judge, and the judge may hand you over to the officer, and you may be thrown into prison. I tell you the truth, you will not get out until you have paid the last penny. MATTHEW 5:25–26

■

JUSTICE AS PRACTICED IN the world is a poor shadow of the real thing. Instead of settling a matter, often the law entangles adversaries in an endless web of claims and counter claims, eating up money, time, and happiness. Instead, Jesus sets before us a stark contrast between seeking worldly justice and living the kingdom ethic that points to a way of life that goes far beyond just fulfilling the simpler aspects of the law. "Settle matters quickly with your adversary who is taking you to court."

SIN BEGINS IN THE HEART

You have heard that it was said, "Do not commit adultery." But I tell you that anyone who looks at a woman lustfully has already committed adultery with her in his heart. If your right eye causes you to sin, gouge it out and throw it away. It is better for you to lose one part of your body than for your whole body to be thrown into hell. And if your right hand causes you to sin, cut it off and throw it away. It is better for you to lose one part of your body than for your whole body to go into hell. MATTHEW 5:27–30

■

JESUS MAKES IT CLEAR that the act of adultery is the offspring of a heart filled with adulterous longings. The law is impotent in restraining the impulses of an unruly heart. If the boundaries erected by governments and religious leaders were truly effective, why would we need the police, courts, and lawyers to enforce their statutes and decrees? Jesus aims at a higher standard by pointing to the source of the problem: individual will. If I want to do something, I will often plunge ahead without considering the consequences. Law cannot restrain me. But Jesus aims at redirecting my desires and appetites to the object of my original love: God Himself.

DIVORCE

It has been said, "Anyone who divorces his wife must give her a certificate of divorce." But I tell you that anyone who divorces his wife, except for marital unfaithfulness, causes her to become an adulteress, and anyone who marries the divorced woman commits adultery. MATTHEW 5:31–32

■

"SO GOD CREATED MAN in his own image, in the image of God he created him; male and female he created them" (Genesis 1:22). After he created them, male and female, he instituted marriage as a way to bond them to build a life together, to raise children together, and to worship God the Creator together. "For this reason a man will leave his father and mother and be united to his wife, and they will become one flesh" (Genesis 2:24). The key word here is "united." The fall in the Garden of Eden fractured the relationship between Adam and Eve, and divorce is one important example of the consequences of the fall. Jesus is referring to the original relationship, not the one marred by sin and dissention. He is talking about restoring the essential goodness of the original purpose of marriage; he is talking about God's higher standard.

DO NOT SWEAR AN OATH AT ALL

Again, you have heard that it was said to the people long ago, "Do not break your oath, but keep the oaths you have made to the Lord." But I tell you, do not swear at all: either by heaven, for it is God's throne; or by the earth, for it is his footstool; or by Jerusalem, for it is the city of the Great King. And do not swear by your head, for you cannot make even one hair white or black. Simply let your "Yes" be "Yes," and your "No," "No"; anything beyond this comes from the evil one. MATTHEW 5:33–37

■

IN OUR MODERN WORLD, a handshake is never enough. A "yes" or a "no" is augmented by either a battery of lawyers and accountants or is modified by innumerable qualifiers. This is the reality we accept; furthermore, we consider it naïve to risk everything on someone's word when his or her intentions are not known. But Jesus is not content to adopt the standards of this world. He focuses on kingdom standards, where the law, as constructed by man, cannot go. Jesus sets a higher standard that is built on a level of integrity that transforms word and action into a single reality: "Simply let your 'Yes' be 'Yes' and your 'No,' 'No'; anything beyond this comes from the evil one."

You have heard that it was said, "Eye for eye, and tooth for tooth." But I tell you, do not resist an evil person. If someone strikes you on the right cheek, turn to him the other also. And if someone wants to sue you and take your tunic, let him have your cloak as well. If someone forces you to go one mile, go with him two miles. Give to the one who asks you, and do not turn away from the one who wants to borrow from you. MATTHEW 5:38–42

■

RULES ARE NECESSARY FOR ordering a decent society. Systems and procedures are necessary for a society to function in ways that promote the general welfare of the people. But rules can easily be corrupted and abused by those in positions of power. It is axiomatic that rules can be used as easily against people as for them. When Jesus says, "Do not resist an evil person," he is not setting forth a new rule. He is giving us a higher standard that is based on foundational principles that support rules. Jesus is always concerned with teaching deeper truths. Here he is saying that rules do not change a person's heart. The principles of a deeper life connected to the kingdom of God bring about genuine transformation, first in the individual, then in families and communities, and ultimately in society itself.

LOVE YOUR ENEMIES

You have heard that it was said, "Love your neighbor and hate your enemy." But I tell you: Love your enemies and pray for those who persecute you, that you may be sons of your Father in heaven. He causes his sun to rise on the evil and the good, and sends rain on the righteous and the unrighteous. MATTHEW 5:43–45

■

IF POLITICIANS ARE CAPABLE of anything, it is swaying large crowds with rhetorical flourishes and visionary pronouncements and promises. Jesus is not of their ilk. He heals individuals, he chose common fishermen to be his followers, and while on earth he tried to avoid crowds and often stole away when people were seeking him. Like John the Baptist, Jesus annoyed and troubled the political and religious authorities of his time. And his teaching follows this same pattern. He does not encourage rebellion. Rather, he deals with each one of us as individuals. He miraculously healed a man with evil spirits and caused a crippled man to walk. He invited a tax collector to dine with him, and he cured a woman who had been suffering for years. He taught in the same way, keeping close to the yearnings and compulsions of the human heart. Most of those who were rich, famous, and powerful in Jesus' time vanished without a trace. But not Jesus. He continues to live in the hearts and minds of people, generation after generation.

BE PERFECT

If you love those who love you, what reward will you get? Are not even the tax collectors doing that? And if you greet only your brothers, what are you doing more than others? Do not even pagans do that? Be perfect, therefore, as your heavenly Father is perfect. MATTHEW 5:46–48

■

JESUS SAYS, "BE PERFECT, therefore, as your heavenly Father is perfect." Why would he set before us an impossibly high standard? Jesus knows that men and women, in their sinful condition, will always be short of perfection. Jesus did not want us to waste our lives wallowing in regret and sorrow. Rather he came to liberate us from that very condition, not to make us perfect, but to help us move toward the Father as we go through this life on earth, always having in view before us the perfect holiness of the Father.

ACTS OF SELF-RIGHTEOUSNESS

Be careful not to do your 'acts of righteousness' before men, to be seen by them. If you do, you will have no reward from your Father in heaven. **MATTHEW 6:1**

■

THE SCREWTAPE LETTERS IS a wickedly unsettling book because it is written from the viewpoint of a lieutenant of the devil himself, who is scheming to undermine a recent convert to Christianity. In one letter, Screwtape writes about the virtue of humility and how to use it to undermine the enemy (the recent convert): "Catch him at the moment when he is really poor in spirit and smuggle into his mind the gratifying reflection, 'By jove! I'm really humble,' and almost immediately pride—pride at his own humility—will appear" (*The Screwtape Letters*). As with humility, so with righteousness: The moment we become conscious of our own righteousness, pride slips in and self-righteousness chases out genuine righteousness.

So when you give to the needy, do not announce it with trumpets, as the hypocrites do in the synagogues and on the streets, to be honored by men. I tell you the truth, they have received their reward in full. But when you give to the needy, do not let your left hand know what your right hand is doing, so that your giving may be in secret. Then your Father, who sees what is done in secret, will reward you. MATTHEW 6:2–4

■

THE KINGDOMS OF THIS earth are but a poor representation of the genuine kingdom that is ruled by the KING of KINGS and the LORD of LORDS (Revelation 17:15). The rich and powerful of this world may give to the poor, but they often do it to show off their generosity and consolidate their temporal power. One of the three temptations Satan offered Jesus was to rule over "all the kingdoms of the world" (Luke 4:5), but what was being presented was a chimera that with time would vanish as if it never existed. Jesus rejected this phony model; instead, he says, give out the goodness and abundance God has bestowed on you. For God sees your acts of generosity and he knows your heart. To act for any reason other than mirroring God's grace is to act outside of the truth of Jesus' teaching.

HOW TO PRAY

And when you pray, do not be like the hypocrites, for they love to pray standing in the synagogues and on the street corners to be seen by men. I tell you the truth, they have received their reward in full. But when you pray, go into your room, close the door and pray to your Father, who is unseen. Then your Father, who sees what is done in secret, will reward you. MATTHEW 6:5–6

■ ◦

IN A VERY DIFFERENT context, Jesus says to Peter, "Get behind me, Satan! You do not have in mind the things of God, but the things of men" (Mark 8:33). In the Sermon on the Mount, Jesus says much the same thing about our motives behind praying. If we pray to impress people with our religious prowess, we are subverting the very reason to pray. Jesus says that prayer is about connecting with God. It is an ongoing conversation, a dialoge where we not only can speak, but we can be spoken to as well. When it comes to prayer, we need to step outside of the discourse and commerce of everyday life so that we can adjust the attitudes of our heart to hear and to be heard, to speak and to be spoken to, not in the normal way of such things, but in the intimate company of God Himself.

And when you pray, do not keep on babbling like pagans, for they think they will be heard because of their many words. Do not be like them, for your Father knows what you need before you ask him. MATTHEW 6:7–8

■

PRAYER IS THE ESSENTIAL link that connects us to God, who is not detached and foreign, but who desires to give each one of us the good things that he planned for us from the very beginning. After David fell into temptation and sin, he implored God to not take his Holy Spirit away because that would be worse than death (Psalm 51:11). God is not impersonal; he knows everything about us, and he wants us to know him. But if we fake it and babble like the pagans and puff ourselves up like the hypocritical religious leaders, we are engaging in mere pretense that in the end leaves us unhappy, alone, and dissatisfied. God is not far away (James 4:8). He is near, and it is through the power of prayer that we can draw ever closer to him. We should be confident that he hears us and longs for our eternal well-being.

THE LORD'S PRAYER

This, then, is how you should pray: "Our Father in heaven, hallowed be your name, your kingdom come, your will be done on earth as it is in heaven." MATTHEW 6:9–10

■

THE LORD'S PRAYER IS so familiar that it is easy to miss its depth and complexity. In the first sentence alone, Jesus includes four declarations. First, he addresses God as "Our Father," not as some stern and unfeeling taskmaster, but as "Daddy," just as a child would address his own loving and protective father. Then he says, "hallowed be your name," which sets this Father apart as holy and perfect and above the sinful and imperfect condition of men and women on earth. Then Jesus prays that God's kingdom will be restored here on earth, replacing the kingdoms that are at war with God and his people. Finally, he prays for the unity that can only exist when the original design takes root here on earth, echoing the harmony that existed at the very beginning when God created the world and all the creatures in it, and he saw that it was very good (Genesis 1:31).

DAILY BREAD

Give us today our daily bread. MATTHEW 6:11

■

IN THIS PLENTIFUL AND prosperous corner of the world, it is too easy to forget what would happen if all the foods we find in markets and restaurants suddenly vanished. It is difficult to imagine a world where this kind of depravation could become a reality, but for many, getting access to food is the harsh reality of daily life. When times are good, it is easy to assume provision from the endless supplies afforded by science and enterprise. But is this a reasonable position? Jesus prays to God for daily provision because he knows that God is the only true provider. As he says elsewhere in the Sermon on the Mount, "Therefore, do not worry about tomorrow, for tomorrow will worry about itself. Each day has enough trouble of its own" (Matthew 6:34). To paraphrase another prayer: "Lord, for tomorrow and its needs I do not pray . . . Please keep me, guide me, love me, Lord, just for today." Recognizing our daily dependence on God is the only way to live each and every day.

FORGIVE

Forgive us our debts, as we also have forgiven our debtors.

MATTHEW 6:12

■

WHETHER WE USE THE word "trespasses," "debts," or "sins" when praying the Lord's Prayer, we are essentially asking God for forgiveness for the countless ways we have fallen away from him. In an earlier encounter, Jesus makes his mission on earth abundantly clear: "It is not the healthy who need a doctor, but the sick. I have not come to call the righteous, but sinners" (Mark 2:17). Paul says "all have sinned and fall short of the glory of God" (Romans 3:23), so when we are praying, "Forgive us," there are no exceptions or exemptions. Everyone needs to ask for God's forgiveness because our sin causes us to betray him time and again. When Paul asks, "Who will rescue me from this body of death," he gives us the answer immediately: "Thanks be to God —through Jesus Christ our Lord!" (Roman 7:24–25) This one line of the Lord's Prayer is liberating because without forgiveness, we will never escape the destructive consequences growing out of our sin-prone nature. But it is not just about us: We need to forgive as God has forgiven us. Just as God's forgiveness cost him dearly, to forgive others as God has forgiven us can be costly. But from an eternal point of view, the cost is worth it.

DELIVER US

And lead us not into temptation, but deliver us from the evil one.
MATTHEW 6:13

■

WHY WOULD GOD LEAD us into temptation? Perhaps it is best to think of this dilemma as fundamental to our relationship with God. Jesus seems to be requesting that God not place him in a situation where he would be tempted to betray God. When Jesus was tempted by the devil three times in the wilderness, he resisted by remaining centered in the Holy Spirit. This prayer acknowledges the existence of an evil one, who wanders the earth looking for people not able to withstand the devil's schemes. Here is the promise for those who believe: "No temptation has seized you except what is common to man. And God is faithful; he will not let you be tempted beyond what you can bear. But when you are tempted, he will also provide a way out so that you can stand up under it" (1 Corinthians 10:13).

When you fast, do not look somber as the hypocrites do, for they disfigure their faces to show men they are fasting. I tell you the truth, they have received their reward in full. But when you fast, put oil on your head and wash your face, so that it will not be obvious to men that you are fasting, but only to your Father, who is unseen; and your Father, who sees what is done in secret, will reward you. MATTHEW 6:16–18

■

WHAT DO YOU HUNGER for? If it is food, you are seeking satisfaction from the bounty of God's beneficence. If we take the provision without acknowledging a debt to the provider, we will continue to hunger and thirst even after we have satiated our temporary need. And so we want more and more. Fasting is a way of keeping our relationship with God and the natural world in balance. Even so, Jesus warns against the imbalance that comes from using the traditional religious practice of fasting to affirm to other men and women our own godliness and righteousness. This serves only to push God away, even as it seems to lift the "hypocrites" up.

Do not store up for yourselves treasures on earth, where moth and rust destroy, and where thieves break in and steal. But store up for yourselves treasures in heaven, where moth and rust do not destroy, and where thieves do not break in and steal. For where your treasure is, there your heart will be also. MATTHEW 6:19–21

■

TREASURE IS A TANTALIZING word. One might think of rugged treasure chests filled with silver and gold coins, pirates, exotic islands, and endless adventure. Or it could be winning the lottery, or living in a luxurious house with an expensive car parked in the front courtyard. But Jesus says treasure is something else: Treasure is the outward manifestation of the inward inclination of the heart. If we spend our time accumulating wealth, then we are permitting that drive to become our ruling passion. Wealth can be a blessing, but when the love of wealth monopolizes all of our attention, then it has the power to separate us from the love of God. It is then that we become like the Rich Young Ruler who cannot abandon his love of wealth and all that it brings him for the love of Christ and all that it could have brought him (Mark 10:17–22).

The eye is the lamp of the body. If your eyes are good, your whole body will be full of light. But if your eyes are bad, your whole body will be full of darkness. If then the light within you is darkness, how great is that darkness! MATTHEW 6:22–23

∎

AT THE VERY BEGINNING of Genesis, God says, "'Let there be light,' and there was light. God saw that the light was good, and he separated the light from the darkness" (Genesis 1:3). But it is the darkness of sin that has separated us from the goodness of the light of God. Elsewhere, Jesus diagnoses the problem this way: "Light has come into the world, but men loved darkness instead of light because their deeds were evil" (John 3:19). Jesus infers that the good eye lets the light of truth pass into the heart, but the bad eye serves as a screen to filter out the goodness of God, leaving us alienated from him. Jesus' mission is to bring the goodness of the light of God into every man and woman's heart: "I am the light of the world. Whoever follows me will never walk in darkness, but will have the light of life" (John 8:12).

HOW CAN YOU SERVE TWO MASTERS?

No one can serve two masters. Either he will hate the one and love the other, or he will be devoted to the one and despise the other. You cannot serve both God and Money. MATTHEW 6:24

■

OFTEN WE ATTEMPT TO avoid the problem of competing loves by pretending no conflict exists, but eventually we come to a fork in the road that requires that we choose one direction or the other. When it comes to the powerful attraction of money and all that wealth can bring us, it is not surprising that the draw of money has an almost spiritual hold on our affections. It is not gold or silver, however, that claims our attention; it is status, power, and the security that money buys that sucks up so much of our affection and time, leaving little room for anything else, including God. "For it is the love of money that is the root of all kinds of evil. Some people eager for money, have wandered from the faith and pierced themselves with many griefs" (1 Timothy 6:10).

WHY DO YOU WORRY?

Therefore I tell you, do not worry about your life, what you will eat or drink; or about your body, what you will wear. Is not life more important than food, and the body more important than clothes? Look at the birds of the air; they do not sow or reap or store away in barns, and yet your heavenly Father feeds them. Are you not much more valuable than they? Who of you by worrying can add a single hour to his life? **MATTHEW 6:25–27**

■

DAVID, THE SHEPHERD BOY, had every reason to worry, because the fate of Israel rested in his hands. Before him stood Goliath, the giant warrior of the Philistines. David was anything but a warrior, and yet he volunteered to battle the fearsome giant who petrified the entire Israel army. Even King Saul dared not take on this seemingly invincible foe. After David rejected Saul's armor for protection, he advanced towards Goliath with nothing but a sling and five smooth stones. The giant mocked him, to which David replied, "You come against me with sword and spear and javelin, but I come against you in the name of the Lord Almighty, the God of the armies of Israel whom you have defied. . . . All those gathered here will know that it is not by sword or spear that the Lord saves; for the battle is the Lord's, and he will give all of you into our hands" (1 Samuel 17:45,47). It is faith that drives out fear and stress and worry. It is living in that faith today that makes the difference. Tomorrow's problems and difficulties can be dealt with then.

And why do you worry about clothes? See how the lilies of the field grow. They do not labor or spin. Yet I tell you that not even Solomon in all his splendor was dressed like one of these. If that is how God clothes the grass of the field, which is here today and tomorrow is thrown into the fire, will he not much more clothe you, O you of little faith? MATTHEW 6:28–30

■

JESUS IS TALKING ABOUT sufficient provision in these verses. He is saying, look around; if God will provide for the flowers of the field and the grass of the meadows, why do you worry that he will not provide for you? We worry, in part, because we have too little faith in the power of God's sufficiency to provide what is needed—truly needed—when it is needed. Our lack of faith expresses itself when we worry that we will not have enough, that God will not provide, and that we need to strive to provide for our own needs. This is why Jesus addresses his listeners as "O you of little faith."

So do not worry, saying, 'What shall we eat?' or 'What shall we drink?' or 'What shall we wear?' For the pagans run after all these things, and your heavenly Father knows that you need them. But seek first his kingdom and his righteousness, and all these things will be given to you as well. MATTHEW 6:31–33

■

THE KINGDOMS OF THIS earth are filled with pagans who pursue a philosophy that can be summed up this way: "Let us eat and drink, for tomorrow we die" (1 Corinthians 15:32). For them, life is fundamentally meaningless; after dealing with the needs of the body, there is only the nothingness of death and oblivion. Jesus says there is a different kingdom that feeds and clothes and attends to the whole person and not just the body. The devil would like to have us believe that his kingdoms here on earth are the only kingdoms to seek, but when tempted by Satan, Jesus declared that man is more than a bundle of physical appetites. "(God) humbled you, causing you to hunger and then feeding you with manna, which neither you nor your fathers had known, to teach you that man does not live on bread alone but on every word that comes from the mouth of the Lord" (Deuteronomy 8:3).

FOCUS ON THE NEEDS OF THE MOMENT

Therefore do not worry about tomorrow, for tomorrow will worry about itself. Each day has enough trouble of its own. MATTHEW 6:34

■

JESUS MAKES A CONCLUDING statement about what he has been teaching: Trust in God and know that he will provide. Paul puts it this way: "Do not be anxious about anything, but in everything by prayer and petition with thanksgiving, present your requests to God. And the peace of God which transcends all understanding, will guard your hearts and your minds in Christ Jesus" (Philippians 4:6–7).

JUDGING

Do not judge, or you too will be judged. For in the same way you judge others, you will be judged, and with the measure you use, it will be measured to you. MATTHEW 7:1–2

■

OFTEN, WHEN WE FIND ourselves being judgmental, we are falling into the trap of assuming full knowledge of a situation when only partial knowledge is possible. Only God can judge from the position of full knowledge, for only "he knows the secrets of the heart" (Psalm 44:21). Though partial knowledge is all that is available to us (1 Corinthians 13:12), it should not be an excuse for abandoning discernment. Jesus warns us not to place ourselves in God's position by assuming superior or complete knowledge. Instead be discerning in all your interactions with people, knowing that wisdom is a gift of God that flows out of a discerning heart (1 Kings 3:10–12).

BLINDNESS

Why do you look at the speck of sawdust in your brother's eye and pay no attention to the plank in your own eye? How can you say to your brother, 'Let me take the speck out of your eye,' when all the time there is a plank in your own eye? You hypocrite, first take the plank out of your own eye, and then you will see clearly to remove the speck from your brother's eye. MATTHEW 7:3–5

■

JESUS USES METAPHOR AND hyperbole to make a point about our willingness to judge others while turning a blind eye to our own flaws and idiosyncratic patterns of behavior. This is the willfulness of our sinful nature at work: Deflect attention from our own individual shortcomings by pointing the finger at others. But holier-than-thou posturing does not deceive Jesus. He knows that accusing and blaming go all the way back to the Garden of Eden when, after disregarding God's one prohibition, the man and woman not only blamed one another for their actions but they blamed God as well. Without redemption, nothing will ever change.

HOW TO USE YOUR GIFTS

Do not give dogs what is sacred; do not throw your pearls to pigs.
If you do, they may trample them under their feet, and then turn
and tear you to pieces. MATTHEW 7:6

■

WHEN JESUS TELLS US to not give what is sacred to dogs, nor cast
pearls before swine, he is drawing on the wisdom of Scripture to
make the point that gifts from God can be easily squandered on
those who refuse to hear and accept the truth. Because his statement
seems harsh and categorical, it might be tempting to read it as an
attack on gender, race, or class. But consider when, as reported in
Matthew and Mark, a Gentile woman pleaded with Jesus to save her
sick daughter, Jesus replied that the Jews must come first: "for it is
not right to take the children's bread and toss it to their dogs" (Mark
7:27). The woman persisted because she had faith that Jesus could
save her daughter, and her faith trumped everything else. Seeing the
strength of her faith, Jesus responded by granting what she begged
for: "For such a reply, you may go; the demon has left your daughter" (Mark 7:29).

ASK, SEEK, KNOCK

Ask and it will be given to you; seek and you will find; knock and the door will be opened to you. For everyone who asks receives; he who seeks finds; and to him who knocks, the door will be opened.
MATTHEW 7:7–8

■

FOR SOME, IT IS a surprise to discover that the Christian life is dynamic at its core; there is nothing static about it. In these verses, Jesus employs three active verbs to help us understand that God is constantly inviting us to walk with him. Jesus commands us to "ask," to "seek," and to "knock." We are being called out of spiritual hibernation and into an ongoing dialogue as we work out God's will in and through our lives. We have been invited into this dynamic relationship with the Lord, but we cannot enter into that life unless we take action by knocking to have the door opened so that we can walk through by the power of the Holy Spirit into the life and relationship God yearns for us to have with him.

SUMMING UP THE LAW AND THE PROPHETS

Which of you, if his son asks for bread, will give him a stone? Or if he asks for a fish, will give him a snake? If you, then, though you are evil, know how to give good gifts to your children, how much more will your Father in heaven give good gifts to those who ask him! So in everything, do to others what you would have them do to you, for this sums up the Law and the Prophets. MATTHEW 7:9–12

■

WHO WILL WIN THE battle for the human heart? It boils down to whom we will follow. Who will we love? Will God be at the center of everything in our lives or will we turn to other substitutes? Can we live in a state of unresolved sin and truly love God at the same time, or are we condemned to live out a life of warring loyalties? Jesus knew that he had come from the Father to finally resolve this battle between Satan and God for the hearts of men and women. If the inclination to sin remains embedded in the human heart, then living by the principles of the Law and the Prophets will be impossible. What Jesus does not say here is that it will be his sacrifice on the cross that will open the door for every man and woman to finally resolve the battles of the heart by committing everything to a genuine relationship with the Lord through the power of the Holy Spirit. Jesus makes it possible for us to begin living out the admonition, "Be holy because I, the Lord your God am holy." (Leviticus 19:2)

Enter through the narrow gate. For wide is the gate and broad is the road that leads to destruction, and many enter through it. But small is the gate and narrow the road that leads to life, and only a few find it. MATTHEW 7:13–14

∎

TIME AND AGAIN, THE Bible reinforces the fact the God gives men and women the gift to choose to follow or rebel, to walk the path that God has laid out for us or to go another way. God made us to be free, but Satan uses that freedom to entangle us in choices that separate us from God. If we choose the path of least resistance, we will end up living outside of the abundant blessings of the kingdom of God. God warned Moses that while he gifted all men and women with the power to choose, he also set forth the consequences that would flow from choosing unwisely: "So be careful to do what the Lord your God has commanded you; do not turn aside to the right or the left. Walk in all the ways that the Lord has commanded you, so that you may live and prosper and prolong your days in the land that you will possess" (Deuteronomy 5:32–33). In order to pass through that narrow gate, we must turn away from serving the idols of this world and choose to place our full allegiance in the one true God. Jesus invites us to do just that.

BEWARE OF FALSE PROPHETS

Watch out for false prophets. They come to you in sheep's clothing, but inwardly they are ferocious wolves. By their fruit you will
recognize them. Do people pick grapes from thorn bushes, or figs
from thistles? Likewise every good tree bears good fruit, but a bad
tree bears bad fruit. A good tree cannot bear bad fruit, and a bad
tree cannot bear good fruit. Every tree that does not bear good
fruit is cut down and thrown into the fire. Thus, by their fruit you
will recognize them. MATTHEW 7:15–20

■

IN OUR OWN TIME, false prophets proliferate using the veneer of
science as their "sheep's clothing" to mask the darker purposes of
their claims to the truth of their idols. Thousands of years ago it was
no different: "From the least to the greatest, all are greedy for gain;
prophets and priests alike, all practice deceit" (Jeremiah 6:13). Jesus
warns us that not all truth tellers are truthful. It is up to us to sift
through counterfeit claims to find that which is authentic. We need
to be observant and discerning, and we need to weigh everything by
the actual "fruit" produced. If we don't, we will be "a reed swayed
by the wind," believing in every new, faddish idea that comes along
instead of the truth that flows from the Word of God.

I NEVER KNEW YOU

Not everyone who says to me, 'Lord, Lord,' will enter the kingdom of heaven, but only he who does the will of my Father who is in heaven. Many will say to me on that day, 'Lord, Lord, did we not prophesy in your name, and in your name drive out demons and perform many miracles?' Then I will tell them plainly, 'I never knew you. Away from me, you evildoers!' MATTHEW 7:21–23

■

HOW WOULD IT FEEL to hear Jesus say, "I never knew you"? We can claim we know Christ and we can even do all kinds of good works in his name, but if we do not do "the will of my Father who is in heaven," there is no authenticity in our claim. We remain in our sins. Following Jesus is not dependent on an outward show of religious fervor or an accumulation of achievements; it is dependent on a heart that yearns to do God's will in everything. "But if we walk in the light as he is in the light, we have fellowship with one another, and the blood of Jesus, his son, purifies us from all sin" (1 John 1:7).

Therefore everyone who hears these words of mine and puts them into practice is like a wise man who built his house on the rock. The rain came down, the streams rose, and the winds blew and beat against that house; yet it did not fall, because it had its foundation on the rock. But everyone who hears these words of mine and does not put them into practice is like a foolish man who built his house on sand. The rain came down, the streams rose, and the winds blew and beat against that house, and it fell with a great crash. MATTHEW 7:24–27

■

JESUS ENDS HIS SERMON with a teaching on the wisdom of building on strong foundations. He is asking us, what is your foundation built on? He reaches back to the wisdom literature of the Scriptures to make a final point about the very nature of the decisions we make in the way we live. Wisdom has its seat in discernment. If we choose to build our lives on the solid foundation of the Word of God, then we will be able to withstand the rains and wind that we will surely experience. But if our foundation is like sand, then, when the adversities of this life come upon us, we will be vulnerable and defenseless. It is not our strength that will ever prevail; it is the Lord's: "I love you, Lord, my strength. The Lord is my rock, my fortress and my deliverer; my God is my rock, in whom I take refuge. He is my shield and the horn of my salvation, my stronghold" (Psalm 18:1–2).

HE TAUGHT WITH AUTHORITY

When Jesus had finished saying these things, the crowds were amazed at his teaching, because he taught as one who had authority, and not as their teachers of the law. MATTHEW 7:28–29

■

WHY WERE THE CROWDS "amazed" by Jesus' teachings? Jesus did not come to them with titles or university degrees; he came without political or religious position; he seemed to emerge out of nowhere, and yet he "taught as one who had authority." What the people sensed was that Jesus taught under the authority of God. And the message he imparted was that the authority given over to Satan by Adam and Eve was about to be won back. Jesus came to reorder the nature of the kingdoms of the world by establishing his kingdom here on earth to replace the counterfeit kingdom erected by Satan. The Sermon on the Mount is the summation of the principles of God's authority on earth. All authority comes from God and flows through his servant believers.

I AM WILLING

When he (Jesus) came down from the mountainside, large crowds followed him. A man with leprosy came and knelt before him and said, "Lord, if you are willing, you can make me clean." Jesus reached out his hand and touched the man. "I am willing," he said. "Be clean!" Immediately he was cured of his leprosy. Then Jesus said to him, "See that you don't tell anyone. But go, show yourself to the priest and offer the gift Moses commanded, as a testimony to them." **MATTHEW 8:1–4**

■

THE SERMON ON THE Mount is where the principles of God are bracketed by the principles of the kingdoms of this world. And what characterizes the kingdoms of this world? Before the sermon began, Jesus was surrounded by those who were "ill with many diseases, those suffering severe pain, the demon-possessed, those having seizures and the paralyzed . . ." (Matthew 5:24). And Matthew tells us that Jesus healed them. After the sermon, Jesus encountered a man with leprosy who said, "Lord, if you are willing, you can make me clean." Jesus was willing and cured the man. Jesus not only enunciated kingdom principles in his sermon, he clearly practiced them as he engaged this needy and alienated world.

I DID NOT EVEN CONSIDER MYSELF WORTHY

When Jesus had finished saying all this in the hearing of the people, he entered Capernaum. There a centurion's servant, whom his
master valued highly, was sick and about to die. The centurion
heard of Jesus and sent some elders of the Jews to him, asking
him to come and heal his servant. When they came to Jesus, they
pleaded earnestly with him, "This man deserves to have you do
this, because he loves our nation and has built our synagogue." So
Jesus went with them. He was not far from the house when the
centurion sent friends to say to him: "Lord, don't trouble yourself,
for I do not deserve to have you come under my roof. That is why
I did not even consider myself worthy to come to you. But say the
word, and my servant will be healed. For I myself am a man under
authority, with soldiers under me. I tell this one, 'Go,' and he goes;
and that one, 'Come,' and he comes. I say to my servant, 'Do this,'
and he does it." When Jesus heard this, he was amazed at him, and
turning to the crowd following him, he said, "I tell you, I have not
found such great faith even in Israel." Then the men who had been
sent returned to the house and found the servant well. LUKE 7:1–10

■

WHY WAS JESUS "AMAZED" at the great faith of the centurion?
Jesus did not miss the contrast between the Roman pagan and the
Jewish citizens of Capernaum. The citizens told Jesus to help the
soldier because "he loves our nation and has built our synagogue."
In other words, they were claiming grace based on works. But Jesus
provided healing based on the man's faith in his (Jesus') power to
heal. The soldier had seen Jesus in action and he had become a believer. He said, "I do not even consider myself worthy to come to
you." The Jewish citizens believed grace could be earned, whereas
the Roman pagan knew that grace is a gift of God.

IN A TOWN CALLED NAIN

Soon afterward, Jesus went to a town called Nain, and his disciples and a large crowd went along with him. As he approached the town gate, a dead person was being carried out—the only son of his mother, and she was a widow. And a large crowd from the town was with her. When the Lord saw her, his heart went out to her and he said, "Don't cry." Then he went up and touched the coffin, and those carrying it stood still. He said, "Young man, I say to you, get up!" The dead man sat up and began to talk, and Jesus gave him back to his mother. They were all filled with awe and praised God. "A great prophet has appeared among us," they said. "God has come to help his people." This news about Jesus spread throughout Judea and the surrounding country. LUKE 7:11–17

■

NAIN IS A SMALL town backed by hills and surrounded by fields that exists to this very day. It is off the beaten path that connects Nazareth and Galilee, so it seems unusual that Jesus would have used this route. But Jesus appeared in this insignificant town at just the right time to perform an astonishing miracle of raising from the dead the only son of a widow. The people understood immediately the significance of what had happened. Remembering the miracles of the great prophets Elijah and Elisha, the people exclaimed, "A great prophet has appeared among us . . . God has come to help his people." Jesus may have been rejected in his hometown, and he was attacked as a threat to the ruling class in Jerusalem, but in this small, out-of-the-way place called Nain, the people saw Jesus for who he really is.

When John heard in prison what Christ was doing, he sent his disciples to ask him, "Are you the one who was to come, or should we expect someone else?" Jesus replied, "Go back and report to John what you hear and see: The blind receive sight, the lame walk, those who have leprosy are cured, the deaf hear, the dead are raised, and the good news is preached to the poor. Blessed is the man who does not fall away on account of me." **MATTHEW 11:2–6**

■

HEROD WAS HOLDING JOHN the Baptist prisoner. John was in a crisis of doubt because he knew it would be only a matter of time before the executioner would appear. He even sent messengers to ask Jesus if he truly is the Messiah. Jesus replied by saying, in effect, "look beyond my words to the evidence," and then he gave six demonstrations of the power of the Holy Spirit at work through him: The blind see, the lame walk, lepers are cured, the deaf hear, the dead are raised, and the good news is preached. Jesus was telling John that he should not give in to despair: "When you proclaimed, 'Look, the Lamb of God, who takes away the sin of the world,' you were proclaiming the truth about me. I am, indeed, the one 'who was to come.'" (John 1:29)

HE IS THE ELIJAH WHO WAS TO COME

As John's disciples were leaving, Jesus began to speak to the crowd about John: "What did you go out into the wilderness to see? A reed swayed by the wind? If not, what did you go out to see? A man dressed in fine clothes? No, those who wear fine clothes are in kings' palaces. Then what did you go out to see? A prophet? Yes, I tell you, and more than a prophet. This is the one about whom it is written: "'I will send my messenger ahead of you, who will prepare your way before you.' Truly I tell you, among those born of women there has not risen anyone greater than John the Baptist; yet whoever is least in the kingdom of heaven is greater than he. From the days of John the Baptist until now, the kingdom of heaven has been subjected to violence, and violent people have been raiding it. For all the Prophets and the Law prophesied until John. And if you are willing to accept it, he is the Elijah who was to come. Whoever has ears, let them hear. MATTHEW 11:7–15

■

JESUS TOLD HIS FOLLOWERS that, despite appearances, the kingdom of heaven is forcefully advancing. It would appear that the kingdom was under pressure of defeat and surrender because John the Baptist, who Jesus claimed was greater than all the prophets, had been imprisoned and was threatened with execution. But Jesus said to not be deceived by appearances, for God is at work to reclaim all his people since mankind's fall. It is through Jesus that God's purpose has reached a momentum that nothing in this world, including Satan, can stop. While the disciples remained mostly in the dark, Jesus knew how the story would turn out: first in apparent defeat, but then in victory over sin and death.

WISDOM IS PROVED RIGHT BY ALL HER CHILDREN

To what, then, can I compare the people of this generation? What are they like? They are like children sitting in the marketplace and calling out to each other: 'We played the flute for you, and you did not dance; we sang a dirge, and you did not cry.' For John the Baptist came neither eating bread nor drinking wine, and you say, 'He has a demon.' The Son of Man came eating and drinking, and you say, 'Here is a glutton and a drunkard, a friend of tax collectors and "sinners."' But wisdom is proved right by all her children."
LUKE 7:31–35

■

JESUS WAS SATURATED IN the knowledge of the Scriptures of his time. He knew the Pentateuch, the Prophets, and the wisdom literature of David and Solomon. And better than anyone, he knew that the source of all wisdom is God Himself. We have heard that Solomon asked God for discernment to help him establish right rule in the kingdom of Israel. So when Jesus says, "wisdom will be proved right by all her children," he is saying that the wisdom that comes from God for what is right and just will be proven right by the fruit that comes from the children of wisdom. Elsewhere, Jesus says that he can do nothing without the Father, and that "I am in the Father, and the Father is in me. The words I say to you are not just my own. Rather it is the Father, living in me, who is doing his work" (John 14:10). Jesus is inseparable from God, and all of God's wisdom abides in him. It is through sharing his Holy Spirit with us that we come to possess God's wisdom. And it is by the fruit of that wisdom that we will be known.

THE DAY OF JUDGMENT WILL COME

Then Jesus began to denounce the cities in which most of his miracles had been performed, because they did not repent. "Woe to you, Korazin! Woe to you, Bethsaida! If the miracles that were performed in you had been performed in Tyre and Sidon, they would have repented long ago in sackcloth and ashes. But I tell you, it will be more bearable for Tyre and Sidon on the day of judgment than for you." MATTHEW 11:20–22

■

JESUS PERFORMED MIRACLES IN Korazin and Bethsaida, but the people did not repent; their godlessness was comparable to the Gentile cities of Tyre and Sidon. But when Jesus speaks of the Day of Judgment, he sounds more like the Old Testament prophet Jeremiah than the "meek and mild" Sunday School Jesus of our present time. Had Jesus decided to suddenly take on the characteristics of a wrathful and judgmental God rather than a loving one? Certainly not. Jesus was stating the truth about the people of those towns. It was not that God had condemned them. The truth is they had condemned themselves by their godless actions, just as the people of Jerusalem condemned themselves in Jeremiah's time, even though they had been repeatedly warned to repent.

All things have been committed to me by my Father. No one knows the Son except the Father, and no one knows the Father except the Son and those to whom the Son chooses to reveal him. Come to me, all you who are weary and burdened, and I will give you rest. Take my yoke upon you and learn from me, for I am gentle and humble in heart, and you will find rest for your souls. For my yoke is easy and my burden is light. MATTHEW 11:27–30

■

AS JESUS IS YOKED to the Father, so we need to be yoked to him. When Jesus says, "No one knows the Son except the Father, and no one knows the Father except the Son," he is saying that he is joined to the Father in everything he does and says. Likewise, for those who choose to follow him, Jesus offers the yoke as a form of apprenticeship. When oxen are yoked together, they have double the strength to pull the load. Furthermore, Jesus offers to be the lead to provide direction and purpose. So as the Father is to Jesus so Jesus will be to us, if we will only accept the offer: "Come to me, all you who are weary and burdened, and I will give you rest. Take my yoke upon you and learn from me, for I am gentle and humble of heart, and you will find rest for your souls."

Now one of the Pharisees invited Jesus to have dinner with him, so he went to the Pharisee's house and reclined at the table. When a woman who had lived a sinful life in that town learned that Jesus was eating at the Pharisee's house, she brought an alabaster jar of perfume, and as she stood behind him at his feet weeping, she began to wet his feet with her tears. Then she wiped them with her hair, kissed them and poured perfume on them. When the Pharisee who had invited him saw this, he said to himself, "If this man were a prophet, he would know who is touching him and what kind of woman she is—that she is a sinner." LUKE 7:36–39

■

THERE IS AN IRONIC juxtaposition in this account of the sinful woman and the self-righteous Pharisee. Jesus was invited to the Pharisee's house for dinner. This might seem unusual because Jesus had no obvious social cache, but word had spread about his miraculous powers of healing. Then, "a woman who had lived a sinful life" entered the picture. She brought an "alabaster jar of perfume," washed Jesus' feet with her tears, dried them with her hair, and then applied the perfume. It is not clear how the woman gained entry to the Pharisee's house—perhaps he secretly knew her—but publically he showed outrage and contempt that Jesus would allow a sinful woman to touch him. It is the nature of self-righteousness to spot sin and shortcomings in others. It is the nature of God to forgive those who genuinely seek forgiveness.

"Two men owed money to a certain moneylender. One owed him five hundred denarii, and the other fifty. Neither of them had the money to pay him back, so he canceled the debts of both. Now which of them will love him more?" Simon replied, "I suppose the one who had the bigger debt canceled." "You have judged correctly," Jesus said. LUKE 7:41–43

■

JESUS ADDRESSED THE PHARISEE, "Simon, I have something to tell you," and then he began to teach through a short parable about debt to illustrate a larger point. Jesus asked, who would love a lender more, the person forgiven a large debt or the one forgiven a small debt? The Pharisee answered, "I suppose the one who had the bigger debt cancelled." "You have judged correctly," Jesus said. It is important to remember that with Jesus anyone can be forgiven, no matter how sinful the person has been. That is the will of God. Even the self-righteous Pharisee can be saved. Whether he applies that answer to his own condition is another matter.

WHO IS THIS WHO EVEN FORGIVES SINS?

Then he turned toward the woman and said to Simon, "Do you see this woman? I came into your house. You did not give me any water for my feet, but she wet my feet with her tears and wiped them with her hair. You did not give me a kiss, but this woman, from the time I entered, has not stopped kissing my feet. You did not put oil on my head, but she has poured perfume on my feet. Therefore, I tell you, her many sins have been forgiven—for she loved much. But he who has been forgiven little loves little." Then Jesus said to her, "Your sins are forgiven." The other guests began to say among themselves, "Who is this who even forgives sins?" Jesus said to the woman, "Your faith has saved you; go in peace."

LUKE 7:44–50

■

THE WOMAN WAS FORGIVEN much because she loved much. When Jesus said to her, "Your faith has saved you; go in peace," he made a theological point that caused him trouble with the religious leaders. Earlier, when Jesus cured the paralytic in the midst of a crowd of people, the teachers of the law who were present said, "He's blaspheming! Who can forgive sins but God?" (Mark 2:7) While the repentant woman gratefully placed her faith in the Lordship of Jesus Christ, Simon the Pharisee refused to acknowledge that Jesus has the power and authority to forgive sins. He remained blinded by his adherence to his identity as a member of the ruling class.

After this, Jesus traveled about from one town and village to another, proclaiming the good news of the kingdom of God. The Twelve were with him, and also some women who had been cured of evil spirits and diseases: Mary (called Magdalene) from whom seven demons had come out; Joanna the wife of Cuza, the manager of Herod's household; Susanna; and many others. These women were helping to support them out of their own means. LUKE 8:1–3

■

IT IS TRUE THAT women were not considered nearly as important as men in biblical times, yet whether it was Mary, Elizabeth, or Anna at the beginning of Luke's account of Jesus' life, or Mary Magdalene, Joanna, or Susanna later when his ministry became public, women are identified as an irreplaceable part to the story. Luke says that these women and others "were helping to support (Jesus and the Twelve) out of their own means." They were not shadowy background figures but prominent players throughout Jesus' ministry and all the way to Golgotha and the establishment of the Church. In our own time we want to categorize women by gender, but Luke focuses on their giftedness and the importance of their participation in the events surrounding the life and ministry of Jesus Christ.

HE IS OUT OF HIS MIND

Then Jesus entered a house, and again a crowd gathered, so that he and his disciples were not even able to eat. When his family heard about this, they went to take charge of him, for they said, "He is out of his mind." And the teachers of the law who came down from Jerusalem said, "He is possessed by Beelzebub! By the prince of demons he is driving out demons." **MARK 3:20–22**

■

JESUS TRAVELED THROUGHOUT THE region of Galilee performing miracles by healing the sick, giving sight to the blind, and even raising a boy from the dead. He did things that proclaimed him to be more than just a prophet or teacher. But his actions stirred up concern even with his own family. They came to take charge of him, for they said, "He is out of his mind." Then some religious leaders slandered him by publically declaring, "The prince of demons possessed him." Who was right? C.S. Lewis said that there could be no neutral ground when it comes to our own response to Jesus. He is either Lord, liar, or lunatic. His family came down on the side of lunatic, and the teachers of the law said that he was a liar because he was possessed by "the father of lies" (John 8:44). But Jesus' actions go far beyond those performed by one who is a teacher or prophet. Later Jesus asked his disciples, "Who do you say that I am?" He is asking us as well. What will it be: Lord, liar, or lunatic?

So Jesus called them and spoke to them in parables: "How can Satan drive out Satan? If a kingdom is divided against itself, that kingdom cannot stand. If a house is divided against itself, that house cannot stand. And if Satan opposes himself and is divided, he cannot stand; his end has come. In fact, no one can enter a strong man's house and carry off his possessions unless he first ties up the strong man. Then he can rob his house." **MARK 3:23–27**

■

KINGDOMS WERE ALL OVER the place in Jesus' time, but did any of them resemble the kingdom of God? Jesus emerged out of nowhere in the early days of his three-year ministry, proclaiming, "The kingdom of God is near" (Mark 1:15). He had quietly invaded the other kingdom—the counterfeit kingdom of Satan—that became possible when the first man and woman gave up their God-given authority to him. Satan's kingdom has been in opposition to God from the beginning. Jesus makes it clear that he has come to destroy Satan's dominion. He says that "from the time of John the Baptist, the kingdom of heaven is forcefully advancing, and forceful men lay hold of it" (Matthew 11:12). We are the foot soldiers who have been authorized by Jesus to establish through the power of the Holy Spirit a new kind of rule based not on subterfuge and domination, but on love, justice, and service. We are under the authority of Christ, through the power of his Holy Spirit, to continue to build, here on earth, the kingdom of God.

Jesus continues, "I tell you the truth, all the sins and blasphemies of men will be forgiven them. But whoever blasphemes against the Holy Spirit will never be forgiven; he is guilty of an eternal sin." He said this because they were saying, "He has an evil spirit."
MARK 3:28–30

■

JESUS SAYS, "WHOEVER BLASPHEMES against the Holy Spirit will never be forgiven; he is guilty of an eternal sin." At this moment the teachers of the law were attacking and rejecting Jesus by claiming he had an evil spirit. But Jesus countered by saying that to blaspheme the Holy Spirit is to reject the true identity of Jesus. To reject Jesus by claiming he has an evil spirit is to reject God, and by doing so we remain in our chronic condition of sin and separation from the God who loves us. "The Father loves the Son and has placed everything in his hands. Whoever believes in the Son has eternal life, but whoever rejects the Son will not see life, for God's wrath remains on him" (John 3:36).

Now Jesus' mother and brothers came to see him, but they were not able to get near him because of the crowd. Someone told him, "Your mother and brothers are standing outside, wanting to see you." He replied, "My mother and brothers are those who hear God's word and put it into practice." LUKE 8:19–21

■

IF MEN AND WOMEN are category builders, Jesus is a category breaker. He asks us to think beyond the normal categories of self or group identification. He refuses to reduce our inherent complexity to what are essentially tribal relationships, such as family, gender, or age. When he says, "My mother and brothers are those who hear God's word and put it into practice," he is cutting across our self-imposed boundaries. He is saying that all people who know the Father and live a life with, through, and in Him are members of his family. He said this even before he began his public ministry, when he remained in Jerusalem after Joseph and Mary left to return home. When they realized their son was not with them, they returned to find him in the Temple with many teachers, impressing them with his extraordinary knowledge. Mary said, "Son, why have you treated us like this? Your father and I have been anxiously searching for you." "Why were you searching for me?" he asked. "Didn't you know I had to be in my Father's house?" (Luke 2:48–49) Jesus understood even then who his real Father is. He sees all relationships through the eyes of his Father.

Then some of the Pharisees and teachers of the law said to him, "Teacher, we want to see a miraculous sign from you." He (Jesus) answered, "A wicked and adulterous generation asks for a miraculous sign! But none will be given it except the sign of the prophet Jonah. For as Jonah was three days and three nights in the belly of a huge fish, so the Son of Man will be three days and three nights in the heart of the earth." MATTHEW 12:38–40

■

THE PHARISEES CONSIDERED THEMSELVES to be the final authority when it came to interpreting the Word of God. But Jesus cut through the pretensions of his inquisitors by saying that those asking for a miraculous sign were indistinguishable from the "wicked and adulterous generation" all around them. The world rather than the Word of God had mastered them. Then Jesus turned to the Book of Jonah to show what was to happen to him. He would be swallowed by death and buried for three days (as Jonah was buried in the belly of a fish in the depths of the sea), and then be raised from the dead and delivered unto life. No one in his presence understood what Jesus was actually prophesying. It was only after Peter and others looked back over their experience with the living Lord that they remembered this prophecy.

BLESSED ARE THOSE WHO
HEAR THE WORD OF GOD AND OBEY IT

"When an evil spirit comes out of a man, it goes through arid places seeking rest and does not find it. Then it says, 'I will return to the house I left.' When it arrives, it finds the house swept clean and put in order. Then it goes and takes seven other spirits more wicked than itself, and they go in and live there. And the final condition of that man is worse than the first." As Jesus was saying these things, a woman in the crowd called out, "Blessed is the mother who gave you birth and nursed you." He replied, "Blessed rather are those who hear the word of God and obey it." LUKE 11:24–28

■

IN GENESIS IT SAYS, "the Lord God formed the man from the dust of the ground and breathed into his nostrils the breath of life, and the man became a living being" (Genesis 2:7). After the fall, however, other spirits entered the hearts of Adam and Eve, and the wickedness and corruption that ensued caused God to grieve over what had become of his creation, for "every inclination of the thoughts of (their hearts were) only evil all the time" (Genesis 6:5). Through this parable of the empty house, Jesus tells us that there is no such thing as a benign empty heart. The human heart needs to be filled up with something, and either it will be the Holy Spirit of God or it will be the "seven other spirits more wicked than (the first spirit), and they will go in and live there."

NINEVEH REPENTED

As the crowds increased, Jesus said, "This is a wicked generation. It asks for a miraculous sign, but none will be given it except the sign of Jonah. For as Jonah was a sign to the Ninevites, so also will the Son of Man be to this generation. The Queen of the South will rise at the judgment with the men of this generation and condemn them; for she came from the ends of the earth to listen to Solomon's wisdom, and now one greater than Solomon is here. The men of Nineveh will stand up at the judgment with this generation and condemn it; for they repented at the preaching of Jonah, and now one greater than Jonah is here." LUKE 11:29–32

■

AGAIN JESUS REFERS TO "this wicked generation." Then he says that no miraculous signs will be given it except the sign of Jonah. What does he mean by this? Nineveh was a large, ancient city known for its wickedness. At first, Jonah refused to go there to preach repentance because he believed there was no way the leaders and citizens of Nineveh would repent and seek reconciliation with God. But the unexpected happened and the king and all the people gave up "their evil and violent ways" (Jonah 3:8) and the city was saved. This is what God is seeking from all generations: Repentance, reconciliation, and new life. God sent one even greater than Jonah to bring restoration to the people of Israel and to all the people of the world.

Jesus spoke all these things to the crowd in parables; he did not say anything to them without using a parable. So was fulfilled what was spoken through the prophet: "I will open my mouth in parables, I will utter things hidden since the creation of the world." MATTHEW 13:34–35

■

HOW DOES GOD COMMUNICATE his story? We know our story: We are born into a family made up of a mother and father, sisters, brothers, relatives, communities, and even nations. But often ours is also a story of conflict and sorrow, sickness and separation. For the world we enter is broken and needs repentance, reconciliation, and restoration. This is where God's story intersects with human history. And that story must be told in the language of the Holy Spirit, which is God's language, the figurative language of metaphor, allegory, and poetry. "This is what we speak, not in words taught us by human wisdom but in the words taught by the Spirit, expressing spiritual truths in spiritual words" (1 Corinthians 2:13). This is the language of the mind and heart of Christ.

GOOD SOIL

Again Jesus began to teach by the lake. The crowd that gathered around him was so large that he got into a boat and sat in it out on the lake, while all the people were along the shore at the water's edge. He taught them many things by parables, and in his teaching said: "Listen! A farmer went out to sow his seed. As he was scattering the seed, some fell along the path, and the birds came and ate it up. Some fell on rocky places, where it did not have much soil. It sprang up quickly, because the soil was shallow. But when the sun came up, the plants were scorched, and they withered because they had no root. Other seed fell among thorns, which grew up and choked the plants, so that they did not bear grain. Still other seed fell on good soil. It came up, grew and produced a crop, multiplying thirty, sixty, or even a hundred times." Then Jesus said, "He who has ears to hear, let him hear." MARK 4:1–9

■

THOUGH WE MAY NOT be farmers or intimately know the cycles of planting and harvesting, we still need not stretch too far to gather the import of what Jesus is teaching. But we do need to slow down a bit so that we can hear God's voice through Jesus' words. Jesus begins by saying, "Listen!" to the crowd that has gathered on the shore of the Sea of Galilee. He wants the people to be fully engaged so that they can hear what God is saying to them through this story of planting and harvesting. Jesus draws a spiritual point from everyday reality. It is as if he is saying that the physical world around us can give us all the examples we need to understand the spiritual principles behind the everyday reality of life, if we will only be attentive.

When he was alone, the Twelve and the others around him (Jesus) asked him about the parables. He told them, "The secret of the kingdom of God has been given to you. But to those on the outside everything is said in parables so that, 'they may be ever seeing but never perceiving, and ever hearing but never understanding; otherwise they might turn and be forgiven!'" Then Jesus said to them, "Don't you understand this parable? How then will you understand any parable?" MARK 4:10–13

■

JESUS WAS PREPARING HIS disciples for ministering to a broken world. He knows that even the chosen people of God turn aside in willful blindness. After being freed from the yoke of slavery in Egypt, after experiencing miracle after miracle in the desert, the Israelites failed time and again to "perceive" and "understand" that the hand of God was guiding them toward freedom. Instead, "They forgot God who saved them, who had done great things in Egypt, miracles in the land of Ham and awesome deeds by the Red Sea" (Psalm 106:21–22). Jesus understood the extreme difficulty of the mission ahead, but he also knows that God is seeking reconciliation with a people who have abandoned him. Jesus wanted his disciples to understand that their mission was to open the hearts of men and women to the true heart of God.

SEED SOWN ALONG THE PATH

The farmer sows the word. Some people are like seed along the path, where the word is sown. As soon as they hear it, Satan comes and takes away the word that was sown in them. **MARK 4:14–15**

■

JESUS REVEALS THAT HE is talking about more than seeds. He clearly states that the seed is a metaphor for the Word of God. God extravagantly sows the earth with his Word, but it does not always land where it can germinate and grow. Sometimes the seed lands on a path where the soil has been hardened by treading feet so that the seed cannot penetrate and have time to grow. Jesus says that Satan can easily find this exposed seed and steal it away. Jesus is saying that many men and women experience the Word of God this way. The seed (or the Word) has not penetrated their hearts, and so it cannot grow. With a heart empty of God's Word, people will, nevertheless, continue to look for solace and identity and so will gather around themselves "a great number of teachers to say what their itching ears want to hear. They will turn their ears away from the truth and turn aside to myths" (2 Timothy 4:3–4).

Others, like seed sown on rocky places, hear the word and at once receive it with joy. But since they have no root, they last only a short time. When trouble or persecution comes because of the word, they quickly fall away. MARK 4:16–17

■

IT IS GOOD TO remember that Jesus was preparing his disciples for a time when "trouble and persecution" would sweep in and test their resolve, even to the point of death. If the Word he planted fell on rocky soil where it could not take root, then at the first sign of adversity, his followers would fall away. And at the moment of true testing, they did fall away. What Jesus is saying here is a prophetic warning, not only to his disciples then, but also to all generations who will face adversity in the days, months, and years to follow.

SEED SOWN AMONG THORNS

Still others, like seed sown among thorns, hear the word; but the worries of this life, the deceitfulness of wealth and the desires for other things come in and choke the word, making it unfruitful.
MARK 4:18–19

■

JESUS GIVES US A three-part warning of what can happen if we are blind to the dangers surrounding us. First, Satan can steal the word, leaving us empty and defenseless. Second, the world with all its troubles and persecutions can scatter us. Finally, the flesh, the powerful desires for the things of this life, such as the desire for wealth, power, and status, can "choke the word, making it unfruitful." The enemy of the Word is a multifaceted deceiver. Jesus was born into a warring environment, and he does not expect anything different for those who love and follow him.

SEED SOWN ON GOOD SOIL

Others, like seed sown on good soil, hear the word, accept it, and produce a crop—thirty, sixty or even a hundred times what was sown. MARK 4:20

■

FINALLY, WHEN THE SEED finds good soil, a crop will be produced as much as one hundred times what was sown. The miracle of the earliest days of the church is one of extraordinary increase. Out of an unlikely assortment of men and women, the church grew exponentially throughout the Mediterranean world. Paul saw himself as a conduit of the Holy Spirit as he travelled from place to place spreading the word of God in the name of Jesus Christ. He fully understood the near impossibility of the task, but neither that nor anything else prevented him from working within the design of fruitfulness God blessed him with. "What is Paul? Only servants, through whom you came to believe—as the Lord has assigned to each his task. I planted the seed, Apollos watered it, but God made it grow" (1 Corinthians 3:5–6).

UNDER A BOWL OR A BED?

He said to them, "Do you bring in a lamp to put it under a bowl or a bed? Instead, don't you put it on its stand? For whatever is hidden is meant to be disclosed, and whatever is concealed is meant to be brought out into the open. If anyone has ears to hear, let him hear. Consider carefully what you hear. With the measure you use, it will be measured to you—and even more. Whoever has will be given more; whoever does not have, even what he has will be taken from him." **MARK 4:21–25**

■

JESUS USES FIGURATIVE LANGUAGE to draw a connection between the spiritual and natural worlds. As he used seed to represent the Word of God in the parable of the sower, so here he uses light to represent the wisdom of God. If you have the light, use it. If you have seed, plant it. If we think only in terms of the natural world, we miss the spiritual reality behind everything. The natural world mimics aspects of the spiritual world. Jesus says, open your eyes and your heart to God's spiritual reality all around you and act on that reality. Paul says the same thing in his prayer to the Ephesians: "may (God) give you the Spirit of wisdom and revelation, so that you may know him better. I pray also that the eyes of your heart may be enlightened in order that you may know the hope to which he has called you . . ." (Ephesians 1:17–18).

THE HARVEST

He also said, "This is what the kingdom of God is like. A man scatters seed on the ground. Night and day, whether he sleeps or gets up, the seed sprouts and grows, though he does not know how. All by itself the soil produces grain—first the stalk, then the head, then the full kernel in the head. As soon as the grain is ripe, he puts the sickle to it, because the harvest has come." **MARK 4:26–29**

■

LIKE THE RELIGIOUS LEADERS of Jesus' time, the modern, scientific "masters of the universe" want to strain miracles out of existence by applying their naturalistic knowledge to the mysteries of the universe, the solar system, and the earth. For them, there is no need to trust in God because God is a human invention, an archaic holdover from an earlier time. But Jesus says it is otherwise. Man did not invent God; God created man, and God has not given up on us, even though we often give up on him. Without God, all explanations come up short. Jesus points to the Creator of all things for understanding the mysteries of this life. He tells us to not trust in our own understanding; rather, trust in God, just as the farmer trusts that the planted seed will produce an abundant crop. Behind all natural phenomena there exists a spiritual reality. Jesus reverses the order of our thinking. The natural world around us is a metaphor for the spiritual reality that has always been and always will be: "God is spirit, and his worshippers must worship in spirit and in truth" (John 4:24).

THE PARABLE OF THE WEEDS

Jesus told them another parable: "The kingdom of heaven is like a man who sowed good seed in his field. But while everyone was sleeping, his enemy came and sowed weeds among the wheat, and went away. When the wheat sprouted and formed heads, then the weeds also appeared. The owner's servants came to him and said, 'Sir, didn't you sow good seed in your field? Where then did the weeds come from?' 'An enemy did this,' he replied. The servants asked him, 'Do you want us to go and pull them up?' 'No,' he answered, 'because while you are pulling the weeds, you may root up the wheat with them. Let both grow together until the harvest. At that time I will tell the harvesters: First collect the weeds and tie them in bundles to be burned; then gather the wheat and bring it into my barn.'" MATTHEW 13:24–30

■

IN THIS PARABLE JESUS introduces the idea of evil existing side by side with good. Just as man was created in the image of God, he is born into sin as a son or daughter of Adam (Psalm 51:5). The enemy has done his work in the night; weeds have been sowed among the wheat, leaving the owner of the field with a dilemma: Should he pull up the good with the bad? The owner answers with discernment. If he acts precipitously, he will destroy both the wheat and the weeds, both the good and the bad. But if he waits until the crops have grown, he will be able to judge correctly. He will harvest the wheat but will bundle the weeds and have them burned. Jesus says judgment will come in God's good time, but judgment, whenever it arrives, will be tempered by discernment.

THE HARVEST IS THE END OF THE AGE

Then he left the crowd and went into the house. His disciples came to him and said, "Explain to us the parable of the weeds in the field." He answered, "The one who sowed the good seed is the Son of Man. The field is the world, and the good seed stands for the sons of the kingdom. The weeds are the sons of the evil one, and the enemy who sows them is the devil. The harvest is the end of the age, and the harvesters are angels." **MATTHEW 13:36–39**

■

THE LANGUAGE JESUS USES to explain his parable of the weeds can create discomfort for many who hear it. He says, "The weeds are the sons of the evil one, and the enemy who sows them is the devil." Part of the problem for us is that Jesus describes the devil as an actual being who is at war with the Son of Man. In our quest to promote our culture of comfort, where conflict is papered over with feel-good thinking, the devil's existence presents an awkward intrusion into the fantasy that the devil himself is a fantasy. C.S. Lewis says that there are two dangers when dealing with the devil: The first is to think too much about him, and the second is to ignore him. Jesus never ignored him, and neither should we.

As the weeds are pulled up and burned in the fire, so it will be at the end of the age. The Son of Man will send out his angels, and they will weed out of his kingdom everything that causes sin and all who do evil. They will throw them into the fiery furnace, where there will be weeping and gnashing of teeth. Then the righteous will shine like the sun in the kingdom of their Father. He who has ears, let him hear. MATTHEW 13:40–43

■

WHEN WE THINK OF God, do we think of him as love or do we think of him as judge? Most of us would prefer to think of him in terms of love because it is comforting to do so. Judgment can precipitate the fear of being punished for some imagined or real crime. Like the guilty fugitive, we are reduced to living haunted lives as we imagine being chased down for unresolved secret crimes. But God's plan permits a way out. We are all under judgment, but we are also subjects of his love. The answer lies in us: Will we be the wheat to be harvested or will we choose to be the weeds that will be pulled up and burned up before the harvest?

Again Jesus said, "What shall we say the kingdom of God is like, or what parable shall we use to describe it? It is like a mustard seed, which is the smallest of all seeds on earth. Yet when planted, it grows and becomes the largest of all garden plants, with such big branches that the birds can perch in its shade." **MARK 4:30–32**

■

AT FIRST GLANCE IT seems strange to hear Jesus compare the kingdom of God to a mustard seed. At that time, the mustard seed was the smallest of the flowering seeds, tiny in comparison to what it would become. But the people expected God's coming kingdom to be like the kingdoms that had sprouted throughout the world, with the only difference being that the warrior king would be in the line of David. The people of Israel were under the control of Rome and its armies and so they were looking for a geopolitical solution to their captivity. Jesus compared the kingdom of God to something that challenged preconceptions of what would save Israel. He did not come as the warrior king but as something as apparently insignificant as a tiny seed that grows dynamically into "the largest of all the garden plants."

LIKE HIDDEN TREASURE

The kingdom of heaven is like treasure hidden in a field. When a
man found it, he hid it again, and then in his joy went and sold all
he had and bought that field. MATTHEW 13:44

■

FOR A SECOND TIME Jesus offers his followers a better way to understand what the kingdom of God is like. Here he tells of a man
who discovers a treasure, hides it, sells all of his own possessions,
and then buys the field where the treasure is hidden. He gives up
everything to gain something of much greater worth. Jim Elliot, a
missionary who lost his life in 1956 while attempting to minister to
the Huaorani Indians in Ecuador, wrote a line in his journal before
his death that beautifully summarizes what Jesus is teaching us:
"He is no fool who gives what he cannot keep to gain that which he
cannot lose."

Again, the kingdom of heaven is like a merchant looking for fine pearls. When he found one of great value, he went away and sold everything he had and bought it. MATTHEW 13:45–46

■

JESUS IS GOING TO great lengths to draw us into his understanding of his mission here on earth. His poetic use of language invites listeners into a story and lets their imaginations develop in a way that is different from a lawyer's argument or a scientist's proof. Jesus teaches about a reality that exists beyond the natural realm, but he uses the natural world to illustrate a spiritual point of great importance. In essence, he says that the kingdom of God must always come first: "So do not worry, saying, 'What shall we eat?' or 'What shall we drink?' or 'What shall we wear?' For the pagans run after all these things, and your heavenly Father knows that you need them. But seek first his kingdom and his righteousness and all these things will be given to you as well" (Matthew 6:32–33).

"Once again, the kingdom of heaven is like a net that was let down into the lake and caught all kinds of fish. When it was full, the fishermen pulled it up on the shore. Then they sat down and collected the good fish in baskets, but threw the bad away. This is how it will be at the end of the age. The angels will come and separate the wicked from the righteous and throw them into the fiery furnace, where there will be weeping and gnashing of teeth. Have you understood all these things?" Jesus asked. "Yes," they replied. He said to them, "Therefore every teacher of the law who has been instructed about the kingdom of heaven is like the owner of a house who brings out of his storeroom new treasures as well as old." MATTHEW 13:47–52

■

JESUS USES THIS PARABLE to contrast two very different kingdoms. The kingdom of heaven might also be called the kingdom of light; it is the providence of God, a place of infinite blessings and goodness that will be fully reestablished on the Day of Judgment. But right now the kingdom of the prince of darkness has set itself up as an alternative kingdom, where people "call evil good, who put darkness for light and light for darkness, who put bitter for sweet and sweet for bitter" (Isaiah 5:20). When Jesus speaks about the good fish being chosen and the bad fish being thrown out, he is referring to the time when those who choose evil over good and darkness over light will receive their just reward. If we choose the kingdom of heaven, we will receive the blessings of eternal life with the Father. But if we choose the kingdom of darkness, we will end up where there is endless "weeping and gnashing of teeth." God never sends anyone to hell. That is our choice because God offers an alternative path to every man and woman; he offers the kingdom of heaven through the cross of his Son, Jesus Christ.

WHO IS THIS?

One day Jesus said to his disciples, "Let us go over to the other side of the lake." So they got into a boat and set out. As they sailed, he fell asleep. A squall came down on the lake, so that the boat was being swamped, and they were in great danger. The disciples went and woke him, saying, "Master, Master, we're going to drown!" He got up and rebuked the wind and the raging waters; the storm subsided, and all was calm. "Where is your faith?" he asked his disciples. In fear and amazement they asked one another, "Who is this? He commands even the winds and the water, and they obey him." LUKE 8:22–25

■

WITH THIS STORY WE move from parable to action. Jesus called his disciples to join him for a voyage across the Sea of Galilee to pagan territory. The disciples must have wondered about the purpose of such a dangerous undertaking, but Jesus showed no fear by falling asleep, even as a squall began to overwhelm the vessel and threaten the lives of everyone in it. The disciples, by contrast, experienced extreme fear as the chaos of the storm-driven sea began to swamp the boat. At the moment of greatest danger, Jesus arose and commanded the winds and the raging waters to be still, and the danger immediately subsided. This was not the last time Jesus demonstrated his authority over the dark forces of this world. The disciples did not understand the meaning of what happened on the Sea of Galilee. They asked, "Who is this?" This question continued to arise all the way to the cross. It is asked even to this very day.

AN AFFLICTED REGION

When he arrived at the other side in the region of the Gadarenes, two demon-possessed men coming from the tombs met him. They were so violent that no one could pass that way. "What do you want with us, Son of God?" they shouted. "Have you come here to torture us before the appointed time?" Some distance from them a large herd of pigs was feeding. The demons begged Jesus, "If you drive us out, send us into the herd of pigs." He said to them, "Go!" So they came out and went into the pigs, and the whole herd rushed down the steep bank into the lake and died in the water. Those tending the pigs ran off, went into the town and reported all this, including what had happened to the demon-possessed men. Then the whole town went out to meet Jesus. And when they saw him, they pleaded with him to leave their region. **MATTHEW 8:28–34**

■

WHY DID THE PEOPLE of the region of the Gadarenes plead with Jesus to leave? On the surface this seems strange because Jesus miraculously cured the two demon-possessed men who terrorized the region. At the same time Jesus gave permission to the afflicting spirits to enter a herd of pigs that then rushed into the Sea of Galilee and drowned. This loss of livestock cost the people of this wild region a great deal of money, forcing them to chose between God and economic wellbeing. The people of the Gadarenes ultimately decided it was better to live among demonic spirits than risk their economic livelihood, and so they sent Jesus away. Much the same thing happened to Paul in Ephesus when those who profited by the business of creating shrines to the god Artemis discovered that Paul was subverting their business by proclaiming, "man-made gods are no gods at all" (Acts 19:28). Here again, the economy of darkness trumped the light of the Spirit of God.

EVERYTHING IS POSSIBLE FOR
ONE WHO BELIEVES

Jesus asked the boy's father, "How long has he been like this?"
"From childhood," he answered. "It has often thrown him into fire
or water to kill him. But if you can do anything, take pity on us
and help us." "'If you can'?" said Jesus. "Everything is possible for
one who believes." MARK 9:21–23

■

JESUS HAS AN UNCANNY ability to speak to our deepest levels of
unbelief. He says, "Everything is possible for one who believes," and
we recoil with our naturalistic preconceptions of what is possible
and what is not. The father had been living with a child afflicted
with what appeared to be epilepsy, and he couched his request for
help with the conditional "if you can" because he despaired of a
miracle. How easy it is to identify with the father's doubt. Our faith
is often circumscribed by the limits of our own idea of the miraculous. When Mary was visited by the angel Gabriel and told what
would take place through her, she replied, "How will this be?" because she was confronted with improbability upon improbability.
The father's doubts and Mary's questions resonate with all of us. We
must grapple with all the reasons for our unbelief. It is a central is-
sue for each one of us.

Immediately the boy's father exclaimed, "I do believe; help me overcome my unbelief!" When Jesus saw that a crowd was running to the scene, he rebuked the impure spirit. "You deaf and mute spirit," he said, "I command you, come out of him and never enter him again." The spirit shrieked, convulsed him violently and came out. The boy looked so much like a corpse that many said, "He's dead." But Jesus took him by the hand and lifted him to his feet, and he stood up. After Jesus had gone indoors, his disciples asked him privately, "Why couldn't we drive it out?" He replied, "This kind can come out only by prayer." MARK 9:24–29

■

DO WE MORTALS SEE as Jesus sees? The answer is yes, but with this exception: Jesus sees in full while we see in part. He walked the same earth that we walk and breathed the same air we breathe, but when he encountered this afflicted son and suffering father, he brought the force and full authority of God into the encounter. The father was powerless to overcome his son's sickness. But with Jesus present, hope flooded back into the father's heart, and he exclaimed, "I do believe . . . !" The father also came to realize that alone he was powerless to bring about the good he hoped for, so he pleaded with Jesus to help him overcome his unbelief. What a profound request! This should be everyone's prayer because until we do overcome our unbelief in the Lordship of Jesus Christ, we will remain vulnerable to every false belief that passes by.

THEY DID NOT UNDERSTAND

They left that place and passed through Galilee. Jesus did not want anyone to know where they were, because he was teaching his disciples. He said to them, "The Son of Man is going to be delivered into the hands of men. They will kill him, and after three days he will rise." But they did not understand what he meant and were afraid to ask him about it. They came to Capernaum. When he was in the house, he asked them, "What were you arguing about on the road?" But they kept quiet because on the way they had argued about who was the greatest. Sitting down, Jesus called the Twelve and said, "Anyone who wants to be first must be the very last, and the servant of all." He took a little child whom he placed among them. Taking the child in his arms, he said to them, "Whoever welcomes one of these little children in my name welcomes me; and whoever welcomes me does not welcome me but the one who sent me." MARK 9:30–37

■

AS JESUS WALKED WITH his disciples, he taught them kingdom principles that starkly contrasted with commonly understood earthly ways of living. The disciples strove to discern who would earn the rank of being first among the followers of Jesus. In our world, it is considered right to strive to be first, whether on the playground, in school and college, or at work. Instead of service and humility, everything comes down to achievement and self-aggrandizement. We race the race to gain the prize that will soon be won by another striver lurking in the wings. In the kingdom of God, we do not need to earn recognition. We are already there; we already belong. We have accepted God's invitation to place our identity in his hands through belief in his Son, Jesus Christ.

DO NOT STOP HIM

"'Teacher,' said John, "we saw someone driving out demons in your name and we told him to stop, because he was not one of us." "Do not stop him," Jesus said. "For no one who does a miracle in my name can in the next moment say anything bad about me, for whoever is not against us is for us. Truly I tell you, anyone who gives you a cup of water in my name because you belong to the Messiah will certainly not lose their reward." **MARK 9:38–41**

■

IF JESUS CONSTANTLY POINTS to the kingdom of God, his disciples often provide a worldly counterpoint. Listen to one of the disciples: "Teacher, we saw someone driving out demons in your name and we told him to stop, because he was not of us." Jesus is not tribal; he does not limit himself to a small inside group. He is not a collector nor is he a possessor of things. He is the opposite, because he is always giving away. Jesus not only represents the kingdom of God here on earth, he lives it. His kingdom is not limited by social identity; he does not exclude anyone who wants to enter. His kingdom is based on the principle of multiplication, not subtraction. So he told his disciples to not exclude those who are seeking a way in, "For no one who does a miracle in my name can in the next moment say anything bad about me, for whoever is not against us is for us."

If anyone causes one of these little ones—those who believe in me—to stumble, it would be better for them if a large millstone were hung around their neck and they were thrown into the sea. If your hand causes you to stumble, cut it off. It is better for you to enter life maimed than with two hands to go into hell, where the fire never goes out. And if your foot causes you to stumble, cut it off. It is better for you to enter life crippled than to have two feet and be thrown into hell. And if your eye causes you to stumble, pluck it out. It is better for you to enter the kingdom of God with one eye than to have two eyes and be thrown into hell, where 'the worms that eat them do not die, and the fire is not quenched.'
MARK 9:42–48

■

EARLIER, JESUS SAID THAT if people are not against us, they must be considered for us, and he continues on to qualify his previous statement by saying, "If anyone causes one of these little ones— those who believe in me—to stumble, it would be better for them if a large millstone where hung around their neck and they were thrown into the sea." This sounds like an exaggeration, but only to the extent that Jesus is accentuating the seriousness of the consequences of misdirecting anyone who has found his or her way to God through belief in His Son. By this statement, Jesus is acknowledging the reality of the spiritual warfare that is always at work in both the earthly and heavenly realms.

DO YOU BELIEVE?

As Jesus went on from there, two blind men followed him, calling out, "Have mercy on us, Son of David!" When he had gone indoors, the blind men came to him, and he asked them, "Do you believe that I am able to do this?" "Yes, Lord," they replied. Then he touched their eyes and said, "According to your faith let it be done to you," and their sight was restored. Jesus warned them sternly, "See that no one knows about this." But they went out and spread the news about him throughout the region. While they were going out, a man who was demon-possessed and could not talk was brought to Jesus. And when the demon was driven out, the man who had been mute spoke. The crowd was amazed and said, "Nothing like this has ever been seen in Israel." But the Pharisees said, "It is by the prince of demons that he drives out demons." MATTHEW 9:27–34

■

AFTER THE CATASTROPHE IN the Garden of Eden, much of mankind was afflicted by blindness to the reality of God and an incapacity to hear God's word. Jesus uses his divine powers to open eyes and ears to the reality of God's love, not only for those afflicted with diseases but to all who turn from sin to follow him. But the Pharisees preferred the darkness of their own condition because they saw Jesus as a threat to their comfortable well-being. It is ironic that they falsely accused Jesus of being an instrument of the devil by using the devil's favorite weapon of subversion: lies.

He went to Nazareth, where he had been brought up, and on the Sabbath day he went into the synagogue, as was his custom. He stood up to read, and the scroll of the prophet Isaiah was handed to him. Unrolling it, he found the place where it is written: "The Spirit of the Lord is on me, because he has anointed me to proclaim good news to the poor. He has sent me to proclaim freedom for the prisoners and recovery of sight for the blind, to set the oppressed free, to proclaim the year of the Lord's favor." Then he rolled up the scroll, gave it back to the attendant and sat down. The eyes of everyone in the synagogue were fastened on him. He began by saying to them, "Today this scripture is fulfilled in your hearing." All spoke well of him and were amazed at the gracious words that came from his lips. "Isn't this Joseph's son?" they asked. LUKE 4:16–22

■

THE RESPONSE OF THE people to Jesus in the synagogue in Nazareth established a recurring pattern that continues to this very day. At first Jesus was praised and admired for his gracious words. He read from Isaiah, and the words of the passage were uplifting and hopeful. The reaction was almost one of pride in the local boy who seemed to be on the road to achieving great things by preaching good news to the poor, by proclaiming freedom for the prisoners and sight for the blind, and by releasing the oppressed. Who wouldn't want to help the poor, feed the hungry, and give sight to the blind? This sounds like a program anyone would embrace. But what if the words Jesus quotes from Isaiah had a cost attached? What if Jesus inferred that those in his presence might not agree so readily if they were being asked to lift their own fingers? We will see that the reaction was not as pleasant when Jesus turned the words of Scripture on those listening in the synagogue.

NO PROPHET IS ACCEPTED
IN HIS HOMETOWN

Jesus said to them, "Surely you will quote this proverb to me: 'Physician, heal yourself!' And you will tell me, 'Do here in your hometown what we have heard that you did in Capernaum.'" "Truly I tell you," he continued, "no prophet is accepted in his hometown." LUKE 4:23–24

■

JESUS QUICKLY REJECTED THE identity imposed upon him by the people of Nazareth. They wanted him to perform the same miracles for them that he performed in Capernaum and elsewhere. But their requests had nothing to do with faith, because the people of Nazareth, including members of his own family, had defined Jesus as nothing more than the kid next door who left town and then returned as a success. They could not escape their firmly fixed idea of the boy who had lived, played, and worked among them. They could not accept his true identity because to them it was too improbable. He is the son of Joseph, not the Son of God. They could not overcome their unbelief, and so when Jesus said, "Today this scripture is fulfilled in your hearing," the crowd had no idea what he was telling them. They too suffered from blindness. They simply could not see the truth.

I assure you that there were many widows in Israel in Elijah's time, when the sky was shut for three-and-a-half years and there was a severe famine throughout the land. Yet Elijah was not sent to any of them, but to a widow in Zarephath in the region of Sidon. And there were many in Israel with leprosy in the time of Elisha the prophet, yet not one of them was cleansed—only Naaman the Syrian. All the people in the synagogue were furious when they heard this. They got up, drove him out of the town, and took him to the brow of the hill on which the town was built, in order to throw him off the cliff. But he walked right through the crowd and went on his way. LUKE 4:25–30

■

LIKE JOHN THE BAPTIST before him, Jesus turned the spotlight on the chronic condition of the people of Nazareth. To illustrate that "no prophet is accepted in his hometown," he referenced two great prophets of Israel—Elijah and Elisha—but he could just as easily have mentioned Samuel, Isaiah, Jeremiah, or even John the Baptist. The people of Israel had strayed from God's path: "There is no one righteous, not even one, there is no one who understands, no one who seeks God" (Romans 3:10–11). The people were blind to their own condition, which is why Jesus' pointed to Zarephath the widow and Naaman the Syrian. Jesus is saying that just as in previous times when the people of Israel rejected God and the prophets he sent, God would reject them as well. And as with the Syrian and the widow, both Gentiles, God reaches beyond his own people to fulfill his promise. The crowd in the synagogue reacted by trying to kill the messenger who had brought a message they did not want to hear.

Jesus went through all the towns and villages, teaching in their synagogues, proclaiming the good news of the kingdom and healing every disease and sickness. When he saw the crowds, he had compassion on them, because they were harassed and helpless, like sheep without a shepherd. Then he said to his disciples, "The harvest is plentiful but the workers are few. Ask the Lord of the harvest, therefore, to send out workers into his harvest field." MATTHEW 9:35–38

■

WHY IS THE HARVEST so plentiful? And why are the workers so scarce? It can be difficult to accept the overarching truth that this broken world (and many of the people who inhabit it) is in opposition to God. To switch allegiance from Satan to Jesus is seemingly to ask for trouble, which is what Jesus' disciples discovered. The workers are few because following Jesus can perhaps lead to some very uncomfortable and even dangerous places.

Then Jesus went around teaching from village to village. Calling the Twelve to him, he began to send them out two by two and gave them authority over impure spirits. These were his instructions: "Take nothing for the journey except a staff—no bread, no bag, no money in your belts. Wear sandals but not an extra shirt. Whenever you enter a house, stay there until you leave that town. And if any place will not welcome you or listen to you, leave that place and shake the dust off your feet as a testimony against them." They went out and preached that people should repent. They drove out many demons and anointed many sick people with oil and healed them. MARK 6:6B–13

■

WHEN JESUS SENT HIS disciples into the world to preach, he instructed them to travel light. For most of us, our inclination is to cram every last conceivable necessity into the most capacious bags available. We can't seem to help ourselves, because we assume that the physical things we take will, in the end, save the day. Jesus says, be counterintuitive; carry light and trust in God. For the Christian, Jesus is advancing important principles for living a productive kingdom-driven life: Do not depend on things. God will provide. He will provide food, money, and even clothing and shelter when needed. Trust in God and do the work he has called you to do with praise and thanksgiving.

I am sending you out like sheep among wolves. Therefore be as shrewd as snakes and as innocent as doves. Be on your guard; you will be handed over to the local councils and be flogged in the synagogues. On my account you will be brought before governors and kings as witnesses to them and to the Gentiles. But when they arrest you, do not worry about what to say or how to say it. At that time you will be given what to say, for it will not be you speaking, but the Spirit of your Father speaking through you. MATTHEW 10:16–20

■

PREVIOUSLY, JESUS WARNED US that enemies of God exist everywhere and will come against us in force. These enemies represent the kingdom of this world, and they will do everything in their power to stop us from advancing the kingdom of God. But Jesus also says that when we go out into the world and encounter opposition even from "friends," we will never be alone. Even the words we speak will not be our own words, but what we speak will be "the Spirit of your father speaking through you."

Brother will betray brother to death, and a father his child; children will rebel against their parents and have them put to death. You will be hated by everyone because of me, but the one who stands firm to the end will be saved. When you are persecuted in one place, flee to another. Truly I tell you, you will not finish going through the towns of Israel before the Son of Man comes.

MATTHEW 10:21–23

■

THE PICTURE JESUS PAINTS of a world of conflict and misery is troubling because we are often taught that following Jesus means a good life and an easier path, even the reward of wealth. But this idea is neither true nor biblical. The truth is that accepting Jesus will complicate your life in many ways and might even bring on expressions of enmity and persecution. We distort the truth of Jesus' teachings when we try to mold them to the prevailing cultural milieu. Jesus promised a hard road, but he also promised "that you will not finish going through the towns of Israel before the Son of Man comes." Jesus always points beyond natural realities to the spiritual reality of the presence of God working through the Holy Spirit to restore men and women to their right relationship with the Father.

WHO IS THE TEACHER? WHO IS THE MASTER?

The student is not above the teacher, nor a servant above his master. It is enough for students to be like their teachers, and servants like their masters. If the head of the house has been called Beelzebul, how much more the members of his household! MATTHEW 10:24–25

■

JESUS CONTINUES TO GIVE instruction with what appears to be a truism. He says that the student is not above his teacher, nor is the servant above his master. But what if the teacher is Satan (Beelzebub)? Satan is the archenemy of God; he tried to subvert Jesus in the wilderness, and his own acolytes have opposed Jesus time and again. Jesus warns the disciples (and us) to look beyond the authority of the position to the nature of the person holding that position. Watch out for imposters; they are liars and deceivers. They are wolves in sheep's clothing. They may seem harmless, but Jesus keeps making the point: Be alert and prepared, because you are behind enemy lines.

Taste and see that the Lord is good; blessed is the one who takes refuge in him. Fear the Lord, you his holy people, for those who fear him lack nothing. PSALM 34:8–9

■

WE HAVE BEEN WALKING in Jesus' footsteps now for six months. For the most part he has been developing his ministry in the regions of Galilee. While he was born in the town of Bethlehem, he returned to Nazareth with Joseph and his mother Mary and remained there for most of his youth, living a very ordinary life. But then around the age of thirty, his public ministry materialized almost instantly. We have been witnesses to his extraordinary power to perform miracles, heal the sick, and give sight to the blind. We have sat amongst his followers on a hillside above the Sea of Galilee as he opened up the mysteries of God's Word for all to hear. But now the focus begins to change as "Jesus resolutely set(s) out for Jerusalem" (Luke 9:51). We will set off with him and witness even more astonishing things as he prepares for the events that lie ahead.

NOT PEACE BUT A SWORD

Whoever acknowledges me before others, I will also acknowledge before my Father in heaven. But whoever disowns me before others, I will disown before my Father in heaven. Do not suppose that I have come to bring peace to the earth. I did not come to bring peace, but a sword. For I have come to turn a man against his father, a daughter against her mother, a daughter-in-law against her mother-in-law—a man's enemies will be the members of his own household. MATTHEW 10:32–36

■

MEET JESUS THE REALIST. He knows that most will not willingly acknowledge him. He came into a needy and broken world, and he said explicitly that the world itself needs healing because at heart it is sick with sin: "It is not the healthy who need a doctor, but the sick. I have not come to call the righteous, but sinners" (Mark 2:17). The world is at war on every level: Families feud, nations battle nations, and God Himself is warred against. Jesus descended into the middle of this maelstrom, and he knows that many will either disbelieve that he came from God or will reject him because he came from God. But not everyone will fight against Jesus; some will turn and accept "the light of the knowledge of the glory of God in the face of Christ" (2 Corinthians 4:6).

WHO IS WORTHY OF ME?

Anyone who loves their father or mother more than me is not worthy of me; anyone who loves their son or daughter more than me is not worthy of me. Whoever does not take up their cross and follow me is not worthy of me. Whoever finds their life will lose it, and whoever loses their life for my sake will find it. MATTHEW 10:37–39

■

IN THIS LIFE THERE are many loves. There are wives, husbands, parents, brothers, sisters, and friends. There is our home and community and nation, and there is even our work. But what is our first love? The second part of the great commandment says: "Love your neighbor as yourself," but this commandment follows the first: "Love the Lord your God with all your heart and with all your soul and with all your mind and with all your strength" (Mark 12:30–31). Genuine love flows directly from our love of God to our families, neighbors, and communities. Never substitute the good for the best. "Whom have I in heaven but you? And earth has nothing I desire besides you. My flesh and my heart may fail, but God is the strength of my heart and my portion forever" (Psalm 73:25–26).

WHAT DOES JESUS MEAN BY "WELCOMES ME"?

Anyone who welcomes you welcomes me, and anyone who welcomes me welcomes the one who sent me. Whoever welcomes a prophet as a prophet will receive a prophet's reward, and whoever welcomes a righteous person as a righteous person will receive a righteous person's reward. And if anyone gives even a cup of cold water to one of these little ones who is my disciple, truly I tell you, that person will certainly not lose their reward. MATTHEW 10:40–42

■

WHEN WE HEAR THE word "connectivity" we often think of the properties of electricity. Without connectivity our computers and appliances would run down and eventually become useless. Here Jesus is simply saying, if someone welcomes you, he welcomes me and also God the Father, who sent me. Jesus uses the word "welcome" to convey a connectedness between a person, a follower of Jesus, Jesus himself, and God. A simple act of kindness or hospitality has cosmic connectivity. We may not always be privy to a full understanding of the consequences of a single act, but we do believe "that in all things God works for the good of those who love him, who have been called according to his purpose" (Romans 8:28).

HEROD: AFRAID OF JOHN?

Now Herod had arrested John and bound him and put him in prison because of Herodias, his brother Philip's wife, for John had been saying to him, "It is not lawful for you to have her." Herod wanted to kill John, but he was afraid of the people, because they considered John a prophet. MATTHEW 14:3–5

■

EVEN BEFORE MARY GAVE birth to Jesus, John was present in the narrative, first in the womb of Elizabeth his mother and then as a prophet attracting large crowds to the Jordan River to hear his proclamation that the time to repent had come. He also came as a witness to testify that one greater than he would soon appear. He said that the one who will follow him "will surpass me because he was before me" (John 1:15). John is considered a prophet in the spirit of Elijah, but once he had fulfilled his mission, he told his disciples, "A man can receive only what is given him from heaven. You yourselves can testify that I said, 'I am not the Christ but am sent ahead of him . . . He must become greater; I must become less'" (John 3:27–28, 30).

A DAUGHTER DANCED

On Herod's birthday the daughter of Herodias danced for the guests and pleased Herod so much that he promised with an oath to give her whatever she asked. Prompted by her mother, she said, "Give me here on a platter the head of John the Baptist." The king was distressed, but because of his oaths and his dinner guests, he ordered that her request be granted and had John beheaded in the prison. His head was brought in on a platter and given to the girl, who carried it to her mother. John's disciples came and took his body and buried it. Then they went and told Jesus. MATTHEW 14:6–12

■

WITH THE BRUTAL MURDER of John the Baptist, we witness the highest level of corrupt political drama imaginable. John had offended the wife of Herod Antipas by publically objecting to her marriage to Herod, because she had been the wife of Herod's living brother, Philip. Finally, through Herodias' insistence, Herod imprisoned John, but he did not execute him. Then, in a moment of drunken folly, Herod promised his wife's daughter that she could have anything she asked for. Herodias seized this moment to exact revenge on her imprisoned nemesis. Salome, the daughter, asked for the head of John on a platter, which put Herod in an impossible position. He had to comply, for to deny the request would have been to put his own position of power in question. So Herodias' lust for revenge was momentarily satisfied. When political power and corruption intersect, human suffering invariably follows.

HEROD FEARED JOHN
HAD COME BACK FROM THE DEAD

King Herod heard about this, for Jesus' name had become well known. Some were saying, "John the Baptist has been raised from the dead, and that is why miraculous powers are at work in him." Others said, "He is Elijah." And still others claimed, "He is a prophet, like one of the prophets of long ago." But when Herod heard this, he said, "John, whom I beheaded, has been raised from the dead!" MARK 6:14–16

∎

THE CRIME THAT COST John the Baptist his life was the crime of proclaiming the truth of God's Word to those who hold political power. John did not deny God to avoid the wrath of a powerful political figure that ultimately cost him his life. Jesus, too, encountered opposition from religious leaders throughout his three-year ministry, but they could not stop him from making his journey to Jerusalem, the seat of political power in Israel. We see both John and Jesus walk through a world steeped in sin and under the protection of the political and religious elites. So naturally, in such a godless place, we should not be surprised that both Jesus and John experienced strong resistance from the very people they came, in very different ways, to save: "Those who hate me without reason, outnumber the hairs of my head; many are my enemies without cause, those who seek to destroy me" (Psalm 69:4).

GIVE THEM SOMETHING TO EAT

When the apostles returned, they reported to Jesus what they had done. Then he took them with him and they withdrew by themselves to a town called Bethsaida, but the crowds learned about it and followed him. He welcomed them and spoke to them about the kingdom of God, and healed those who needed healing. Late in the afternoon the Twelve came to him and said, "Send the crowd away so they can go to the surrounding villages and countryside and find food and lodging, because we are in a remote place here." He replied, "You give them something to eat." They answered, "We have only five loaves of bread and two fish—unless we go and buy food for all this crowd." (About five thousand men were there.) LUKE 9:10–14

■

THE APOSTLES EXCITEDLY RETURNED to Jesus to report on all the things that had happened since they had been sent out. But then Jesus notched it up several levels. They went with Jesus to a remote place near the small town of Bethsaida, but crowds of people followed, causing a crisis. Thousands of people gathered to hear Jesus teach about the kingdom of God, and, for those in need, to experience the miracle of healing. When the apostles sensed the danger of the moment, they advised Jesus to send the people to the surrounding villages for food. The apostles performed miracles themselves, but here their minds reverted to seeking commonsense solutions for earth-bound problems like hunger. They forgot their own history of the exodus from Egyptian slavery, where God intervened supernaturally to supply all the food and drink necessary for survival. The apostles had not fully embraced the truth that all things are possible for God and that he will provide the means. Jesus stretched the boundaries of the possible to overcome the seeming impossibility of the momentary crisis.

TO TAKE, TO BLESS, TO BREAK, TO GIVE

(About five thousand men were there.) But he said to his disciples, "Have them sit down in groups of about fifty each." The disciples did so, and everyone sat down. Taking the five loaves and the two fish and looking up to heaven, he gave thanks and broke them. Then he gave them to the disciples to distribute to the people. They all ate and were satisfied, and the disciples picked up twelve basketfuls of broken pieces that were left over. LUKE 9:14–17

■

WITH HIS FEEDING THE five thousand, Jesus shows us that we are dependent creatures. We may flee from this reality, but that does not make our dependence any less real. After conception, we are dependent on our mother's body to sustain our life, and after our birth, we are helpless without the loving protection of our parents. On a larger plain, there could be no life without the sustaining warmth of the sun. In the natural world, interdependence is searched out by scientists who want to discover the secrets behind why the world operates as it does. It turns out, though, that Jesus is that searched-for connection. But he cannot be found if we limit the search to just naturalistic phenomena and explanation. The natural world in all its beauty and complexity is a reflection of the reality of the presence of God everywhere, just as we are creatures who reflect the image of God, not in our form but in our divinely shaped nature, as it was originally given to us.

LORD, SAVE ME!

. . . and the boat was already a considerable distance from land, buffeted by the waves because the wind was against it. Shortly before dawn Jesus went out to them, walking on the lake. When the disciples saw him walking on the lake, they were terrified. "It's a ghost," they said, and cried out in fear. But Jesus immediately said to them, "Take courage! It is I. Don't be afraid." "Lord, if it's you," Peter replied, "tell me to come to you on the water." "Come," he said. Then Peter got down out of the boat, walked on the water and came toward Jesus. But when he saw the wind, he was afraid and, beginning to sink, cried out, "Lord, save me!" Immediately Jesus reached out his hand and caught him. "You of little faith," he said, "why did you doubt?" And when they climbed into the boat, the wind died down. Then those who were in the boat worshiped him, saying, "Truly you are the Son of God." **MATTHEW** 14:24–33

∎

IF WE HAD BEEN among the disciples, would we have said with Peter, "You are the Christ" (Mark 9:29)? Alternatively, would we have said from the storm-tossed boat, "It's a ghost"? The disciples wavered because they were confronted with something that defied common sense and natural law. Men do not walk on water, nor do they feed five thousand people with a few fish and some bread. The disciples were often clueless when it came to accepting Jesus' true identity, even though they were with him almost all the time. As with the disciples, we need to cast aside our willingness to believe in almost anything as a substitute for believing in the Lordship of Jesus Christ. Our human nature demands that we believe, "It's a ghost." Only when the eyes of our hearts open up to the true identity of Jesus will we say, "It's the Lord."

THE WORK OF GOD

Once the crowd realized that neither Jesus nor his disciples were there, they got into the boats and went to Capernaum in search of Jesus. When they found him on the other side of the lake, they asked him, "Rabbi, when did you get here?" Jesus answered, "Very truly I tell you, you are looking for me, not because you saw the signs I performed but because you ate the loaves and had your fill. Do not work for food that spoils, but for food that endures to eternal life, which the Son of Man will give you. For on him God the Father has placed his seal of approval." Then they asked him, "What must we do to do the works God requires?" Jesus answered, "The work of God is this: to believe in the one he has sent." JOHN 6:24–29

■

"THE WORK OF GOD is this: to believe in the one he has sent." This statement sounds so simple, but consider its implications. One must begin with God: Do we believe he exists, and do we believe he created the heavens and the earth and everything in it? Do we believe that he created human beings in his own image, and do we believe he placed them in an abundant garden where they would have dominion and be able to exercise their own free will with but one exception? And do we believe that the woman and the man were deceived into disobedience and by doing so introduced alienation from God through sin that has carried on through all generations, even to the present day? And finally, do we believe that Jesus Christ is the only Son of God who was sent into this conflicted world to reconcile all men and women to God the Father through the shedding of his blood on a cross? The rulers, authorities, and powers of this dark world would have us believe in anything but the Lordship of Jesus Christ. To believe that Jesus is the Son of God is very real work because so much of the world has lined up against that belief.

THE TRUE BREAD FROM HEAVEN

So they asked him, "What sign then will you give that we may see it and believe you? What will you do? Our ancestors ate the manna in the wilderness; as it is written: 'He gave them bread from heaven to eat.'" Jesus said to them, "Very truly I tell you, it is not Moses who has given you the bread from heaven, but it is my Father who gives you the true bread from heaven. For the bread of God is the bread that comes down from heaven and gives life to the world." "Sir," they said, "always give us this bread." **JOHN 6:30–34**

■

AS WITH MATTHEW, MARK, and Luke, John tells the story of Jesus, but with a discernable difference: the language of John's Gospel is figurative and poetic. Rather than saying that God will satisfy our physical hunger and thirst, Jesus says, "It is my Father who gives you the true bread from heaven." Jesus uses language to suggest that he is speaking about something much more important than mere bread. He says that God will provide life through his Son, who is the perfect expression of the heart and mind of God Himself. Just as he told the Samaritan woman that the water he offers is a "spring of water welling up to eternal life," (John 4:14), the bread from heaven "comes down from heaven and gives life to the world." This figurative use of language is the way that Jesus indicates the presence of the Holy Spirit of God in all things. The language of man, taken alone, is insufficient to communicate the majesty and mystery of God: "Oh, the depth of the riches of the wisdom and knowledge of God! How unsearchable his judgments, and his paths beyond tracing out!" (Romans 11:33) John not only tells us what happens, he shows us through Jesus' use of language how the living Spirit of God is the animating reality behind life itself.

I AM THE BREAD OF LIFE

Then Jesus declared, "I am the bread of life. Whoever comes to me will never go hungry, and whoever believes in me will never be thirsty. But as I told you, you have seen me and still you do not believe. All those the Father gives me will come to me, and whoever comes to me I will never drive away. For I have come down from heaven not to do my will but to do the will of him who sent me. And this is the will of him who sent me, that I shall lose none of all those he has given me, but raise them up at the last day. For my Father's will is that everyone who looks to the Son and believes in him shall have eternal life, and I will raise them up at the last day." JOHN 6:35–40

■

WHEN MOSES ENCOUNTERED GOD in the desert, he asked God what he should say when asked who sent him. God replied, "I AM WHO I AM. This is what you are to say to the Israelites: 'I AM has sent me to you'" (Exodus 3:14). By saying, "I am the bread of life," Jesus connects himself directly to the sustainer of all life. There is no equivocation here. Jesus boldly proclaims his direct kinship to God the Father, and by doing so, he subjects himself to the accusation that he is a blasphemer. Jesus reinforces this claim by saying, "For I have come down from heaven not to do my will but to do the will of him who sent me." At the same time, he tells us directly the purpose of the Father in sending him: "For my Father's will is that everyone who looks to the Son and believes in him shall have eternal life, and I shall raise them up at the last day."

THIS BREAD IS MY FLESH

At this the Jews there began to grumble about him because he said, "I am the bread that came down from heaven." They said, "Is this not Jesus, the son of Joseph, whose father and mother we know? How can he now say, 'I came down from heaven'?" "Stop grumbling among yourselves," Jesus answered. "No one can come to me unless the Father who sent me draws them, and I will raise them up at the last day. It is written in the Prophets: 'They will all be taught by God.' Everyone who has heard the Father and learned from him comes to me. No one has seen the Father except the one who is from God; only he has seen the Father. Very truly I tell you, the one who believes has eternal life. I am the bread of life. Your ancestors ate the manna in the wilderness, yet they died. But here is the bread that comes down from heaven, which anyone may eat and not die. I am the living bread that came down from heaven. Whoever eats this bread will live forever. This bread is my flesh, which I will give for the life of the world." JOHN 6:41–51

■

HOW DO YOU IDENTIFY yourself? Is it by name? Or is it by your association to family or community or even to work or wealth? It is easy for any of us to fall into the identity others have foisted upon us, but this is not the case with Jesus. He does not allow himself to be wedged into any of the normal reductionist categories. Just the opposite: Jesus constantly reframes his identity beyond the normal definitions of family and town. He wants us to see that he existed with the Father in heaven prior to the incarnation. He is the Son, and he is on a life-saving mission. Later, in Jerusalem, he confirms this relationship with the Father when he prays, "Father, glorify me in your presence with the glory I had with you before the world began" (John 17:5).

A DIFFICULT TEACHING

Jesus said to them, "Very truly I tell you, unless you eat the flesh of the Son of Man and drink his blood, you have no life in you. Whoever eats my flesh and drinks my blood has eternal life, and I will raise them up at the last day. For my flesh is real food and my blood is real drink. Whoever eats my flesh and drinks my blood remains in me, and I in them. Just as the living Father sent me and I live because of the Father, so the one who feeds on me will live because of me. This is the bread that came down from heaven. Your ancestors ate manna and died, but whoever feeds on this bread will live forever." He said this while teaching in the synagogue in Capernaum. JOHN 6:53–59

■

IF JESUS' INTENT IS to startle, then he succeeds when he says, "Whoever eats my flesh and drinks my blood remains in me, and I in them." It is important to remember, though, that Jesus often speaks figuratively. This is an instance where he is prefiguring the Eucharist, where the bread is the body of Christ and the wine his blood. Jesus says that we need to ingest this bread and this wine to become one with him, just as he is one with the Father. "Just as the living Father sent me and I live because of the Father, so the one who feeds on me will live because of me."

On hearing it, many of his disciples said, "This is a hard teaching. Who can accept it?" Aware that his disciples were grumbling about this, Jesus said to them, "Does this offend you? Then what if you see the Son of Man ascend to where he was before! The Spirit gives life; the flesh counts for nothing. The words I have spoken to you—they are full of the Spirit and life. Yet there are some of you who do not believe." For Jesus had known from the beginning which of them did not believe and who would betray him. He went on to say, "This is why I told you that no one can come to me unless the Father has enabled them." From this time many of his disciples turned back and no longer followed him. "You do not want to leave too, do you?" Jesus asked the Twelve. Simon Peter answered him, "Lord, to whom shall we go? You have the words of eternal life. We have come to believe and to know that you are the Holy One of God." JOHN 6:60–69

■

HERE WE CONCLUDE a series of passages from the Gospel of John that seem to set Jesus apart from many of his followers. These followers said, in effect, that Jesus is a crazy man speaking of crazy things, and they were put off by it. They could no longer follow him, and so they left. It is no different today. Jesus is truly revolutionary. He asks each of us to do the most uncomfortable thing in this world: Break from our past allegiances and follow him. It is hard, very hard, and we become exhausted trying to overcome our predisposition not to follow. But despite this, Jesus says, "Come to me, all you who are weary and burdened, and I will give you rest. Take my yoke upon you and learn from me, for I am gentle and humble in heart, and you will find rest for your souls. For my yoke is easy and my burden is light" (Matthew 11:28–30). Peter was right when he asked, "Lord, to whom shall we go?" He asked not only for himself, but for us too.

The Pharisees and some of the teachers of the law who had come from Jerusalem gathered around Jesus and saw some of his disciples eating food with hands that were defiled, that is, unwashed. (The Pharisees and all the Jews do not eat unless they give their hands a ceremonial washing, holding to the tradition of the elders. When they come from the marketplace they do not eat unless they wash. And they observe many other traditions, such as the washing of cups, pitchers and kettles.) So the Pharisees and teachers of the law asked Jesus, "Why don't your disciples live according to the tradition of the elders instead of eating their food with defiled hands?" He replied, "Isaiah was right when he prophesied about you hypocrites; as it is written: 'These people honor me with their lips, but their hearts are far from me. They worship me in vain; their teachings are merely human rules.' You have let go of the commands of God and are holding on to human traditions."
MARK 7:1–8

■

ONCE AGAIN, JESUS MAKES a distinction that if applied will lead to a truly God-centered life. Jesus says, quoting Isaiah, that the religious leaders have replaced the commands of God with human traditions. He calls them hypocrites because they force their rules on the people but don't live by them themselves: "'These people honor me with their lips, but their hearts are far from me'" (Isaiah 29:13). The leaders had departed so far from God's path that they transformed God's principles for a better life into a set of impossible rules and regulations of a burdened life.

NULLIFYING THE WORD OF GOD

And Jesus continued, "You have a fine way of setting aside the commands of God in order to observe your own traditions! For Moses said, 'Honor your father and mother,' and, 'Anyone who curses their father or mother is to be put to death.' But you say that if anyone declares that what might have been used to help their father or mother is Corban (that is, devoted to God)—then you no longer let them do anything for their father or mother. Thus you nullify the word of God by your tradition that you have handed down. And you do many things like that." MARK 7:9–13

■

AS WE CONTINUE IN this passage from Mark's Gospel, we see Jesus elaborate on his teaching on the liberating nature of God's law. The law was given to guide all troubled and blinded people back to the better way, but over time, as Jesus points out, man's traditions began to become substitutes for God's Word. Jesus came from God to reestablish what has always been true: God created men and women with the free will to accept God's gift of love or to reject it. But with rejection comes tragic consequences, which all of us struggle with every day. Human traditions do not liberate, but they can enslave. Jesus does not want to abolish the law; he has come to fulfill it, and by doing so, he offers everyone a pathway to true freedom (Matthew 5:17–20).

OUT OF THE HEART

Again Jesus called the crowd to him and said, "Listen to me, everyone, and understand this. Nothing outside a person can defile them by going into them. Rather, it is what comes out of a person that defiles them." After he had left the crowd and entered the house, his disciples asked him about this parable. "Are you so dull?" he asked. "Don't you see that nothing that enters a person from the outside can defile them? For it doesn't go into their heart but into their stomach, and then out of the body." (In saying this, Jesus declared all foods clean.) He went on: "What comes out of a person is what defiles them. For it is from within, out of a person's heart, that evil thoughts come—sexual immorality, theft, murder, adultery, greed, malice, deceit, lewdness, envy, slander, arrogance and folly. All these evils come from inside and defile a person."
MARK 7:14–23

■

NEARLY ALL THE GREAT poets and writers, from Shakespeare to Dostoyevsky to Tolstoy, draw their inspiration from biblical truth discovered in passages like this one. Jesus provides us with an insight into the condition of the broken human heart, where all kinds of evil inclinations bubble over into evil thoughts that lead to destructive action. This condition, untreated, is fatal. Jesus came to cauterize the human heart so that out of such a heart will flow thoughts and passions that mirror God's thoughts and passions. It is for this purpose that God sent Jesus into the world. The peace Jesus speaks of is not a political or societal peace, it is the peace that Paul proclaims in his letter to the Romans: "What a wretched man that I am! Who will rescue me from this body of death? Thanks be to God—through Jesus Christ our Lord!" (Romans 7:24–25)

Jesus left there and went along the Sea of Galilee. Then he went up on a mountainside and sat down. Great crowds came to him, bringing the lame, the blind, the crippled, the mute and many others, and laid them at his feet; and he healed them. The people were amazed when they saw the mute speaking, the crippled made well, the lame walking and the blind seeing. And they praised the God of Israel. MATTHEW 15:29–31

■

THE CONTRAST IS STARK. The setting is the Sea of Galilee, a place of sweeping beauty with low-lying mountains that surround the sea and a breeze that cools the land. Into such a place came people who were lame, blind, crippled, and mute to be healed by the one who came to heal all. The broken condition of man, with all of its suffering, is out of place here. It was not meant to be this way. The place and the people were meant to be in harmony with one another, and so Jesus performed the miracle of healing. The mute spoke, the crippled were made well, the lame walked, and the blind were given sight. "And they praised the God of Israel." Once again, Jesus revealed through his power to heal that he is all about the restoration of the true kingdom, where harmony exists between God and man.

A WICKED AND ADULTEROUS GENERATION

The Pharisees and Sadducees came to Jesus and tested him by asking him to show them a sign from heaven. He replied, "When evening comes, you say, 'It will be fair weather, for the sky is red,' and in the morning, 'Today it will be stormy, for the sky is red and overcast.' You know how to interpret the appearance of the sky, but you cannot interpret the signs of the times. A wicked and adulterous generation looks for a sign, but none will be given it except the sign of Jonah." Jesus then left them and went away.

MATTHEW 16:1–4

■

IN CONTRAST TO THE vision of God's kingdom that we experienced on the mountainside above the Sea of Galilee, we now see Jesus confronted by the ruling class. These were the people who expropriated all the levers of power and misused that power to take over the system for their own advantage. Jesus challenged their authority by saying that while they may have knowledge and even natural wisdom born of experience, they cannot see clearly because they look at all things through the eyes of the world they are immersed in. They had no spiritual discernment because they were part of a "wicked and adulterous generation." Spiritual discernment means that any knowledge and wisdom one possesses is always exercised in cooperation with God. The ruling Pharisees and Sadducees were in opposition to Jesus, and therefore they were in opposition to God.

WHO DO YOU SAY I AM?

Once when Jesus was praying in private and his disciples were with him, he asked them, "Who do the crowds say I am?" They replied, "Some say John the Baptist; others say Elijah; and still others, that one of the prophets of long ago has come back to life." "But what about you?" he asked. "Who do you say I am?" Peter answered, "God's Messiah." LUKE 9:18–21

■

"BUT WHAT ABOUT YOU? Who do you say I am?" Peter answered the question, but have we? Christianity is not about groups or denominations, it is built on an individual's belief that Jesus is the Messiah, the Anointed One of God. This belief is the building block of the church, and the power of this belief moves the corporate body of the church to reach out to the world, near and far, to proclaim the truth that Jesus Christ is Lord. As Jesus called his disciples to follow even before belief could become the springboard to action, so too we are called so that through our belief in Jesus as Lord, we can act with the authority of the Holy Spirit in a world that needs to hear and know the truth.

He then began to teach them that the Son of Man must suffer many things and be rejected by the elders, the chief priests and the teachers of the law, and that he must be killed and after three days rise again. He spoke plainly about this, and Peter took him aside and began to rebuke him. But when Jesus turned and looked at his disciples, he rebuked Peter. "Get behind me, Satan!" he said. "You do not have in mind the concerns of God, but merely human concerns." **MARK 8:31–33**

■

ONE MOMENT PETER WAS inspired to proclaim Jesus "God's Messiah," but then in another he went off the rails, causing Jesus to rebuke him. What happened? Peter had his own preconception of what God's Messiah was meant to be. Peter believed that the Messiah had come to liberate Israel from the iron yoke of Roman domination, but Jesus corrected Peter by saying he had reduced Jesus to a narrow, human understanding of the Messiah's mission. Peter may have been thinking of Daniel's revelation, but Jesus pointed to the suffering servant of Isaiah when he said, "the Son of Man must suffer many things and be rejected . . ." Peter moved from brilliant insight to missing the mark completely, which should serve as a cautionary tale for anyone who believes they have the inside track in discerning the mind of God by using "mere human concerns" as the basis for interpretation.

Then he called the crowd to him along with his disciples and said: "Whoever wants to be my disciple must deny themselves and take up their cross and follow me. For whoever wants to save their life will lose it, but whoever loses their life for me and for the gospel will save it. What good is it for someone to gain the whole world, yet forfeit their soul? Or what can anyone give in exchange for their soul? If anyone is ashamed of me and my words in this adulterous and sinful generation, the Son of Man will be ashamed of them when he comes in his Father's glory with the holy angels." And he said to them, "Truly I tell you, some who are standing here will not taste death before they see that the kingdom of God has come with power." **MARK 8:34–9:1**

∎

IT IS DIFFICULT FOR us to hear these words: "Whoever wants to be my disciple must deny themselves and take up their cross and follow me." Our culture, from our families and communities to our finest institutions, preaches of pathways that promote self-advancement and self-actualization. If their assumption is that this life is the only game in town, then they might be right. But Jesus sees beyond this narrow understanding of life and death on Earth. He is thinking beyond the City of Man to the City of God. As inhabitants of this Earth, Jesus wants us to balance the necessities of this life with the necessities of the next.

About eight days after Jesus said this, he took Peter, John and James with him and went up onto a mountain to pray. As he was praying, the appearance of his face changed, and his clothes became as bright as a flash of lightning. Two men, Moses and Elijah, appeared in glorious splendor, talking with Jesus. They spoke about his departure, which he was about to bring to fulfillment at Jerusalem. Peter and his companions were very sleepy, but when they became fully awake, they saw his glory and the two men standing with him. As the men were leaving Jesus, Peter said to him, "Master, it is good for us to be here. Let us put up three shelters—one for you, one for Moses and one for Elijah." (He did not know what he was saying.) While he was speaking, a cloud appeared and covered them, and they were afraid as they entered the cloud. A voice came from the cloud, saying, "This is my Son, whom I have chosen; listen to him." When the voice had spoken, they found that Jesus was alone. The disciples kept this to themselves and did not tell anyone at that time what they had seen.

LUKE 9:28–36

■

IN EXODUS, MOSES WENT to the mountain to receive the Law. Elijah received the Word of God on Horeb, the mountain of God (1 Kings 19). Here on the Mount of Transfiguration in the company of Moses and Elijah, Jesus was commissioned and strengthened to go forward with God's mission. He received everything he would need, and the voice of God proclaimed to Peter, John, and James, "This is my Son, whom I have chosen; listen to him." This is a turning point. Next Jesus set his sights on another high place, called Golgotha, where he will glorify God by giving his own life for many.

When they came to the crowd, a man approached Jesus and knelt before him. "Lord, have mercy on my son," he said. "He has seizures and is suffering greatly. He often falls into the fire or into the water. I brought him to your disciples, but they could not heal him." "You unbelieving and perverse generation," Jesus replied, "how long shall I stay with you? How long shall I put up with you? Bring the boy here to me." Jesus rebuked the demon, and it came out of the boy, and he was healed at that moment. Then the disciples came to Jesus in private and asked, "Why couldn't we drive it out?" He replied, "Because you have so little faith. Truly I tell you, if you have faith as small as a mustard seed, you can say to this mountain, 'Move from here to there,' and it will move. Nothing will be impossible for you." MATTHEW 17:14–20

■

INTERESTINGLY, JESUS' CLAIM THAT through faith we can move mountains may not be quite as outlandish as it first sounds. Herod, the great and brutal king of Israel, was known in his time as a prolific builder. He built the seaside city of Caesarea to honor Caesar, his political master in Rome, and he also built many other buildings and temples. But one of his greatest projects was a fortress that he called Herodium. It still stands today outside of Bethlehem, and is not far from Jerusalem itself. Herod had to literally move a mountain to construct this fortress. It stands as the highest point in the vicinity, and it would have been known to the people of Jesus' time. Rather than use hyperbole to make his point, Jesus may have drawn his example from a very real event of recent history where a mountain was moved by the will of one man who had the political and financial power to move it. The power to move mountains is even truer in the kingdom of God.

They left that place and passed through Galilee. Jesus did not want anyone to know where they were, because he was teaching his disciples. He said to them, "The Son of Man is going to be delivered into the hands of men. They will kill him, and after three days he will rise." But they did not understand what he meant and were afraid to ask him about it. They came to Capernaum. When he was in the house, he asked them, "What were you arguing about on the road?" But they kept quiet because on the way they had argued about who was the greatest. MARK 9:30–32

■

THE DISCIPLES SEEMED LOST when Jesus said that he would be delivered into the hands of men, be killed by them, and then after three days rise. Could it be that their perplexity grew out of Jesus identifying himself as the "Son of Man"? While Isaiah identified the Messiah as the Suffering Servant, Daniel described this "son of man" as a conquering warrior: "In my vision at night I looked, and there before my eyes was one like a son of man, coming with the clouds of heaven . . . He was given authority, glory and sovereign power; all peoples, nations and men of every language worshipped him" (Daniel 7:13–14). If this was the lens the disciples used to identify Jesus as the Messiah, then it is understandable why they were confused. They glossed over Isaiah's Messiah, who would come as the Suffering Servant (Isaiah 53). Jesus says the Suffering Servant must come first, then there will be a second coming at the end of times, which is described in both Daniel and Revelation. The disciples narrowed the Son of Man to their own interpretation, leaving aside the more complete picture. Their narrow lens distorted their understanding of what was actually happening.

WHO IS THE GREATEST?

An argument started among the disciples as to which of them would be the greatest. Jesus, knowing their thoughts, took a little child and had him stand beside him. Then he said to them, "Whoever welcomes this little child in my name welcomes me; and whoever welcomes me welcomes the one who sent me. For it is the one who is least among you all who is the greatest." LUKE 9:46–48

■

THE ARGUMENT AMONG THE disciples about who would be considered the greatest represents the world's point of view on almost every subject. We strive for money, position, and awards so that others will officially see the greatness that we see in ourselves. Jesus told his disciples plainly that this striving is upside down. The world can offer all kinds of recognition, just as Satan attempted to offer Jesus all the kingdoms of this world. But the kingdom of heaven is not about awards; it is about grace. It is not about what we do; it is about what animates what we do. After the resurrection, Jesus restored Peter by asking a very simple question three times: "Do you truly love me?" (John 21:16) He was not asking if Peter truly loved these other disciples or even himself. He was asking the one essential question everyone must eventually answer: Do you love the Lord your God with all your heart, with all your soul, with all your strength, and with all your mind?

He took a little child whom he placed among them. Taking the child in his arms, he said to them, "Whoever welcomes one of these little children in my name welcomes me; and whoever welcomes me does not welcome me but the one who sent me." "Teacher," said John, "we saw someone driving out demons in your name and we told him to stop, because he was not one of us." "Do not stop him," Jesus said. "For no one who does a miracle in my name can in the next moment say anything bad about me, for whoever is not against us is for us. Truly I tell you, anyone who gives you a cup of water in my name because you belong to the Messiah will certainly not lose their reward." MARK 9:36–41

■

C.S. LEWIS MUST HAVE been thinking of this passage when he wrote, "There must be a real giving up of the self . . . As long as your own personality is what you are bothering about you are not going to Him at all. The very first step is to try to forget about the self altogether" (*Mere Christianity*). Jesus continues to teach kingdom principles. The disciples fell into the trap of tribal exclusion. They said that if someone was not part of the group, then that person must be against them. Jesus cut through this artificially constructed barrier by saying, "whoever is not against us is for us." Jesus is all about inclusion; he wants no one to miss the chance for salvation.

GOD IS NOT WILLING
THAT ANY SHOULD PERISH

What do you think? If a man owns a hundred sheep, and one of them wanders away, will he not leave the ninety-nine on the hills and go to look for the one that wandered off? And if he finds it, truly I tell you, he is happier about that one sheep than about the ninety-nine that did not wander off. In the same way your Father in heaven is not willing that any of these little ones should perish.
MATTHEW 18:12–14

■

IN JESUS' TIME, WHEN a shepherd contracted to take care of a flock, it was implicitly agreed that he would be responsible for returning eighty percent of the number he began with. It was understood that some would be lost, some stolen, and some eaten by predators. Only in the rarest of cases would a shepherd leave the ninety-nine to look for one lost sheep. But God is not like the contract shepherd; he will leave the safe ones to seek and find the one lost sheep, and so it is for each one of us. The church was built for seeking lost sheep, and Jesus is the model. He excluded no one who sought to be healed. The beggar called out, "Lord, have mercy on me, a sinner," and Jesus restored his sight. The church operates on this model as well; it is the one institution that exists for its "not yet" members. Jesus' command for each and every one of us as members of his body is "go and seek the lost."

After this, Jesus went around in Galilee. He did not want to go about in Judea because the Jewish leaders there were looking for a way to kill him. But when the Jewish Festival of Tabernacles was near, Jesus' brothers said to him, "Leave Galilee and go to Judea, so that your disciples there may see the works you do. No one who wants to become a public figure acts in secret. Since you are doing these things, show yourself to the world." For even his own brothers did not believe in him. Therefore Jesus told them, "My time is not yet here; for you any time will do. The world cannot hate you, but it hates me because I testify that its works are evil. You go to the festival. I am not going up to this festival, because my time has not yet fully come." After he had said this, he stayed in Galilee. JOHN 7:1–9

■

BY DECLARING, "MY TIME has not yet fully come," Jesus told his followers (and us) that he does not operate on his own. He must wait on his Father's word. Many times before Jesus said, "I go where the Father is going, I do what the Father does and I say what the Father is saying." Jesus sees himself completely woven into his Father's narrative and will do his Father's will only when the Father commands him to act. If Jesus is commanded to wait, he will wait; if commanded to go, he will go. Apart from the Father he can do nothing.

JESUS APPOINTED SEVENTY-TWO

After this the Lord appointed seventy-two others and sent them two by two ahead of him to every town and place where he was about to go. He told them, "The harvest is plentiful, but the workers are few. Ask the Lord of the harvest, therefore, to send out workers into his harvest field. Go! I am sending you out like lambs among wolves. Do not take a purse or bag or sandals; and do not greet anyone on the road." LUKE 10:1–4

∎

JESUS COMMISSIONED SEVENTY-TWO DISCIPLES to go out into a forbidding world that he compares to a place where wolves prey upon lambs. Jesus was also looking ahead to the time when others must labor in the fields of the lost. He not only commissioned the seventy-two, but also all who believe in him from that time to this: "Ask the Lord of the harvest, therefore, to send out workers into his harvest field." But it is not just about workers; it is about you and me. The workers are few; the harvest is plentiful; the time is now.

I HAVE GIVEN YOU AUTHORITY

The seventy-two returned with joy and said, "Lord, even the demons submit to us in your name." He replied, "I saw Satan fall like lightning from heaven. I have given you authority to trample on snakes and scorpions and to overcome all the power of the enemy; nothing will harm you. However, do not rejoice that the spirits submit to you, but rejoice that your names are written in heaven." At that time Jesus, full of joy through the Holy Spirit, said, "I praise you, Father, Lord of heaven and earth, because you have hidden these things from the wise and learned, and revealed them to little children. Yes, Father, for this is what you were pleased to do." LUKE 10:17–21

■

IT IS HARD TO avoid the truth that evil exists in the world. Jesus gives us a brief glimpse of how evil came to be when he says, "I saw Satan fall like lightening from heaven." Through multiple passages in the Bible, we can reconstruct a picture of what happened even before the creation of mankind. We know that Satan was an angel, that he had followers, that he rebelled against God, that he was banished from heaven, and that he fell to earth, where he began to plot his own restoration. As an angel of God, Satan existed before God created Adam and Eve and he existed before Eden. Satan entered Eden to frustrate and destroy on earth what he could not destroy in heaven. Jesus was sent to earth to do just the opposite: He came to restore the broken relationship between men and women and God. By saying that he saw Satan fall from heaven, Jesus is clearly identifying himself as the Son of God. He was there before time, as we understand it, existed.

Jesus then left that place and went into the region of Judea and across the Jordan. Again crowds of people came to him, and as was his custom, he taught them. MARK 10:1

■

AS LONG AS JESUS stayed in Galilee, he did not represent an extraordinary threat to the religious authorities. But then he crossed the Jordan and entered Judea, and the crowds followed him. While the Pharisees and Sadducees did not make themselves known here, it did not take long for Jesus to attract their attention. As long as he appeared to be an itinerate preacher, they dismissed him as nothing more problematic than an irritating nobody. But as he drew near to Jerusalem, their dismissive attitude was transformed into concern, and once they perceived him as a threat, they pulled all the levers of political power to bring him down.

As they were walking along the road, a man said to him, "I will follow you wherever you go." Jesus replied, "Foxes have dens and birds have nests, but the Son of Man has no place to lay his head." He said to another man, "Follow me." But he replied, "Lord, first let me go and bury my father." Jesus said to him, "Let the dead bury their own dead, but you go and proclaim the kingdom of God." Still another said, "I will follow you, Lord; but first let me go back and say goodbye to my family." Jesus replied, "No one who puts a hand to the plow and looks back is fit for service in the kingdom of God." LUKE 9:57–62

■

WHAT DOES IT MEAN to be a disciple? Jesus does not give us the answer we may want to hear. It is easy to say, "I am a Christian," but what if being a Christian means giving up the comforts of home or family? What if it means being called into an entirely new identity, where we cannot rely on the experiences of the past or the dreams of the future but must embrace the present moment with the life that Christ has called us to live? "Foxes have dens and birds have nests, but the Son of Man has no place to lay his head." This is exactly what discipleship might look like to any of us. If this is uncomfortable, then we might re-examine the things we truly value as we live the life we have been given.

WHO IS HE?

However, after his brothers had left for the Feast, he went also, not publicly, but in secret. Now at the Feast the Jews were watching for him and asking, "Where is that man?" Among the crowds there was widespread whispering about him. Some said, "He is a good man." Others replied, "No, he deceives the people." But no one would say anything publicly about him for fear of the Jews.
JOHN 7:10–13

■

HERE IS A QUESTION that has challenged people from Christ's time to our own: Who is this man? Jesus asked his own disciples, "Who do you say I am?" (Mark 9:29) In Jerusalem, controversy swirled around Jesus. Some called him a good man while others called him a deceiver. The Gospel writers were not afraid to report that during the time of his ministry, as many opposed and dismissed him as embraced him. At one point even his own mother and brothers came to believe he might be unbalanced (Mark 3:31-35), and at another, the adoring crowds tried to make him an earthly king by force (John 6:15). But we need to ask, would it be any different today? Would we recognize him and praise him, or would we dismiss him as a charlatan, or even worse?

Not until halfway through the festival did Jesus go up to the temple courts and begin to teach. The Jews there were amazed and asked, "How did this man get such learning without having been taught?" Jesus answered, "My teaching is not my own. It comes from the one who sent me. Anyone who chooses to do the will of God will find out whether my teaching comes from God or whether I speak on my own. Whoever speaks on their own does so to gain personal glory, but he who seeks the glory of the one who sent him is a man of truth; there is nothing false about him. Has not Moses given you the law? Yet not one of you keeps the law. Why are you trying to kill me?" "You are demon-possessed," the crowd answered. "Who is trying to kill you?" JOHN 7:14–20

■

AT FIRST, JESUS DID not reveal himself in Jerusalem. He went up to the city from Galilee anonymously. But once there he went to the southern entrance of the temple and began to speak to the crowds. The people were amazed because, though not well known, he spoke as one with authority. While all the religious leaders and rabbis had earned their credentials through the official schools, Jesus claimed his authority from a very different source: "My teaching is not my own. It comes from the one who sent me . . . Whoever speaks on his own does so to gain personal glory, but he who seeks the glory of the one who sent him is a man of truth; there is nothing false about him." To those listening, including some of the religious leaders, this claim bordered on blasphemy. Furthermore, Jesus knew what was in their hearts and confronted them about it: "Why are you trying to kill me?" It will soon become clear that he was reading them right.

HE SENT ME

Then Jesus, still teaching in the temple courts, cried out, "Yes, you know me, and you know where I am from. I am not here on my own authority, but he who sent me is true. You do not know him, but I know him because I am from him and he sent me." At this they tried to seize him, but no one laid a hand on him, because his hour had not yet come. Still, many in the crowd believed in him. They said, "When the Messiah comes, will he perform more signs than this man?" JOHN 7:28–31

■

THE GOSPELS PRESENT US with a mystery: Who is this man? The people of his own time were confounded by a man who performed astonishing miracles but who did not meet their expectations of what the savior of Israel would be like. Was he a prophet in the tradition of Elijah and Elisha? Was he the long-anticipated Messiah, the anointed one in the line of David? Or was he a crazy man who probably needed to be locked away? Then there were the miracles that many witnessed, including some in the crowd. Whatever the crowd thought, Jesus remained certain of his own identity and teaching. And he did not take personal credit; instead he made an even more audacious claim: "I am not here on my own authority, but him who sent me is true. You do not know him, but I know him because I am from him and he sent me."

RIVERS OF LIVING WATER WILL FLOW

The Pharisees heard the crowd whispering such things about him. Then the chief priests and the Pharisees sent temple guards to arrest him. Jesus said, "I am with you for only a short time, and then I am going to the one who sent me. You will look for me, but you will not find me; and where I am, you cannot come." The Jews said to one another, "Where does this man intend to go that we cannot find him? Will he go where our people live scattered among the Greeks, and teach the Greeks? What did he mean when he said, 'You will look for me, but you will not find me,' and 'Where I am, you cannot come'?" On the last and greatest day of the festival, Jesus stood and said in a loud voice, "Let anyone who is thirsty come to me and drink. Whoever believes in me, as Scripture has said, rivers of living water will flow from within them." By this he meant the Spirit, whom those who believed in him were later to receive. Up to that time the Spirit had not been given, since Jesus had not yet been glorified. JOHN 7:32–39

■

JESUS TOLD THE SAMARITAN woman at the well, "God is spirit" (John 4:24). At the very beginning of Genesis we are told, "Now the earth was formless and empty, darkness was over the surface of the deep, and the Spirit of God was hovering over the waters" (Genesis 1:2). And after he sinned and prayed for forgiveness, David pleaded with God, "Do not cast me from your presence or take your Holy Spirit from me" (Psalm 51:11). So when Jesus says, "Whoever believes in me, as Scripture has said, rivers of living water will flow from within them," he means the Spirit of God who will be received later by those who believe in him. God is Spirit, but with sin, we lost access to the Spirit of God. Without that Spirit, we are nothing but "a mere phantom as (we) go to and fro" (Psalm 39:6). Jesus knows men and women thirst for the Holy Spirit. He came to earth to open the way to life through his life.

THE PEOPLE WERE DIVIDED BECAUSE OF JESUS

On hearing his words, some of the people said, "Surely this man is the Prophet." Others said, "He is the Messiah." Still others asked, "How can the Messiah come from Galilee? Does not Scripture say that the Messiah will come from David's descendants and from Bethlehem, the town where David lived?" Thus the people were divided because of Jesus. Some wanted to seize him, but no one laid a hand on him. JOHN 7:40–44

■

A DISPUTE AROSE: SOME said Jesus was a prophet, others said he must be the Messiah, and another, educated in the Scriptures, said he couldn't be the Messiah because he is from Galilee and not from David's birthplace. Confusion reigned because Jesus did not fit into any of the boxes people built for him. What was true then is true today. It is hard to see people and events clearly because we tend to see through a multitude of lenses that filter reality into preconceived ideas that allow us to define the world in our own narrow terms. So if Jesus does not fit, we can filter him in a number of ways that will not discomfort us. We can say he was a wise man or a prophet and we would be right as far as those definitions go, but if we filter out the mystery that is at the very center of the Jesus encounter, then we reduce Jesus to something right-sized for humans but completely out of focus as the Son of God.

Finally the temple guards went back to the chief priests and the Pharisees, who asked them, "Why didn't you bring him in?" "No one ever spoke the way this man does," the guards replied. "You mean he has deceived you also?" the Pharisees retorted. "Have any of the rulers or of the Pharisees believed in him? No! But this mob that knows nothing of the law—there is a curse on them." Nicodemus, who had gone to Jesus earlier and who was one of their own number, asked, "Does our law condemn a man without first hearing him to find out what he has been doing?" They replied, "Are you from Galilee, too? Look into it, and you will find that a prophet does not come out of Galilee." JOHN 7:45–52

■

IT IS IMPORTANT TO note that the chief priests and the Pharisees were knowledgeable men; they knew their theology, but they did not know enough. Through their study and tradition, they knew that the Messiah would be in the line of David and would be born in Bethlehem. But everything else they claimed to know was based on hearsay and assumptions. They heard that Jesus came from Nazareth, but this was not where he was born. Ironically, their partial knowledge made the case that Jesus was the Messiah because he was of the line of David and was born in Bethlehem. But the chief priests were not looking for the truth; they were concocting reasons to arrest and condemn a man whom they perceived to be a threat to their power and privilege. To them, Jesus was a potentially dangerous troublemaker.

But Jesus went to the Mount of Olives. At dawn he appeared again in the temple courts, where all the people gathered around him, and he sat down to teach them. The teachers of the law and the Pharisees brought in a woman caught in adultery. They made her stand before the group and said to Jesus, "Teacher, this woman was caught in the act of adultery. In the Law Moses commanded us to stone such women. Now what do you say?" They were using this question as a trap, in order to have a basis for accusing him. But Jesus bent down and started to write on the ground with his finger. When they kept on questioning him, he straightened up and said to them, "Let any one of you who is without sin be the first to throw a stone at her." Again he stooped down and wrote on the ground. At this, those who heard began to go away one at a time, the older ones first, until only Jesus was left, with the woman still standing there. Jesus straightened up and asked her, "Woman, where are they? Has no one condemned you?" "No one, sir," she said. "Then neither do I condemn you," Jesus declared. "Go now and leave your life of sin." JOHN 8:1–11

■

THE TRAP SET FOR Jesus by the teachers of the law and the Pharisees was cunning because it put Jesus in an untenable position between two irreconcilable laws. If he said the woman caught in adultery must be stoned, then he was defying a Roman law that did not permit the Jewish people to carry out death sentences. If he did not condemn her, he would have been accused of disregarding Jewish law. Instead of arguing for or against a particular outcome, Jesus wrote in the sand with his finger. What he wrote is not known—it could have been the three words of condemnation recorded in the Book of Daniel or it could have been something else—but whatever the actual words were, they put the fear of God in the hearts of the accusers, and they slowly slinked away, understanding that the finger was pointing directly at them.

I AM THE LIGHT OF THE WORLD

When Jesus spoke again to the people, he said, "I am the light of the world. Whoever follows me will never walk in darkness, but will have the light of life." The Pharisees challenged him, "Here you are, appearing as your own witness; your testimony is not valid." Jesus answered, "Even if I testify on my own behalf, my testimony is valid, for I know where I came from and where I am going. But you have no idea where I come from or where I am going. You judge by human standards; I pass judgment on no one. But if I do judge, my decisions are true, because I am not alone. I stand with the Father, who sent me. In your own Law it is written that the testimony of two witnesses is true. I am one who testifies for myself; my other witness is the Father, who sent me." JOHN 8:12–18

■

HOW DO WE KNOW something is true? How do we validate a declaration? Truth can be hard to determine. Sometimes the evidence is unclear or there are contradictory claims. Proverbs says, "The first to present his case seems right, 'til another comes forward and questions him" (Proverbs 18:17). If we did not experience an event ourselves, we must depend on the credibility of witnesses, and this goes to the heart of how we respond to the accounts of Jesus' life, death, and resurrection. Are the witnesses credible? Luke tells us that while he was not a direct witness, he carefully investigated everything from the beginning to provide an orderly account so that the reader might know the certainty of the things that have been taught (Luke 1:3–4). In the Gospel of John, we are told that John the Baptist was sent by God to be a witness to testify about Jesus so that "through him all men might believe" (John 1:7). Down through the ages there have been countless witnesses who put aside personal well-being in order to testify to the truth of the Lordship of Jesus Christ.

YOU WILL INDEED DIE IN YOUR SINS

Once more Jesus said to them, "I am going away, and you will look for me, and you will die in your sin. Where I go, you cannot come." This made the Jews ask, "Will he kill himself? Is that why he says, 'Where I go, you cannot come'?" But he continued, "You are from below; I am from above. You are of this world; I am not of this world. I told you that you would die in your sins; if you do not believe that I am he, you will indeed die in your sins." JOHN 8:21–24

■

SO MUCH OF THE drama of the Gospels is summarized by a distinction Jesus made to the Pharisees who gathered around him. He said to them, "You are from below; I am from above. You are of this world; I am not of this world." By "world" Jesus is not just speaking about the globe we live on; he is talking about a world system that has been set up against the world God originally created. The Pharisees moved against Jesus because they were interwoven into this system through sin. The worldly system is Satan's counterfeit kingdom. Jesus understood what he was up against just as clearly as he understood that the Pharisees and their followers were foot soldiers of the enemy. Jesus defined who the enemy is; he also declared who he is.

"Who are you?" they asked. "Just what I have been telling you from the beginning," Jesus replied. "I have much to say in judgment of you. But he who sent me is trustworthy, and what I have heard from him I tell the world." They did not understand that he was telling them about his Father. So Jesus said, "When you have lifted up the Son of Man, then you will know that I am he and that I do nothing on my own but speak just what the Father has taught me. The one who sent me is with me; he has not left me alone, for I always do what pleases him." Even as he spoke, many believed in him. JOHN 8:25–30

■

THEY ASKED, "WHO ARE you?" This question was repeated time and again and came from responses of amazement, wonder, doubt, and fear, and few were satisfied with the answers they got. Some speculated that Jesus was a prophet like the prophets of old; others believed he was a teacher filled with the wisdom of the ages; still others concluded he was a trouble-maker with political designs. They simply could not believe that Jesus was anything but a mere mortal. John reported that many believed, but many more did not, which created even more turmoil and confusion. And through all of this, Jesus was steadfast in claiming oneness with the Father: "The one who has sent me is with me; he has not left me alone." Jesus promises this same comfort to those who believe.

WHY IS MY LANGUAGE NOT CLEAR TO YOU?

Jesus said, "You are doing the works of your own father." "We are not illegitimate children," they protested. "The only Father we have is God Himself." Jesus said to them, "If God were your Father, you would love me, for I have come here from God. I have not come on my own; God sent me. Why is my language not clear to you? Because you are unable to hear what I say. You belong to your father, the devil, and you want to carry out your father's desires. He was a murderer from the beginning, not holding to the truth, for there is no truth in him. When he lies, he speaks his native language, for he is a liar and the father of lies." JOHN 8:41–44

IN THE SECOND AND third chapters of Genesis, the devil used a question to plant seeds of doubt in the mind of Eve. God had established one clear prohibition in the Garden of Eden: ". . . you must not eat from the tree of the knowledge of good and evil, for when you eat of it you will surely die" (Genesis 2:16). The devil, knowing what God said, asked a seemingly simple question: "Did God really say, 'You must not eat from any tree in the garden?'" (Genesis 3:1) Notice the subtle twist of the truth, converting one particular tree into all trees in the garden. Later, when Satan tempted Jesus in the wilderness, he did the same thing: he changed a word or two to subvert the truth, much as propagandists do today. Jesus says the native language of Satan is the lie, for it is through the corruption of language that the liar can successfully achieve his nefarious purposes. The first lie came from Satan, and it is through that lie that he succeeded in separating men and women from God.

"You are not yet fifty years old," they said to him, "and you have seen Abraham!" "Very truly I tell you," Jesus answered, "before Abraham was born, I am!" At this, they picked up stones to stone him, but Jesus hid himself, slipping away from the temple grounds. JOHN 8:57–59

■

JESUS' STATEMENT WAS SIMPLE: "Before Abraham was born, I am!" Why did this cause the people to try to stone him? On one level, Jesus made a statement that seems to make no sense: How could he exist before Abraham when Abraham lived 2,000 years earlier? If Jesus existed before Abraham, then that could mean only one thing: Before Abraham, before Adam, and even before the creation of the world, Jesus existed with God and the Holy Spirit. He even used the revealed name of God, "I am." Jesus did not leave much room for misinterpretation and so his enemies rose up, as they would again and again, from that time until this, to try to kill him.

WHO IS MY NEIGHBOR?

On one occasion an expert in the law stood up to test Jesus. "Teacher," he asked, "what must I do to inherit eternal life?" "What is written in the Law?" he replied. "How do you read it?" He answered, "'Love the Lord your God with all your heart and with all your soul and with all your strength and with all your mind'; and, 'Love your neighbor as yourself.'" "You have answered correctly," Jesus replied. "Do this and you will live." But he wanted to justify himself, so he asked Jesus, "And who is my neighbor?"
LUKE 10:25–29

∎

IS THE "EXPERT IN the law" really looking for an answer? Luke says this man asked the question to test Jesus, which means he was hoping that Jesus would be tripped up by his answer. But Jesus parried with another question: What does Scripture say? The expert answered by saying you must love God completely, and you must love your neighbor. "And who is my neighbor?" the expert asked. This led Jesus to tell a parable that would show the expert of the law just how hard it is to actually love your neighbor.

In reply Jesus said, "A man was going down from Jerusalem to Jericho, when he was attacked by robbers. They stripped him of his clothes, beat him and went away, leaving him half dead. A priest happened to be going down the same road, and when he saw the man, he passed by on the other side. So too, a Levite, when he came to the place and saw him, passed by on the other side. But a Samaritan, as he traveled, came where the man was; and when he saw him, he took pity on him. He went to him and bandaged his wounds, pouring on oil and wine. Then he put the man on his own donkey, brought him to an inn and took care of him. The next day he took out two denarii and gave them to the innkeeper. 'Look after him,' he said, 'and when I return, I will reimburse you for any extra expense you may have.' Which of these three do you think was a neighbor to the man who fell into the hands of robbers?" The expert in the law replied, "The one who had mercy on him." Jesus told him, "Go and do likewise." LUKE 10:30–37

■

WHO IS MY NEIGHBOR? In this parable, we are told of three travelers who have a chance to show compassion to a man who has been robbed and left for dead. You would expect the priest and the Levite to stop and help, but they don't. They pass by because they do not want to be inconvenienced by this unfortunate circumstance. Then a Samaritan happens by and he crosses over to aid the injured man. The natural reaction by the Jewish audience to the Samaritan being the good neighbor must have been disbelief. Impossible! Samaritans are the lowest of the low according to general opinion. But Jesus does not reduce his definition of a good neighbor to tribal and family characteristics. He defines neighbor from a kingdom of God perspective. What does it really mean to be a good neighbor? Jesus says it means being able to put aside provincial considerations in order to cross boundaries. It means casting aside individual imperatives to help someone who might be experiencing pain and trouble, even when doing so may be an inconvenience. The Good Samaritan accepts the inconvenience, for there is a higher call. He crosses the road and puts his own journey on hold to help, just as Jesus gives help to all of us who need his comfort and aid.

MARTHA, MARTHA

As Jesus and his disciples were on their way, he came to a village where a woman named Martha opened her home to him. She had a sister called Mary, who sat at the Lord's feet listening to what he said. But Martha was distracted by all the preparations that had to be made. She came to him and asked, "Lord, don't you care that my sister has left me to do the work by myself? Tell her to help me!" "Martha, Martha," the Lord answered, "you are worried and upset about many things, but few things are needed—or indeed only one. Mary has chosen what is better, and it will not be taken away from her." LUKE 10:38–42

■

MARY AND MARTHA INVITED Jesus into their home, but they chose different roles for the occasion. While Martha played the traditional part by preparing and serving food, Mary, like a student, sat at Jesus' feet absorbing his words. Mary's choice was unorthodox because women in the culture of that time rarely were given the opportunity to sit at the teacher's feet. Martha objected and complained that Mary was not conforming to her traditional role. Jesus, as often happens, provided an unexpected response. "Martha, Martha . . . you are worried and upset about many things, but few things are needed—or indeed only one. Mary has chosen what is better, and it will not be taken away from her." At that moment Mary chose to live outside of the cultural norm but within God's design. Martha's role is good, but Mary's role of being a student of the Lord is even better.

Then Jesus said to them, "Suppose you have a friend, and you go to him at midnight and say, 'Friend, lend me three loaves of bread; a friend of mine on a journey has come to me, and I have no food to offer him.' And suppose the one inside answers, 'Don't bother me. The door is already locked, and my children and I are in bed. I can't get up and give you anything.' I tell you, even though he will not get up and give you the bread because of friendship, yet because of your shameless audacity he will surely get up and give you as much as you need. So I say to you: Ask and it will be given to you; seek and you will find; knock and the door will be opened to you. For everyone who asks receives; the one who seeks finds; and to the one who knocks, the door will be opened." LUKE 11:5–10

■

A CHURCH BUILDING CAN be a refuge from the turmoil of everyday life. In the city, the relentless feeling of chaos often overwhelms our sense of well-being and we seek to escape the frantic collision of people and noise by ducking into the cool, calm of a church, where noise is seemingly barricaded outside the walls of the sanctuary. Jesus is calling us time and again to descend from whatever perch we are resting on to enter the everyday clamor of a needy world. And he tells us that in this world we need to be bold and audacious. We need to meet the dynamic restlessness of a dying world with a dynamic relationship with God through the power of the Holy Spirit. Jesus reminds us that we are not alone. We are to pray boldly and trust broadly. That is where we will find peace, knowing that through Christ, God has forged an unbreakable bond with us as we pursue his purpose for us and for his kingdom to come.

Someone in the crowd said to him, "Teacher, tell my brother to divide the inheritance with me." Jesus replied, "Man, who appointed me a judge or an arbiter between you?" Then he said to them, "Watch out! Be on your guard against all kinds of greed; life does not consist in an abundance of possessions." And he told them this parable: "The ground of a certain rich man yielded an abundant harvest. He thought to himself, 'What shall I do? I have no place to store my crops.' Then he said, 'This is what I'll do. I will tear down my barns and build bigger ones, and there I will store my surplus grain. And I'll say to myself, 'You have plenty of grain laid up for many years. Take life easy; eat, drink and be merry." But God said to him, 'You fool! This very night your life will be demanded from you. Then who will get what you have prepared for yourself?' This is how it will be with whoever stores up things for themselves but is not rich toward God." LUKE 12:13–21

■

MANY THREADS OF JESUS' teachings come together in this passage. Jesus does not condemn the accumulation of wealth, but he does condemn greed that might be understood as preserving that which has been gained for one's own gratification. He reminds us that life does not consist of an abundance of possessions, and often those who accumulate much become parsimonious when it comes to spending for purposes beyond self. So the rich man ends up with fat bank accounts, large estates, and fancy cars, but then is faced with the realization that all of it can vanish in an instant. Here, God calls the rich man a fool because his life was wasted in getting and not giving. He disregarded the existence of God by saying the full purpose of everything is gratifying the appetites for the things of this world: "Take life easy; eat, drink and be merry," he says. But God says, "You fool! This very night your life will be demanded of you." And Jesus concludes, "This is how it will be with whoever stores up things for themselves but is not rich toward God."

I have come to bring fire on the earth, and how I wish it were already kindled! But I have a baptism to undergo, and what constraint I am under until it is completed! Do you think I came to bring peace on earth? No, I tell you, but division. From now on there will be five in one family divided against each other, three against two and two against three. They will be divided, father against son and son against father, mother against daughter and daughter against mother, mother-in-law against daughter-in-law and daughter-in-law against mother-in-law. LUKE 12:49–53

■

WHAT DOES JESUS MEAN when he says that he will bring division, even within families? This statement might rub contemporary followers the wrong way, but it is not a new notion. From the earliest days of his ministry to his final prayer for his disciples, Jesus spoke of a world at war with God. In the Beatitudes he says, "Blessed are you when people insult you, persecute you and falsely say all kinds of evil against you because of me" (Matthew 5:11). There is no question about the condition of the world; opposition to God is prevalent and powerful. Paul preached that we must put on the "full armor of God," because the enemy of God is a powerful force operating in the shadows to obliterate the light. Immediately before his arrest, Jesus prayed to the Father to protect the disciples: "I have given them your word and the world has hated them, for they are not of the world any more than I am of the world. My prayer is not that you take them out of the world but that you protect them from the evil one" (John 17:14–15).

He said to the crowd: "When you see a cloud rising in the west, immediately you say, 'It's going to rain,' and it does. And when the south wind blows, you say, 'It's going to be hot,' and it is. Hypocrites! You know how to interpret the appearance of the earth and the sky. How is it that you don't know how to interpret this present time? Why don't you judge for yourselves what is right? As you are going with your adversary to the magistrate, try hard to be reconciled on the way, or your adversary may drag you off to the judge, and the judge turn you over to the officer, and the officer throw you into prison. I tell you, you will not get out until you have paid the last penny." LUKE 12:54–59

■

THE WORLD OBSESSES OVER forecasting the weather. The word "forecast" means to tell or predict that something will take place that has yet to happen. Jesus told the crowd that they lived in blind ignorance: "How is it that you don't know how to interpret this present time?" He then followed this question with what appears to be a non sequitur, but it is not. He is saying that all of our actions, current and past, will have consequences that from God's perspective are predictable and inevitable. We need to apply the same kind of attention to the principles of everyday living as we do to interpreting the on-coming weather. For in the end, everything we do will come under judgment, both the good and the bad.

As he went along, he saw a man blind from birth. His disciples asked him, "Rabbi, who sinned, this man or his parents, that he was born blind?" "Neither this man nor his parents sinned," said Jesus, "but this happened so that the works of God might be displayed in him. As long as it is day, we must do the works of him who sent me. Night is coming, when no one can work. While I am in the world, I am the light of the world." After saying this, he spit on the ground, made some mud with the saliva, and put it on the man's eyes. "Go," he told him, "wash in the Pool of Siloam" (this word means "Sent"). So the man went and washed, and came home seeing. JOHN 9:1–7

■

JESUS DOES NOT MINCE words. He makes a bold claim: "I am the light of the world," echoing the first words of God as recorded in Genesis: "Let there be light." By claiming to be the light of the world, Jesus links himself directly to the source of all life, and John reinforces this connection in the opening passage of his Gospel: "Through him all things were made; without him nothing was made that has been made. In him was life, and that life was the light of men. The light shines in the darkness, but the darkness has not understood it" (John 1:3–5). Jesus took some mud, the raw material of life, and he animated it with his saliva and gave the light of vision to the man born blind. John recorded an actual event that happened—Jesus gave sight to a blind man—but we can see more than a physical event that happened as reported. The story of creation, the fall of man, and God's plan for restoration are all there to see for anyone willing to open their own eyes.

I AM THE GATE

All who have come before me are thieves and robbers, but the sheep have not listened to them. I am the gate; whoever enters through me will be saved. They will come in and go out, and find pasture. The thief comes only to steal and kill and destroy; I have come that they may have life, and have it to the full. JOHN 10:8–10

■

WHAT DOES JESUS MEAN when he declares, "I am the gate"? On one level he is referring to a gate to a sheep pen. The pen itself was enclosed for protection, but there was a gate that the sheep could go through in order to get in or out of the pen. The shepherd served as steward and protector; the sheep could not leave, nor could predators break in without the shepherd allowing it to happen. Jesus also uses the image of the gate figuratively. He says that he stands at the gate as our Shepherd, and no one can enter or leave without his assent. Again, Jesus affirms his authority as Lord even though he is using an illustration drawn from every day life: ". . . whoever enters through me will be saved."

I am the good shepherd. The good shepherd lays down his life for the sheep. The hired hand is not the shepherd and does not own the sheep. So when he sees the wolf coming, he abandons the sheep and runs away. Then the wolf attacks the flock and scatters it. The man runs away because he is a hired hand and cares nothing for the sheep. I am the good shepherd; I know my sheep and my sheep know me—just as the Father knows me and I know the Father—and I lay down my life for the sheep. I have other sheep that are not of this sheep pen. I must bring them also. They too will listen to my voice, and there shall be one flock and one shepherd. JOHN 10:11–16

■

ISRAEL WAS THIRSTING FOR a Good Shepherd, one who would take care of the flock and not abandon them when it was inconvenient or dangerous. Ezekiel, the great prophet of the Old Testament, spoke of the "shepherds" of his day who had led Israel astray. God said to Ezekiel, "Tell them the Lord says, 'Woe to the shepherds of Israel who only take care of themselves! Should not the shepherds take care of the flocks? You have not strengthened the weak or healed the sick or bound up the injured . . . You have treated them harshly and brutally'" (Ezekiel 34:2,4). Jesus is the Good Shepherd; he cares for the sheep and will look after them because, "I know my sheep and my sheep know me—just as the Father knows me and I know the Father—and I lay down my life for the sheep."

WHY LISTEN TO HIM?

"The reason my Father loves me is that I lay down my life—only to take it up again. No one takes it from me, but I lay it down of my own accord. I have authority to lay it down and authority to take it up again. This command I received from my Father." The Jews who heard these words were again divided. Many of them said, "He is demon-possessed and raving mad. Why listen to him?" But others said, "These are not the sayings of a man possessed by a demon. Can a demon open the eyes of the blind?" JOHN 10:17–21

■

THE RESPONSE TO JESUS has always been mixed, even from the beginning of his life on earth. Herod, the great king of Israel, responded to the news of Jesus' birth by plotting to kill him at the first opportunity. The shepherds in the fields near Bethlehem, hearing the good news of the birth of the Christ child, put everything aside so they could worship him: "The shepherds returned, glorifying and praising God for all the things they had heard and seen, which were just as they had been told" (Luke 2:20). To this day, those who stand in opposition respond to Jesus by lying about him or reducing him to just another teacher or minor prophet. The shepherds, though, believed what they heard and acted on it.

Then Jesus went through the towns and villages, teaching as he made his way to Jerusalem. Someone asked him, "Lord, are only a few people going to be saved?" He said to them, "Make every effort to enter through the narrow door, because many, I tell you, will try to enter and will not be able to. Once the owner of the house gets up and closes the door, you will stand outside knocking and pleading, 'Sir, open the door for us.' But he will answer, 'I don't know you or where you come from.' Then you will say, 'We ate and drank with you, and you taught in our streets.' But he will reply, 'I don't know you or where you come from. Away from me, all you evildoers!'" LUKE 13:22–27

■

JESUS SLOWLY MADE HIS way through towns and villages as he moved toward Jerusalem. In one place he was asked a question: Are only a few people going to be saved? He gave an answer that is not easy to accept because he inferred that the choice between heaven and hell is ours to make. God desires that everyone choose to enter through the narrow door, but not everyone will. Jesus says, "Make every effort to enter through the narrow door, because many, I tell you, will try to enter and will not be able to." Jesus is that narrow door, but if those trying to get through reject him, then it will not be possible to enter.

THERE WILL BE WEEPING THERE

There will be weeping there, and gnashing of teeth, when you see Abraham, Isaac and Jacob and all the prophets in the kingdom of God, but you yourselves thrown out. People will come from east and west and north and south, and will take their places at the feast in the kingdom of God. Indeed there are those who are last who will be first, and first who will be last. LUKE 13:28–30

■

THE JEWISH LEADERS RECEIVED Jesus' message as a challenge to their traditions and authority. Jesus did not deny the foundations of their traditions; he explicitly referenced the patriarchs—Abraham, Isaac, and Jacob—as already being in the kingdom of God, but then he said that those in charge have sought not so much God, but position and power. Furthermore, Gentiles and many others "from east and west and north and south will take their places at the feast in the kingdom of God." And when Jesus said, "there are those who are last who will be first, and first who will be last," he was speaking directly to the arrogance and insularity of the Jewish leaders who were the ultimate excluders. Jesus was saying: Beware or you will discover too late that you will be among those who are being cast out.

Jerusalem, Jerusalem, you who kill the prophets and stone those sent to you, how often I have longed to gather your children together, as a hen gathers her chicks under her wings, and you were not willing. Look, your house is left to you desolate. For I tell you, you will not see me again until you say, 'Blessed is he who comes in the name of the Lord.' MATTHEW 23:37–39

■

IF THERE IS ONE word to describe Jesus' lament over Jerusalem, it is anguish. Jerusalem, once a shining city on a hill, had descended into a hive of corruption and godlessness. Jesus' own words echo the words of Jeremiah, who mourned the great descent and destruction of David's royal city: "How deserted lies the city, once so full of people! How like a widow is she, who once was great among the nations! She who was queen among the provinces has now become a slave" (Lamentations 1:1). Jesus was uttering prophetic words because while the city he was approaching was teeming with people and activity, soon enough it would lie deserted and ruined, as it had been once before, because its rulers and the people had abandoned God.

Large crowds were traveling with Jesus, and turning to them he said: "If anyone comes to me and does not hate father and mother, wife and children, brothers and sisters—yes, even their own life— such a person cannot be my disciple. And whoever does not carry their cross and follow me cannot be my disciple." LUKE 14:25–27

■

IT IS EASY TO fix our attention on Jesus' startling use of the word "hate" because it seems so thoroughly out of character. But Jesus intends to startle, both those who were with him then and us today. He says that in comparison to our commitment to God and his calling, our familial affections might seem like hate. But implicit in our radical commitment to God, where God is above everything, is the necessity to live out that commitment with our children, our spouse, and the people we come into contact with everyday. "And the second is like it: 'Love your neighbor as yourself.' All the Law and the Prophets hang on these two commandments" (Matthew 22:39–40). Jesus wants his followers to never forget, however, which commandment comes first: "Love the Lord your God with all your heart and with all your soul and with all of your mind. This is the first and greatest commandment" (Matthew 22:37–38).

PERSEVERANCE

Suppose one of you wants to build a tower. Won't you first sit down and estimate the cost to see if you have enough money to complete it? For if you lay the foundation and are not able to finish it, everyone who sees it will ridicule you, saying, 'This person began to build and wasn't able to finish.' LUKE 14:28–30

■

JESUS CONTINUES TO EMPHASIZE that God comes before everything else. For many of us that is difficult enough, but Jesus raises the bar even further by telling us to count the cost of discipleship. Jesus knew that many who would come after him would soften the message, but Jesus will never mislead us. He is saying that if you accept the call to follow God, wherever that might lead, there will be a cost as well as a blessing. Accepting the call means we choose to accept a reconfigured heart where God is first, others are next, and we are third.

THE COST OF DISCIPLESHIP

Or suppose a king is about to go to war against another king. Won't he first sit down and consider whether he is able with ten thousand men to oppose the one coming against him with twenty thousand? If he is not able, he will send a delegation while the other is still a long way off and will ask for terms of peace. In the same way, those of you who do not give up everything you have cannot be my disciples. Salt is good, but if it loses its saltiness, how can it be made salty again? It is fit neither for the soil nor for the manure pile; it is thrown out. 'Whoever has ears to hear, let them hear.' LUKE 14:31–35

■

IN SPEAKING ABOUT DISCIPLESHIP, why does Jesus use the analogy of a king suing for peace when he recognizes the opposing king will defeat him? The connection between kings and disciples might not be evident to us at first, but it would have made sense to his disciples. Jesus was teaching them that discipleship is about abandoning yourself to another kind of King, one of far greater power and importance than a king with twenty thousand troops. Surrender to the true King, abandon yourself, and come, follow, and learn a whole new way of living. The king with ten thousand men acted wisely; likewise, the disciple who gives his life over to Christ has embraced the wisdom of living through and for the Lord.

I HAVE FOUND MY LOST COIN

I HAVE FOUND MY LOST COIN

Or suppose a woman has ten silver coins and loses one. Doesn't she light a lamp, sweep the house and search carefully until she finds it? And when she finds it, she calls her friends and neighbors together and says, 'Rejoice with me; I have found my lost coin.' In the same way, I tell you, there is rejoicing in the presence of the angels of God over one sinner who repents. LUKE 15:8–10

■

LUKE RECOUNTS THREE PARABLES, one after another, about being lost. In all three Jesus emphasizes that God will put everything aside to find and restore the thing of value that was lost, even without counting the cost. Why does the woman celebrate when one coin is found? Or why is the shepherd so joyful when the lost sheep is finally found? Jesus tells these stories because he wants us to know that we have a "Prodigal God" who will go to the furthest lengths for "one sinner who repents."

SEPTEMBER 3

246

THE YOUNGER SON

Jesus continued: "There was a man who had two sons. The younger one said to his father, 'Father, give me my share of the estate.'
So he divided his property between them. Not long after that, the
younger son got together all he had, set off for a distant country
and there squandered his wealth in wild living. After he had spent
everything, there was a severe famine in that whole country, and
he began to be in need. So he went and hired himself out to a
citizen of that country, who sent him to his fields to feed pigs. He
longed to fill his stomach with the pods that the pigs were eating,
but no one gave him anything." LUKE 15:11–16

■

THIS PARABLE BEGINS WITH a son asking his father for his share
of the father's estate. This is an odd request because inheritance is
usually passed on after the death of the parent. But not here: The
father divides the property between the two sons without objection.
This generous act is also unusual because the father accedes to the
request by gifting each son, the older as well as the younger. We
know what happens next: The younger son squanders everything
that he was given and ends up more impoverished than the farm
hands around him. He lost everything—his inheritance, his self-
respect, and his family. His actions left him alienated and full of
despair. In many ways, the younger son represents the level of despair experienced by many who have experienced alienation from
the grace of a "Prodigal God."

THE PRODIGAL FATHER

When he came to his senses, he said, 'How many of my father's hired servants have food to spare, and here I am starving to death! I will set out and go back to my father and say to him: Father, I have sinned against heaven and against you. I am no longer worthy to be called your son; make me like one of your hired servants.' So he got up and went to his father. But while he was still a long way off, his father saw him and was filled with compassion for him; he ran to his son, threw his arms around him and kissed him. The son said to him, 'Father, I have sinned against heaven and against you. I am no longer worthy to be called your son.' But the father said to his servants, 'Quick! Bring the best robe and put it on him. Put a ring on his finger and sandals on his feet. Bring the fattened calf and kill it. Let's have a feast and celebrate. For this son of mine was dead and is alive again; he was lost and is found.' So they began to celebrate. LUKE 15:17–24

■

SO FAR THE STORY of the lost son has followed a conventional path. The son wastes the gift of the father in wild living, leaving him in a state of want and despair. His last hope is to return home and attempt to work off his shame and his debt. But here the story takes an unexpected turn. Instead of the father banishing the son in anger, he runs to him and welcomes him back into the family. The son repents by saying, "Father, I have sinned against heaven and against you," and he has no expectation of restoration. But this father celebrates his son's return by lavishly accepting him back into the family as if the son had returned from the dead: "Let's have a feast and celebrate, for this son of mine was dead and is alive again; he was lost and is found."

Meanwhile, the older son was in the field. When he came near the house, he heard music and dancing. So he called one of the servants and asked him what was going on. 'Your brother has come,' he replied, 'and your father has killed the fattened calf because he has him back safe and sound.' The older brother became angry and refused to go in. So his father went out and pleaded with him. But he answered his father, 'Look! All these years I've been slaving for you and never disobeyed your orders. Yet you never gave me even a young goat so I could celebrate with my friends. But when this son of yours who has squandered your property with prostitutes comes home, you kill the fattened calf for him!' LUKE 15:25–30

■

NOW THE OLDER BROTHER makes an appearance. He becomes angry and accusatory and refuses to join the celebration. Why? The parable opens by saying the father "divided his property between them." The older son received his inheritance as well, but unlike his younger brother, he did not toss everything away in wild living. The good son continued to live prudently, but over time he became arrogant and self-righteous. Instead of saying with his younger brother, "I have sinned against heaven and against you," he turns the tables on the father and more or less says, "Father, your behavior is an offense to me." His self-righteousness has distorted his right reason, leaving him in as great a state of spiritual poverty as was his brother's physical poverty. The older son has been a good son in relation to family and work, but he harbors a false belief that his righteousness could be earned through works alone. Compared to the behavior of his younger brother, he has done all the right things, but his heart is full of anger and false pride. Clearly, he has not experienced the transformative power of grace, for if he had, he, too, would have accepted his lost brother with the joy of the father.

'My son,' the father said, 'you are always with me, and everything I have is yours. But we had to celebrate and be glad, because this brother of yours was dead and is alive again; he was lost and is found.' LUKE 15:31–32

■

TIM KELLER, IN HIS book *The Prodigal God*, shifts the focus away from the two sons to a God who is so abundantly generous in his capacity to love and forgive that he can cover a huge spectrum of man's sinful and godless behavior, from profligate living to miserly self-righteousness. The older son is a good person and has lived by the letter of the law, whereas the younger son has lived far outside of the boundaries of that law. But the father does not prefer one son to the other because he loves them both and wants them to love him. The deep well of gratitude expressed by the younger son is cause for celebration, just as the mere existence of the older son causes the father to say, "Everything I have is yours." Both sons are sinners; neither can earn their way back to the father. This father's grace is so wide and deep and high that his love can encompass those who think they deserve his love and those who do not.

Now on his way to Jerusalem, Jesus traveled along the border between Samaria and Galilee. As he was going into a village, ten men who had leprosy met him. They stood at a distance and called out in a loud voice, "Jesus, Master, have pity on us!" When he saw them, he said, "Go, show yourselves to the priests." And as they went, they were cleansed. One of them, when he saw he was healed, came back, praising God in a loud voice. He threw himself at Jesus' feet and thanked him—and he was a Samaritan. Jesus asked, "Were not all ten cleansed? Where are the other nine? Has no one returned to give praise to God except this foreigner?" Then he said to him, "Rise and go; your faith has made you well." LUKE 17:11–19

■

THE SAMARITAN WOMAN AT the well (John 4) was an outcast in a community of outcasts. The Good Samaritan (Luke 10) stepped in where a Levite and a priest did not. And of the ten lepers, only the Samaritan "came back, praising God in a loud voice" and thanked Jesus for healing him. Even though the leper was a Samaritan, he recognized Jesus for who he is, which is why Jesus said, "Rise and go; your faith has made you well." There is more than a hint here that the healing power of Jesus will extend far beyond the tribes and territories of Israel. Jesus has not come just for the Jew or even the outcast Samaritan, but for all who are lost and need the healing hand of God—Gentile and Jew alike.

Then Jesus told his disciples a parable to show them that they should always pray and not give up. He said: "In a certain town there was a judge who neither feared God nor cared what people thought. And there was a widow in that town who kept coming to him with the plea, 'Grant me justice against my adversary.' For some time he refused. But finally he said to himself, 'Even though I don't fear God or care what people think, yet because this widow keeps bothering me, I will see that she gets justice, so that she won't eventually come and attack me!'" LUKE 18:1–5

■

THIS PARABLE IS NOT just a story about a persistent widow or an uncaring judge: It is about you and me and prayer. Luke says at the outset that Jesus tells this parable to show that we should always pray and never give up. Prayer is not about instant gratification. It is a continuous petition, because God will answer prayer on his time, even if we plead that he come right away. Jesus says that we should persist and always be prepared for God's blessings to come, even if they come when least expected.

JUSTICE WILL PREVAIL

And the Lord said, "Listen to what the unjust judge says. And will not God bring about justice for his chosen ones, who cry out to him day and night? Will he keep putting them off? I tell you, he will see that they get justice, and quickly. However, when the Son of Man comes, will he find faith on the earth?" LUKE 18:6–8

■

THE EARTHLY JUDGE, WHO neither feared God nor cared what people thought, stands in contrast to God, who loves to bring blessings. Yet even the earthly judge relented and gave the widow justice. Jesus is telling his disciples (and us) something about the nature of God Himself. When Israel was enslaved by the Egyptians, Scripture says, "God heard their groans and he remembered his covenant with Abraham, with Isaac and with Jacob. So God looked on the Israelites and was concerned about them" (Exodus 2:24–25). God was operating on his own time, but to the Israelites, God might have seemed as heartless and uncaring as the godless judge. At the right time, though, God called Moses from the desert to return to his people to liberate them from slavery under the Egyptians. With Jesus, the Gospel of John repeats again and again, "his time had not yet come." Persist because God does hear your prayers.

Some Pharisees came to him to test him. They asked, "Is it lawful for a man to divorce his wife for any and every reason?" "Haven't you read," he replied, "that at the beginning the Creator 'made them male and female,' and said, 'For this reason a man will leave his father and mother and be united to his wife, and the two will become one flesh'? So they are no longer two, but one flesh. Therefore what God has joined together, let no one separate." MAT-THEW 19:3–6

■

THE PHARISEES DID NOT come to learn from Jesus but to challenge him. They were minimalists who were attempting to jam the fullness of life into intellectual, theological, and cultural containers of their own making. But Jesus did not fall into their legalistic trap. He took them back to God's original design. God created men and women for relationship with him and with one another, where the "two will become one flesh." He made them male and female and then united them to become one flesh. Out of this union of husband and wife comes the structure of family. Jesus then says, because this structure is part of God's design of uniting the two to become one, God's original design supersedes the legalistic rules that were designed for the broken world of sin and death.

IT WAS NOT THIS WAY FROM THE BEGINNING

"Why then," they asked, "did Moses command that a man give his wife a certificate of divorce and send her away?" Jesus replied, "Moses permitted you to divorce your wives because your hearts were hard. But it was not this way from the beginning. I tell you that anyone who divorces his wife, except for sexual immorality, and marries another woman commits adultery." The disciples said to him, "If this is the situation between a husband and wife, it is better not to marry." Jesus replied, "Not everyone can accept this word, but only those to whom it has been given. For there are eunuchs who were born that way, and there are eunuchs who have been made eunuchs by others—and there are those who choose to live like eunuchs for the sake of the kingdom of heaven. The one who can accept this should accept it." MATTHEW 19:7–12

■

THE PHARISEES TURNED TO Moses as the final authority on marriage and divorce, but Jesus made a distinction that goes to the heart of the matter. He said that Moses allowed for divorce because "your hearts are hard." The rules governing divorce were designed to bring order to a people who were verging on chaos and disorder. But even when people disregard the rules, we must keep in mind God's principles behind the rules. God built men and women for relationship within the context of marriage and family. Marriage has a higher, God-originated purpose behind it, and the behavior of rule-breakers and others should not undermine God's higher purpose, even when sin and sexual immorality threaten to obliterate it.

WHY DO YOU CALL ME GOOD?

As Jesus started on his way, a man ran up to him and fell on his knees before him. "Good teacher," he asked, "what must I do to inherit eternal life?" "Why do you call me good?" Jesus answered. "No one is good—except God alone. You know the commandments: 'You shall not murder, you shall not commit adultery, you shall not steal, you shall not give false testimony, you shall not defraud, honor your father and mother.'" "Teacher," he declared, "all these I have kept since I was a boy." Jesus looked at him and loved him. "One thing you lack," he said. "Go, sell everything you have and give to the poor, and you will have treasure in heaven. Then come, follow me." **MARK 10:17–21**

■

THERE IS GREAT IRONY in Jesus' response to the young man's question: "Why do you call me good? No one is good—except God alone." The young man was looking for cheap grace. In essence, he was saying, I have done everything commanded of men—I have followed the law and have lived an exemplary life. He was not really asking; he was proclaiming his own goodness and saying that he had earned his right to eternal life. But Jesus knew the young man's heart; he knew that the young man's wealth and comfort had become his idol and that relinquishing his material well-being overwhelmed his desire for "treasure in heaven." Just as the young man could not "see" who he was addressing as "good teacher," so he could not see beyond the "good" that wealth brings compared to the "better" that God offers for all eternity.

THE DISCIPLES WERE AMAZED

At this the man's face fell. He went away sad, because he had great wealth. Jesus looked around and said to his disciples, "How hard it is for the rich to enter the kingdom of God!" The disciples were amazed at his words. But Jesus said again, "Children, how hard it is to enter the kingdom of God! It is easier for a camel to go through the eye of a needle than for someone who is rich to enter the kingdom of God." The disciples were even more amazed, and said to each other, "Who then can be saved?" Jesus looked at them and said, "With man this is impossible, but not with God; all things are possible with God." **MARK 10:22–27**

■

THE DISCIPLES SEEMED TO believe that there is a correlation between the blessings of wealth and the righteousness that leads to eternal life. But Jesus says the opposite is true: Wealth can often be a snare and a diversion that closes us off from eternal life. Wealth buys nothing but power and position: No one can earn their way into the kingdom of God, not even kings and princes. It is the grace of God that makes possible what is otherwise impossible for men and women. "For it is by grace you have been saved, through faith—and this is not from yourselves, it is a gift of God—not by works, so that no one can boast" (Ephesians 2:8–9).

WE HAVE LEFT EVERYTHING TO FOLLOW YOU!

Then Peter spoke up, "We have left everything to follow you!" "Truly I tell you," Jesus replied, "no one who has left home or brothers or sisters or mother or father or children or fields for me and the Gospel will fail to receive a hundred times as much in this present age: homes, brothers, sisters, mothers, children and fields—along with persecutions—and in the age to come eternal life. But many who are first will be last, and the last first." **MARK** 10:28–31

■

JESUS WAS NOT COMBATTING the Pharisees here; he was teaching his followers about the sacrifices and rewards of following him. He was reinforcing something he said in the Sermon on the Mount: Do not worry about what you will eat or drink or wear; the Father knows what you will need. "But seek first his kingdom and his righteousness, and all these things will be given to you as well. Therefore do not worry about tomorrow, for tomorrow will worry about itself. Each day has enough trouble of its own" (Matthew 6:33–34).

JUSTIFIED BEFORE GOD

To some who were confident of their own righteousness and looked down on everyone else, Jesus told this parable: "Two men went up to the temple to pray, one a Pharisee and the other a tax collector. The Pharisee stood by himself and prayed: 'God, I thank you that I am not like other people—robbers, evildoers, adulterers—or even like this tax collector. I fast twice a week and give a tenth of all I get.' But the tax collector stood at a distance. He would not even look up to heaven, but beat his breast and said, 'God, have mercy on me, a sinner.' I tell you that this man, rather than the other, went home justified before God. For all those who exalt themselves will be humbled, and those who humble themselves will be exalted." LUKE 18:9–14

■

ARE YOU THE PHARISEE or are you the tax collector? There is a good test that will help uncover the answer. The next time you do a good thing, try to discern your reason for doing it. The Pharisee is proud of his "goodness." He said, "I fast twice a week and I give a tenth of all I get." These are good things; no one would deny it. But contrast this attitude with that of the tax collector. He comes before the Lord in total humility. He will not even look up to heaven but simply pleads, "God, have mercy on me, a sinner." The Pharisee thanks God for helping him to be better than all those other sinners out there. He puffs himself up, not seeing that by doing so, he is succumbing to the sin of pride. He does the right thing for the wrong reason, whereas the tax collector humbles himself before God, hoping that God is gracious and forgiving, even to a sinner like him. David was a truly great king because he did not pretend to be exempt from judgment. He prayed, "Have mercy on me, O God, according to your unfailing love, according to your great compassion blot out my transgressions . . . Against you, you only, have I sinned and done what is evil in your sight" (Psalm 51:1,3).

LET THE LITTLE CHILDREN COME TO ME

People were bringing little children to Jesus for him to place his hands on them, but the disciples rebuked them. When Jesus saw this, he was indignant. He said to them, "Let the little children come to me, and do not hinder them, for the kingdom of God belongs to such as these. Truly I tell you, anyone who will not receive the kingdom of God like a little child will never enter it." And he took the children in his arms, placed his hands on them and blessed them. MARK 10:13–16

■

JESUS USED THE SIMPLE faith of a little child to show his own disciples what genuine faith actually looks like. Like a child, we are dependent on the Father. He will protect us, guide us, and love us. When we put our faith in money, or position, or even family and friends, we become dependent on our own ingenuity, position, and power, all of which will certainly fail us at some point. This is what David meant when he said, "The Lord is with me; I will not be afraid. It is better to take refuge in the Lord than to trust in humans. It is better to take refuge in the Lord than to trust in princes" (Psalm 118:6, 8–9).

THE DISCIPLES
DID NOT UNDERSTAND ANY OF THIS

Jesus took the Twelve aside and told them, "We are going up to Jerusalem, and everything that is written by the prophets about the Son of Man will be fulfilled. He will be delivered over to the Gentiles. They will mock him, insult him and spit on him; they will flog him and kill him. On the third day he will rise again." The disciples did not understand any of this. Its meaning was hidden from them, and they did not know what he was talking about. LUKE 18:31–34

■

JESUS KNEW HIS FOLLOWERS were misreading his mission. They saw him as the one who would reestablish the glorious throne of David. Jesus would be the fulfillment of God's promise that David's line will be established forever (Psalm 89:3–4). But Jesus opened another vista for them; one they had not been able to see because they had their hearts set on a different kind of Messiah. Jesus refers to the prophet Isaiah in describing what will soon take place in Jerusalem. His disciples may have known this prophecy, but their own hope blinded them from seeing the connection to Jesus: "Surely he took up our pain and bore our suffering, yet we considered him punished by God, stricken by him, and afflicted. But he was pierced for our transgressions, he was crushed for our iniquities; the punishment that brought us peace was on him and by his wounds we are healed" (Isaiah 53:4–5).

WHAT IS IT YOU WANT?

Then the mother of Zebedee's sons came to Jesus with her sons and, kneeling down, asked a favor of him. "What is it you want?" he asked. She said, "Grant that one of these two sons of mine may sit at your right and the other at your left in your kingdom." "You don't know what you are asking," Jesus said to them. "Can you drink the cup I am going to drink?" "We can," they answered. Jesus said to them, "You will indeed drink from my cup, but to sit at my right or left is not for me to grant. These places belong to those for whom they have been prepared by my Father." MAT-THEW 20:20–23

■

JAMES AND JOHN WERE the sons of Zebedee. Along with Peter they formed an informal inner circle among the followers of Jesus. But they seemed to want public recognition of their close relationship with Jesus, and so they sent their mother to him to seek privileged positions in the coming kingdom. Whether or not the brothers were referring to an earthly or heavenly kingdom is not certain, but Jesus made his meaning clear by stating that to drink the cup he would be drinking comes with a cost, even to the point of death. John and James still did not fully understand the import of what Jesus was telling them, but soon enough the cost of discipleship became brutally clear to them and many others.

I DID NOT COME TO BE SERVED, BUT TO SERVE

When the ten heard about this, they were indignant with the two brothers. Jesus called them together and said, "You know that the rulers of the Gentiles lord it over them, and their high officials exercise authority over them. Not so with you. Instead, whoever wants to become great among you must be your servant, and whoever wants to be first must be your slave—just as the Son of Man did not come to be served, but to serve, and to give his life as a ransom for many." MATTHEW 20:24–28

■

When the ten other disciples learned that John and James had lobbied for a preferred position, they became indignant. Why? Were they also infected by the same inclination to earn or win a preferred place in Jesus' kingdom? The truth is that all the disciples used worldly standards of comparison to define their identity within the group. They were bound by a system of hierarchy where one's identity is wrapped up in one's title or position. But Jesus rejected this system and instead declared a new order for his kingdom. The mainspring of his kingdom is the inverse of the worldly system. In Jesus' kingdom, we are servants to our Master and do his will, not our own, "just as the Son of Man did not come to be served, but to serve, and to give his life as a ransom for many."

Then they came to Jericho. As Jesus and his disciples, together with a large crowd, were leaving the city, a blind man, Bartimaeus (which means "son of Timaeus"), was sitting by the roadside begging. When he heard that it was Jesus of Nazareth, he began to shout, "Jesus, Son of David, have mercy on me!" Many rebuked him and told him to be quiet, but he shouted all the more, "Son of David, have mercy on me!" Jesus stopped and said, "Call him." So they called to the blind man, "Cheer up! On your feet! He's calling you." Throwing his cloak aside, he jumped to his feet and came to Jesus. "What do you want me to do for you?" Jesus asked him. The blind man said, "Rabbi, I want to see." "Go," said Jesus, "your faith has healed you." Immediately he received his sight and followed Jesus along the road. MARK 10:46–52

■

JESUS' REPUTATION AS A miracle worker must have preceded him to Jericho because the blind man, Bartimaeus, called out to him, "Jesus, Son of David, have mercy on me!" By calling Jesus "Son of David," it is possible that Bartimaeus was identifying Jesus as the Messiah. Jesus' followers tried to shun the man, but he persisted, and so Jesus said, "Call him." Jesus had found a man of faith who wanted to see after spending a lifetime in darkness. Jesus did not do anything; he merely granted sight to the man, saying: "Go, your faith has healed you." Bartimaeus displayed a radical faith; he believed that God restores sight miraculously and that Jesus is the one who God promised would sit on David's throne. That faith healed him.

While they were listening to this, he went on to tell them a parable, because he was near Jerusalem and the people thought that the kingdom of God was going to appear at once. He said: "A man of noble birth went to a distant country to have himself appointed king and then to return. So he called ten of his servants and gave them ten minas. 'Put this money to work,' he said, 'until I come back.' But his subjects hated him and sent a delegation after him to say, 'We don't want this man to be our king.' He was made king, however, and returned home. Then he sent for the servants to whom he had given the money, in order to find out what they had gained with it. The first one came and said, 'Sir, your mina has earned ten more.' 'Well done, my good servant!' his master replied. 'Because you have been trustworthy in a very small matter, take charge of ten cities.' The second came and said, 'Sir, your mina has earned five more.' His master answered, 'You take charge of five cities.' LUKE 19:11–19

■

LUKE TELLS US THAT Jesus approached Jerusalem and that "the people thought that the kingdom of God was going to appear at once." This parable is told to keep the focus on what God is actually going to do and how he intends to do it. In the parable, the noble man goes off to "a distant country" to be appointed king. His subjects, however, do not want him to return as king. They prefer to live without him. But before he leaves, he chooses ten servants to look after his kingdom while he is gone. After he returns, he asks the servants what they have done with the minas he has given them. The first two have done well and are rewarded proportionally. But as we will learn, not everyone who says "'Lord, Lord,' will enter the kingdom of heaven" (Matthew 7:21).

"Then another servant came and said, 'Sir, here is your mina; I have kept it laid away in a piece of cloth. I was afraid of you, because you are a hard man. You take out what you did not put in and reap what you did not sow.' His master replied, 'I will judge you by your own words, you wicked servant! You knew, did you, that I am a hard man, taking out what I did not put in, and reaping what I did not sow? Why then didn't you put my money on deposit, so that when I came back, I could have collected it with interest?' Then he said to those standing by, 'Take his mina away from him and give it to the one who has ten minas.' 'Sir,' they said, 'he already has ten!' He replied, 'I tell you that to everyone who has, more will be given, but as for the one who has nothing, even what they have will be taken away. But those enemies of mine who did not want me to be king over them— bring them here and kill them in front of me.'" LUKE 19:20–27

■

NOW WE COME TO the third servant of the parable. He falsely claims that he knows the nature of his master. He says that his master is a hard man who takes away what he did not put in and reaps what he did not sow. But we have seen the master reward the previous two servants by giving them much more than the amount they returned to their master. The third servant acted out of fear based on a wrong assumption. He buried the mina because he could not be sure that he would be able to preserve what he had been given and did not want to suffer punishment for poor stewardship. How often are we immobilized by the fear of consequences or failure? We translate risk into probability and therefore are tempted to do nothing. This kind of behavior directly results from either no faith or low faith. Fruitfulness requires a certain level of risk. It is faith itself that neutralizes uncertainty and is the mainspring of action. The third servant was unfruitful because he "knew" his master was a hard man and this "knowledge" inhibited him from acting. If he had allowed faith to drive out fear, he then could have put his mina to work, just as the other two servants had done.

INCREASE OUR FAITH!

Jesus said to his disciples: "Things that cause people to stumble are bound to come, but woe to anyone through whom they come. It would be better for them to be thrown into the sea with a millstone tied around their neck than to cause one of these little ones to stumble. So watch yourselves. If your brother or sister sins against you, rebuke them; and if they repent, forgive them. Even if they sin against you seven times in a day and seven times come back to you saying 'I repent,' you must forgive them." The apostles said to the Lord, "Increase our faith!" LUKE 17:1–5

■

QUOTING FROM LEVITICUS, PETER writes, "Be holy, because I (the Lord your God) am holy" (Leviticus 19:2). God is holy; we are not, but in so many ways we strive to attain holiness while disregarding the thing that holds us back. If we remain captive to sin, even if our sin seems harmless or inconsequential, we cannot escape the invisible chains that bind. Jesus says that if someone repents, you must forgive. He goes further: "Even if they sin against you seven times a day and seven times come back to you saying 'I repent,' you must forgive them." If we truly desire to draw closer to God, we must accept the fact that sin has infected everyone. If we ask, God will forgive us our sins as he has promised and he will keep on forgiving as long as we sincerely repent. What God is willing to do, we must be willing to do as well. Then Peter's call to us to be holy will begin to move from a possibility to an attainable probability.

Now a man named Lazarus was sick. He was from Bethany, the village of Mary and her sister Martha. (This Mary, whose brother Lazarus now lay sick, was the same one who poured perfume on the Lord and wiped his feet with her hair.) So the sisters sent word to Jesus, "Lord, the one you love is sick." When he heard this, Jesus said, "This sickness will not end in death. No, it is for God's glory so that God's Son may be glorified through it." Now Jesus loved Martha and her sister and Lazarus. So when he heard that Lazarus was sick, he stayed where he was two more days, and then he said to his disciples, "Let us go back to Judea." JOHN 11:1–7

■

LAZARUS WAS THE BROTHER of Mary and Martha, who Jesus had visited in Bethany several times. Bethany was a small village that rested on a hill across the Kidron Valley from Jerusalem itself. When Jesus learned that Lazarus was sick, he did not act immediately by leaving for Bethany, but rather he made a statement that foreshadowed what would happen in Jerusalem during Passover. He said, "This sickness will not end in death. No, it is for God's glory so that God's Son may be glorified through it." The disciples did not understand what he meant by this, but we know that he was not only referring to the death of Lazarus and the miracle he would perform through him, but also Calvary, where he himself would die "so that the Son may be glorified through it."

"But Rabbi," they said, "a short while ago the Jews there tried to stone you, and yet you are going back?" Jesus answered, "Are there not twelve hours of daylight? Anyone who walks in the daytime will not stumble, for they see by this world's light. It is when a person walks at night that they stumble, for they have no light." After he had said this, he went on to tell them, "Our friend Lazarus has fallen asleep; but I am going there to wake him up." His disciples replied, "Lord, if he sleeps, he will get better." Jesus had been speaking of his death, but his disciples thought he meant natural sleep. So then he told them plainly, "Lazarus is dead, and for your sake I am glad I was not there, so that you may believe. But let us go to him." Then Thomas (also known as Didymus) said to the rest of the disciples, "Let us also go, that we may die with him." JOHN 11:8–16

■

WHY DO THE DISCIPLES seem so dense? Jesus did speak figuratively when he said that Lazarus had "fallen asleep," which might be understood as natural rest, but they also knew that Jesus had performed many miracles. He had given sight to the blind, healed the lame, and fed thousands with a few pieces of bread and some fish. The truth is that we see Jesus very differently than they did. The world had never seen anyone like him before. The resurrection had not yet taken place, and the disciples had the optics of a world circumscribed by natural events. Their ability to understand what Jesus was saying had not yet been transformed by the experience of the resurrected Lord. And so Thomas merely resigned himself to follow Jesus to a martyr's death. He uttered brave words, but those words missed the point.

On his arrival, Jesus found that Lazarus had already been in the tomb for four days. Now Bethany was less than two miles from Jerusalem, and many Jews had come to Martha and Mary to comfort them in the loss of their brother. When Martha heard that Jesus was coming, she went out to meet him, but Mary stayed at home. "Lord," Martha said to Jesus, "if you had been here, my brother would not have died. But I know that even now God will give you whatever you ask." Jesus said to her, "Your brother will rise again." Martha answered, "I know he will rise again in the resurrection at the last day." Jesus said to her, "I am the resurrection and the life. The one who believes in me will live, even though they die; and whoever lives by believing in me will never die. Do you believe this?" JOHN 11:17–26

■

MARTHA'S BROTHER LAZARUS HAD died and been buried. If there was any hope of saving him, that hope was lost by the time Jesus arrived. He was too late, and Martha nearly rebuked him when she said, "If you had been here, my brother would not have died." But then she threw a curve ball by adding, "But I know that even now God will give you whatever you ask." Martha believed that Jesus was a man of God, but whether that belief extended to believing her brother would be awakened from the sleep of death was doubtful. Jesus turned the tables on her by declaring that he himself was the resurrection and the life. He brought future hope into the present by saying that God had granted him the power even to restore life. "I am the resurrection and the life. The one who believes in me will live, even though they die; and whoever lives by believing in me will never die. Do you believe this?"

". . . and whoever lives by believing in me will never die. Do you believe this?" "Yes, Lord," she replied, "I believe that you are the Messiah, the Son of God, who is to come into the world." After she had said this, she went back and called her sister Mary aside. "The Teacher is here," she said, "and is asking for you." When Mary heard this, she got up quickly and went to him. Now Jesus had not yet entered the village, but was still at the place where Martha had met him. When the Jews who had been with Mary in the house, comforting her, noticed how quickly she got up and went out, they followed her, supposing she was going to the tomb to mourn there. When Mary reached the place where Jesus was and saw him, she fell at his feet and said, "Lord, if you had been here, my brother would not have died." JOHN 11:26–32

■

MARTHA PROGRESSED FROM "LORD, if you had been here" to "I believe that you are the Messiah, the Son of God, who is to come into the world." She went from mild accusation to belief by being in the presence of Jesus. When Mary learned that Jesus had arrived, she dropped everything and went out to meet him, but when she found him, she too offered a mild rebuke: "Lord, if you had been here, my brother would not have died." Death had not only torn Lazarus from his family, it had created a slight rift between the two sisters and Jesus. But Jesus had come on a mission to reveal that he is the resurrected life. Before he left for Bethany he said, "Our friend Lazarus has fallen asleep; but I am going there to wake him up." Jesus used sleep as a metaphor because he knew that "whoever lives by believing in me will never die." He would wake Lazarus from the sleep of death, and soon enough he would show, through his own death, that he is indeed the "resurrection and the life."

JESUS WEPT

When Jesus saw her weeping, and the Jews who had come along with her also weeping, he was deeply moved in spirit and troubled. "Where have you laid him?" he asked. "Come and see, Lord," they replied. Jesus wept. Then the Jews said, "See how he loved him!" But some of them said, "Could not he who opened the eyes of the blind man have kept this man from dying?" Jesus, once more deeply moved, came to the tomb. It was a cave with a stone laid across the entrance. "Take away the stone," he said. "But, Lord," said Martha, the sister of the dead man, "by this time there is a bad odor, for he has been there four days." JOHN 11:33–39

■

AS FAR BACK AS Genesis, we are told that God grieved because mankind had rejected him: "The Lord saw how great man's wickedness on the earth had become, and that every inclination of the thoughts of his heart was only evil all the time" (Genesis 6:5). Though God's grief led to a desire to "wipe mankind, whom I have created, from the face of the earth," he relented and called upon Noah to build an ark that carried mankind into the future. Here Jesus wept just as God wept because death (which is the penalty for sin) had brought pain and sorrow to those who loved Lazarus. As long as Satan reigns, this life will be lived in the "valley of the shadow of death" (Psalm 23:4), but Jesus came to change that condition once and for all. "I will turn their mourning into gladness; I will give them comfort and joy instead of sorrow" (Jeremiah 31:13).

Then Jesus said, "Did I not tell you that if you believe, you will see the glory of God?" So they took away the stone. Then Jesus looked up and said, "Father, I thank you that you have heard me. I know that you always hear me, but I said this for the benefit of the people standing here, that they may believe that you sent me." When he had said this, Jesus called in a loud voice, "Lazarus, come out!" The dead man came out, his hands and feet wrapped with strips of linen, and a cloth around his face. Jesus said to them, "Take off the grave clothes and let him go." JOHN 11:40–44

■

TRY TO IMAGINE BEING there when Jesus cried out, "Lazarus, come out!" Wouldn't you wonder if this was some kind of trick? Wouldn't this challenge everything you knew about life and death? Lazarus had been in the grave for four days. Martha warned Jesus not to have the stone removed because the decomposition would have caused a bad odor. And yet Lazarus came out bound up in grave clothes, and we are left either to believe what John reports or reject this account as impossible. The news of Lazarus' resurrection reached those in positions of authority in Jerusalem, causing the religious leaders to redouble their efforts to bring Jesus down. The forces that led to Calvary were set in motion.

Therefore many of the Jews who had come to visit Mary, and had seen what Jesus did, believed in him. But some of them went to the Pharisees and told them what Jesus had done. Then the chief priests and the Pharisees called a meeting of the Sanhedrin. "What are we accomplishing?" they asked. "Here is this man performing many signs. If we let him go on like this, everyone will believe in him, and then the Romans will come and take away both our temple and our nation." JOHN 11:45–48

■

THE RAISING OF LAZARUS was the match that lit the fuse. As Martha and Mary celebrated the return of their brother, the Pharisees called an emergency meeting of the Sanhedrin in Jerusalem to discuss the threat Jesus posed. They were afraid Jesus would attract an even larger following, bringing about the potential for greater unrest in the population. Their power rested on pleasing the Roman occupiers, and they were afraid they would lose everything if they allowed Jesus to go unchecked, and ". . . then the Romans will come and take away both our temple and our nation."

IT IS BETTER FOR YOU THAT ONE MAN DIE FOR THE PEOPLE

Then one of them, named Caiaphas, who was high priest that year, spoke up, "You know nothing at all! You do not realize that it is better for you that one man die for the people than that the whole nation perish." He did not say this on his own, but as high priest that year he prophesied that Jesus would die for the Jewish nation, and not only for that nation but also for the scattered children of God, to bring them together and make them one. JOHN 11:49–52

■

IRONICALLY, CAIAPHAS, THE HIGH priest, inadvertently revealed God's greater purpose when he said, "it is better for you that one man die for the people than that the whole nation perish." What Caiaphas intended for evil, God intends for good. It is God's plan that his Son is the sacrifice for the sin of many—one for all: "He sacrificed for their sins once for all when he offered himself" (Hebrews 7:27). Just as God found a ram as a substitute for Abraham's son Isaac (Genesis 22), so God sent his Son, not to save the temple or the nation, but to offer life through the sacrifice of his own, so that all who believe might live.

So from that day on they plotted to take his life. Therefore Jesus no longer moved about publicly among the people of Judea. Instead he withdrew to a region near the wilderness, to a village called Ephraim, where he stayed with his disciples. When it was almost time for the Jewish Passover, many went up from the country to Jerusalem for their ceremonial cleansing before the Passover. They kept looking for Jesus, and as they stood in the temple courts they asked one another, "What do you think? Isn't he coming to the festival at all?" But the chief priests and the Pharisees had given orders that anyone who found out where Jesus was should report it so that they might arrest him. JOHN 11:53–57

■

HIS TIME HAD NOT yet come, so Jesus retreated to the village of Ephraim. The crowds gathering in Jerusalem for Passover were waiting in expectation for Jesus to appear, but the Pharisees had issued orders for his arrest. The forces at work at this moment were intense. An air of high expectation hovered over the scene as if something monumental was about to happen. But whatever the people and the Pharisees expected, it had no resemblance to what God was about to bring about. It was as if the world rested on a hinge, with one door about to close and another open.

As he approached Jerusalem and saw the city, he wept over it and said, "If you, even you, had only known on this day what would bring you peace—but now it is hidden from your eyes. The days will come upon you when your enemies will build an embankment against you and encircle you and hem you in on every side. They will dash you to the ground, you and the children within your walls. They will not leave one stone on another, because you did not recognize the time of God's coming to you." LUKE 19:41–44

■

A CITY THAT HAS abandoned God is a city at risk of complete ruin. Jesus wept because he foresaw what would take place in the not-distant future when the Roman forces cast down even the vast stonewalls of the temple. But Jesus also heard the cries of anguish and fear that had once filled the streets of David's city as the Babylonian armies invaded and destroyed the ancient Jerusalem where God had been worshipped and welcomed. In the words of Jeremiah: "Zion will be plowed like a field, Jerusalem will become a heap of rubble, the temple hill a mound overgrown with thickets" (Jeremiah 26:18). Jesus wept because the city of God had once again declined into just another city of man, where the people and their leaders were blind and deaf to the dangers of their dire condition.

Six days before the Passover, Jesus came to Bethany, where Lazarus lived, whom Jesus had raised from the dead. Here a dinner was given in Jesus' honor. Martha served, while Lazarus was among those reclining at the table with him. Then Mary took about a pint of pure nard, an expensive perfume; she poured it on Jesus' feet and wiped his feet with her hair. And the house was filled with the fragrance of the perfume. JOHN 12:1–3

■

THE SCENE WAS SET in Bethany, a small town on a hill across the Kidron Valley from Jerusalem and the temple. Below, on the side of the hill, were rows and rows of graves of whitewashed stones. Jesus was the guest of honor in the house of Martha, Mary, and Lazarus; they were celebrating the miraculous return of the brother who was dead but now alive. Then, unexpectedly, Mary took a pint of expensive perfume and poured it on Jesus' feet, and in complete humility she wiped his feet with her hair. What possessed Mary to do this act of adoration? It was as if the Holy Spirit had taken hold of her and told her to do this for Jesus as a sign of what was soon to take place.

JUDAS OBJECTED

But one of his disciples, Judas Iscariot, who was later to betray him, objected, "Why wasn't this perfume sold and the money given to the poor? It was worth a year's wages." He did not say this because he cared about the poor but because he was a thief; as keeper of the money bag, he used to help himself to what was put into it. "Leave her alone," Jesus replied. "It was intended that she should save this perfume for the day of my burial." JOHN 12:4–7

■

MARY HAD TAKEN AN expensive perfume and unexpectedly poured it on the one who had raised her brother from the dead. What Mary did was not generous in the normal sense; it was an act of worship, appropriate in ways that she could not fully imagine. But at the same time Judas Iscariot looked on in stunned exasperation. What Mary expended in worship, Judas saw as waste. Worse than that, it was revealed that he had been secretly stealing from the money used to support Jesus and the disciples. Judas was self-righteously scolding Mary out of guilt rather than concern for the well-being of Jesus and his followers. Judas had succumbed to temptation, and his greed led to a desperate place.

THE LEADERS PLOTTED AGAINST
LAZARUS AS WELL

Meanwhile a large crowd of Jews found out that Jesus was there and came, not only because of him but also to see Lazarus, whom he had raised from the dead. So the chief priests made plans to kill Lazarus as well, for on account of him many of the Jews were going over to Jesus and believing in him. JOHN 12:9–11

■

ON THE SURFACE EVERYTHING in the city seemed normal, but behind closed doors men were plotting to smother the crisis before things got out of hand. Word had spread among the people that a great miracle had taken place, and they wanted to see for themselves that Lazarus was indeed alive. The religious leaders saw this clear expression of the power of God as a threat to their own control. The people of Jerusalem were "going over to Jesus and believing in him." And so the Jewish leaders, who were forever concerned about keeping their Roman masters contented, decided not only to rid themselves of Jesus, but also to destroy the evidence of his miracles by killing Lazarus as well.

YOU WILL FIND A COLT TIED THERE

As they approached Jerusalem and came to Bethphage and Bethany at the Mount of Olives, Jesus sent two of his disciples, saying to them, "Go to the village ahead of you, and just as you enter it, you will find a colt tied there, which no one has ever ridden. Untie it and bring it here. If anyone asks you, 'Why are you doing this?' say, 'The Lord needs it and will send it back here shortly.'" They went and found a colt outside in the street, tied at a doorway. As they untied it, some people standing there asked, "What are you doing, untying that colt?" They answered as Jesus had told them to, and the people let them go. When they brought the colt to Jesus and threw their cloaks over it, he sat on it. MARK 11:1–7

■

MARK SEEMS TO BE telling a simple story here. Jesus approached Jerusalem for the final time and asked two of his disciples to go on an unusual mission. They were to go to a village just ahead, find a colt that had never been ridden, and bring it to him. This is where the story becomes interesting. Everything happened just as Jesus said it would. Furthermore, the owner of the colt allowed the disciples to take it. But unknown to everyone but Jesus, he asked for the colt to fulfill a five-hundred-year-old prophecy: "See the king comes to you, righteous and having salvation, gentle and riding on a donkey, on a colt, the foal of a donkey . . . He will proclaim peace to the nations, His rule will extend from sea to sea and from the River to the ends of the earth" (Zechariah 9:9–10). It is here where the present moment, the historical moment, and the prophetic moment reveal in a powerful way the identity and purpose of Jesus Christ.

Many people spread their cloaks on the road, while others spread branches they had cut in the fields. Those who went ahead and those who followed shouted, "Hosanna!" "Blessed is he who comes in the name of the Lord!" "Blessed is the coming kingdom of our father David!" "Hosanna in the highest heaven!" Jesus entered Jerusalem and went into the temple courts. He looked around at everything, but since it was already late, he went out to Bethany with the Twelve. MARK 11:8–11

■

HE CAME THROUGH THE gates of Jerusalem, not as a triumphant warrior, but as Isaiah's "suffering servant," on a colt. The people shouted "Hosanna" as if half expecting King David to appear to reclaim his birthright. But it was another sort of Messiah who had returned to Jerusalem to die. Jesus knew why he was there, but the people had no idea what was about to take place. The savior they envisioned was a military leader who would release them from the political bondage imposed by the Romans, but Jesus came on a very different mission. This is how Isaiah describes this King of Kings and Lord of Lords: "Surely he took up our infirmities and carried our sorrows, yet we considered him stricken by God, smitten by him, and afflicted. But he was pierced for our transgressions, he was crushed for our iniquities; the punishment that brought us peace was upon him, and by his wounds we are healed" (Isaiah 53:4–5). This is the one who entered Jerusalem triumphantly that day.

Jesus entered the temple courts and drove out all who were buying and selling there. He overturned the tables of the money changers and the benches of those selling doves. "It is written," he said to them, "'My house will be called a house of prayer,' but you are making it 'a den of robbers.'" The blind and the lame came to him at the temple, and he healed them. But when the chief priests and the teachers of the law saw the wonderful things he did and the children shouting in the temple courts, "Hosanna to the Son of David," they were indignant. "Do you hear what these children are saying?" they asked him. "Yes," replied Jesus, "have you never read, 'From the lips of children and infants you, Lord, have called forth your praise'?" And he left them and went out of the city to Bethany, where he spent the night. MATTHEW 21:12–17

■

JESUS ENTERED JERUSALEM, THE city of David, to find the temple courts teeming with people getting and spending, while the temple itself loomed over the scene as a rebuke to all who pursued mammon and not God. How far the people had fallen. David said about the temple, "Open for me the gates of righteousness, I will enter and give thanks to the Lord. This is the gate of the Lord through which the righteous may enter. I will give thanks, for you answered me, you have become my salvation" (Psalm 118: 19–21). But Jesus called it a "den of robbers," echoing the words of the prophet Jeremiah, "Will you steal and murder, commit adultery and perjury, burn incense to Baal and follow other gods you have not known, and then come and stand before me at this house, which bears my Name, and say, 'We are safe'—safe to do all these detestable things? Has this House, which bears my Name, become a den of robbers to you?" (Jeremiah 7:9–11) The people had drifted into a dangerous disregard for God, even in the courtyard of the temple.

WE WOULD LIKE TO SEE JESUS

Now there were some Greeks among those who went up to worship at the festival. They came to Philip, who was from Bethsaida in Galilee, with a request. "Sir," they said, "we would like to see Jesus." Philip went to tell Andrew; Andrew and Philip in turn told Jesus. Jesus replied, "The hour has come for the Son of Man to be glorified. Very truly I tell you, unless a kernel of wheat falls to the ground and dies, it remains only a single seed. But if it dies, it produces many seeds. Anyone who loves their life will lose it, while anyone who hates their life in this world will keep it for eternal life. Whoever serves me must follow me; and where I am, my servant also will be. My Father will honor the one who serves me. JOHN 12:20–26

■

AT MANY DIFFERENT TIMES throughout the Gospel of John we are told that Jesus' time had not yet come. Jesus told his mother at Cana that "My time has not yet come" (John 2:4). And when he is teaching in the temple area, John says, "no one seized him, because his time had not yet come" (John 8:20). But now, after his entry into Jerusalem on a colt, Jesus acknowledged to Philip that, "the hour has come for the Son of Man to be glorified." But by this Jesus did not mean the time had come for him to be crowned king like any other monarch. Jesus meant that the time had come for him to die by being lifted up on a cross. Philip may have been puzzled by this reply, but Jesus knew exactly what it meant when he said, "the hour had come." The mission and the moment were about to fuse.

"Now my soul is troubled, and what shall I say? 'Father, save me from the hour'? No, it was for this very reason I came to this hour. Father, glorify your name!" Then a voice came from heaven, "I have glorified it, and will glorify it again." The crowd that was there and heard it said it had thundered; others said an angel had spoken to him. Jesus said, "This voice was for your benefit, not mine. Now is the time for judgment on this world; now the prince of this world will be driven out. And I, when I am lifted up from the earth, will draw all people to myself." He said this to show the kind of death he was going to die. The crowd spoke up, "We have heard from the Law that the Messiah will remain forever, so how can you say, 'The Son of Man must be lifted up'? Who is this 'Son of Man'?" Then Jesus told them, "You are going to have the light just a little while longer. Walk while you have the light, before darkness overtakes you. Whoever walks in the dark does not know where they are going. Believe in the light while you have the light, so that you may become children of light." When he had finished speaking, Jesus left and hid himself from them. JOHN 12:27–36

■

FINALLY, AFTER ALL THOSE times when we heard that Jesus' time had not yet come, it has come. Jesus confirmed that his hour had arrived: "No, it was for this very reason I came to this hour." Should he try to avoid it? Jesus answered that question with a question of his own: Should he ask the Father to save him from this hour? Jesus had already answered these questions many times before when he told people that he could do nothing without the Father. While the people around him thought they heard thunder or perhaps angels speaking to him, Jesus heard the voice of the Father confirming the purpose and cosmic importance of the mission. Rather than the temptation to be saved from completing the mission, Jesus received confirmation that he is to glorify the name of the Father. The voice said, "I have glorified it and will glorify it again." God will glorify his name through the Son, who will begin the end of the reign of "the prince of this world." Jesus understood exactly what this means; his own followers and the people surrounding him hadn't a clue.

Even after Jesus had performed so many signs in their presence, they still would not believe in him. This was to fulfill the word of Isaiah the prophet: "Lord, who has believed our message and to whom has the arm of the Lord been revealed?" JOHN 12:37–38

■

IF MANY IN JESUS' own time did not believe, why do we think it would be any different today? If his closest followers had their doubts, why would we be dismissive when we come upon a doubter? In this age, where the scientific method is deified and technological innovation is a manifestation of science's power, why are we surprised when we hear that many no longer accept the truth of the Bible? The fact is that Christ has always been under attack, since the time of his own birth. Yet despite the skepticism of our own times, faith in Jesus Christ is alive in every corner of the world. People everywhere have answered Jesus' question to Peter, "But who do you say I am?" with "You are the Christ of God" (Mark 8:29).

For this reason they could not believe, because, as Isaiah says elsewhere, "He has blinded their eyes and hardened their hearts, so they can neither see with their eyes, nor understand with their hearts, nor turn—and I would heal them." Isaiah said this because he saw Jesus' glory and spoke about him. Yet at the same time many even among the leaders believed in him. But because of the Pharisees they would not openly acknowledge their faith for fear they would be put out of the synagogue; or they loved human praise more than praise from God. JOHN 12:39–43

■

WHAT BARS US FROM belief? Isaiah refers to intellectual blindness and a cold and hardened heart. John mentions the social or financial cost because "they loved human praise more than the praise from God." Perhaps we believe, like squirrels, that our acorn of belief will be safe if we bury it. But if our belief matters to us, if it is important enough to bury like a treasure, why can't we bring ourselves to live our faith in the open? Is it as true now as it was in Jesus' own time that we actually love human praise more than praise from God? If we profess Christ, do we proclaim him? Or do we bury our belief in him like that acorn, anticipating there will be a time and place to dig it up again?

Then Jesus cried out, "Whoever believes in me does not believe in me only, but in the one who sent me. The one who looks at me is seeing the one who sent me. I have come into the world as a light, so that no one who believes in me should stay in darkness. If anyone hears my words but does not keep them, I do not judge that person. For I did not come to judge the world, but to save the world. There is a judge for the one who rejects me and does not accept my words; the very words I have spoken will condemn them at the last day." JOHN 12:44–48

■

EARLIER JESUS SAYS, "GOD did not send his Son into the world to condemn the world, but to save the world through him" (John 3:17). The world Jesus entered was shrouded in darkness. God did not need to judge it because it stood judged already. Jesus goes on to say that mankind has abandoned love of God for love of darkness: "but men loved darkness instead of light because their deeds were evil. Everyone who does evil hates the light and will not come into the light for fear their deeds will be exposed" (John 3:20). Jesus came to change all of that because he has "come into the world as a light, so that no one who believes in me should stay in darkness." Simply put, Jesus came to reverse the order of loves. Rather than the love of self, or friends, or things, Jesus came to restore love of God as our primary love that then radiates out to love for others before love of self.

I DID NOT SPEAK ON MY OWN

For I did not speak on my own, but the Father who sent me commanded me to say all that I have spoken. I know that his command leads to eternal life. So whatever I say is just what the Father has told me to say. JOHN 12:49–50

■

JESUS MAKES WHAT MIGHT appear to be a wild claim, but it is wild only if he is not the Son of God. While the Jews were trying to adhere to the spoken Word, Jesus came as the living Word—the exact representation on earth of God the Father. The Son speaks what the Father commands him to say and so perfectly reveals the Father through this dynamic relationship. The Father is perfectly revealed by his Son through the Holy Spirit as if they existed together eternally in complete harmony.

A FRUITLESS FIG TREE

The next day as they were leaving Bethany, Jesus was hungry. Seeing in the distance a fig tree in leaf, he went to find out if it had any fruit. When he reached it, he found nothing but leaves, because it was not the season for figs. Then he said to the tree, "May no one ever eat fruit from you again." And his disciples heard him say it. MARK 11:12–14

∎

As JESUS LEFT BETHANY to return to the temple in Jerusalem, he came upon a fig tree that had leaves but no fruit. Spring was not the season for the tree to produce figs, but Jesus was hungry and the tree did not serve its purpose. Jesus' cursing of the tree may seem disproportional, but consider that Jesus may have been using the tree as an example to make a spiritual statement. In Jesus' time the fig tree was a symbol for Israel, a land that had abandoned the God of the patriarchs and had become unfruitful. The nation had been cursed, occupied by foreign armies, and presided over by corrupt leaders. Jesus may have been using the fig tree as a symbol of God's judgment, even as God was moving toward removing that curse through what Jesus would do on the cross.

A WITHERED FIG TREE

In the morning, as they went along, they saw the fig tree withered from the roots. Peter remembered and said to Jesus, "Rabbi, look! The fig tree you cursed has withered!" "Have faith in God," Jesus answered. "Truly I tell you, if anyone says to this mountain, 'Go, throw yourself into the sea,' and does not doubt in their heart but believes that what they say will happen, it will be done for them. Therefore I tell you, whatever you ask for in prayer, believe that you have received it, and it will be yours. And when you stand praying, if you hold anything against anyone, forgive them, so that your Father in heaven may forgive you your sins." **MARK** 11:20–25

■

THE DISCIPLES WERE AMAZED that the fig tree actually withered one day after Jesus cursed it. But Jesus simply asked, why are you so surprised? Faith is audacious, and when you pray, audacious things are possible. At the same time, Jesus is not saying that God will answer every prayer and petition in just the way we want him to. In fact, we may find that God seems to be silent for a time because the time may not be right. Jesus continuously prayed to God, always knowing that in the end it must be God's will, not his (or our) will, that needs to be done. So pray boldly but trust broadly, because "we know that in all things God works for the good of those who love him, who have been called according to his purpose" (Romans 8:25).

WHO GAVE YOU THIS AUTHORITY?

One day as Jesus was teaching the people in the temple courts and proclaiming the good news, the chief priests and the teachers of the law, together with the elders, came up to him. "Tell us by what authority you are doing these things," they said. "Who gave you this authority?" He replied, "I will also ask you a question. Tell me: John's baptism—was it from heaven, or of human origin?" They discussed it among themselves and said, "If we say, 'From heaven,' he will ask, 'Why didn't you believe him?' But if we say, 'Of human origin,' all the people will stone us, because they are persuaded that John was a prophet." So they answered, "We don't know where it was from." Jesus said, "Neither will I tell you by what authority I am doing these things." LUKE 20:1–8

■

THE CHIEF PRIESTS AND teachers of the law stepped forward to question Jesus' authority to teach the people in the temple courts. They approached with confidence because they held the institutional authority of the temple itself. They had all the credentials that conferred power and protection upon them. Yet somehow they felt threatened because the people were listening to Jesus. Jesus responded to the priests and teachers with his own question, which forced them to answer, "We don't know." The irony here is that the very nature of the question cut through the pretense of the authority of the priests and teachers. If their authority was from God, they would have known the answer and not worried about the opinion of the people. All authority comes from God, including John's baptism. The religious leaders corrupted the authority they held for their own purposes. The authority God gave to John the Baptist had threatened the political order of things and therefore was destroyed. Now they saw Jesus as another threat to their power.

DOING A FATHER'S WILL

"What do you think? There was a man who had two sons. He went to the first and said, 'Son, go and work today in the vineyard.' 'I will not,' he answered, but later he changed his mind and went. Then the father went to the other son and said the same thing. He answered, 'I will, sir,' but he did not go. Which of the two did what his father wanted?" "The first," they answered. Jesus said to them, "Truly I tell you, the tax collectors and the prostitutes are entering the kingdom of God ahead of you. For John came to you to show you the way of righteousness, and you did not believe him, but the tax collectors and the prostitutes did. And even after you saw this, you did not repent and believe him." MATTHEW 21:28–32

■

JESUS CONTINUED TO ADDRESS the chief priests and teachers of the law. He told a story of two sons: One pretends to do the right thing but then does the opposite, while the other at first refuses to do the right thing but then ends up obeying. Jesus aimed this parable directly at those who questioned his authority. Then he added insult to injury by saying that their pretensions to righteousness belied their disbelief in the righteousness of John the Baptist. Jesus further offended them by saying that the lowest of the low— prostitutes and tax collectors—who believed John the Baptist would enter the kingdom of God ahead of them. Belief is not based on outward appearances; according to Jesus, an authentic desire to repent and turn your heart over to Jesus in joyful surrender is the only pathway to abiding in the will of God.

A LOADED QUESTION

Later they sent some of the Pharisees and Herodians to Jesus to catch him in his words. They came to him and said, "Teacher, we know that you are a man of integrity. You aren't swayed by others, because you pay no attention to who they are; but you teach the way of God in accordance with the truth. Is it right to pay the imperial tax to Caesar or not? Should we pay or shouldn't we?" But Jesus knew their hypocrisy. "Why are you trying to trap me?" he asked. "Bring me a denarius and let me look at it." They brought the coin, and he asked them, "Whose image is this? And whose inscription?" "Caesar's," they replied. Then Jesus said to them, "Give back to Caesar what is Caesar's and to God what is God's." And they were amazed at him. MARK 12:13–17

■

JESUS WAS NOT DECEIVED by the flattering words of the Pharisees and Herodians. While they may have changed their tactics, they had not changed their intention. Their speech might have been as smooth as butter, but war against Jesus remained very much in their hearts (Psalm 55:21). Jesus knew this because he was not deceived by men and the things that corrupt them: "for he knew all men. He did not need man's testimony about man, for he knew what was in a man" (John 2:24–25). In answer to their loaded question, he asked for a coin, looked at it, and said, "Whose image is this?" When the Pharisees said Caesar's, he simply replied, "Give back to Caesar what is Caesar's and to God what is God's." The irony here is that the Pharisees and Herodians had given what is God's to Caesar as well, betraying God for the rewards of personal position and power.

SUMMING UP THE LAW AND THE PROPHETS

One of the teachers of the law came and heard them debating. Noticing that Jesus had given them a good answer, he asked him, "Of all the commandments, which is the most important?" "The most important one," answered Jesus, "is this: 'Hear, O Israel: The Lord our God, the Lord is one. Love the Lord your God with all your heart and with all your soul and with all your mind and with all your strength.' The second is this: 'Love your neighbor as yourself.' There is no commandment greater than these." **MARK** 12:28–31

■

JESUS DISTILLED THE HUNDREDS of laws, rules, and regulations into two commandments, one drawn from Deuteronomy and the other from Leviticus. By giving just two commandments, he is not saying that all the other laws are rendered obsolete; rather, he is pronouncing the two basic principles that are foundational for all the rules and regulations that came after God gave Moses the Ten Commandments, which are themselves built on the two commandments that Jesus gives us.

"Well said, teacher," the man replied. "You are right in saying that God is one and there is no other but him. To love him with all your heart, with all your understanding and with all your strength, and to love your neighbor as yourself is more important than all burnt offerings and sacrifices." When Jesus saw that he had answered wisely, he said to him, "You are not far from the kingdom of God." And from then on no one dared ask him any more questions. MARK 12:32–34

■

THIS PARTICULAR TEACHER OF the law was an honest broker, a striver for the truth. He genuinely wanted Jesus to give an answer to his question, and he was not disappointed by what he heard. But then Jesus moved from the truth of his answer to the question of how to apply that truth. He said, "You are not far from the kingdom of God." By this he meant that knowing you should love the Lord your God is not the same as acting on that knowledge. Knowing is only the first step in acting in a way that will further the kingdom here and now. The commandment to love God and neighbor seems so simple; when we actually live it every day, we come to experience the harmonious beauty that radiates from this core into God's own purpose and design for building the kingdom that is to come.

A RIDDLE

While the Pharisees were gathered together, Jesus asked them, "What do you think about the Messiah? Whose son is he?" "The son of David," they replied. He said to them, "How is it then that David, speaking by the Spirit, calls him 'Lord'? For he says, 'The Lord said to my Lord: 'Sit at my right hand until I put your enemies under your feet.' If then David calls him 'Lord,' how can he be his son?" MATTHEW 22:41–45

■

JESUS ASKED THE PHARISEES a seemingly simple question: "What do you think about the Messiah? Whose son is he?" The Pharisees gave the partially correct answer: "The Son of David." This answer is true, but their answer was far too bound up by earthly chronology. Jesus reveals that the Messiah both precedes David and comes after David. He is from the beginning, but he will take earthly form as a descendant of David (Psalm 132:11). Immediately before his arrest, Jesus prayed this prayer with his disciples: "And now, Father, glorify me in your presence with the glory I had with you before the world began" (John 17:5). The Pharisees understood how life unfolds in its natural order, but to see the full dimensions of the mystery of God's purpose as revealed in Jesus Christ was simply beyond their capacity to believe.

While all the people were listening, Jesus said to his disciples, "Beware of the teachers of the law. They like to walk around in flowing robes and love to be greeted with respect in the market-places and have the most important seats in the synagogues and the places of honor at banquets. They devour widows' houses and for a show make lengthy prayers. These men will be punished most severely." LUKE 20:45–47

■

BEHIND JESUS' DOUBLE-EDGED WARNING was an implicit under-standing of God-directed leadership. Jesus warned the disciples not to emulate the corrupt ruling class because their thirst for the prerequisites of rule had led them away from God. Jesus warned the leaders themselves that they were only serving themselves by stealing from widows and loudly uttering vaporous prayers that served no other purpose than to strengthen their hold on political and religious power. Jesus offers a radical substitute for this earth-bound notion of leadership. Jesus' model is based on the central idea that we must serve God in whatever capacity we have been gifted and called. Jesus told his disciples, "the Son of Man did not come to be served, but to serve, and to give his life as a ransom for many" (Matthew 20:28). Jesus sets forth God's own model for lead-ership, and he tells us to beware of everything else.

Jesus left the temple and was walking away when his disciples came up to him to call his attention to its buildings. "Do you see all these things?" he asked. "Truly I tell you, not one stone here will be left on another; everyone will be thrown down." As Jesus was sitting on the Mount of Olives, the disciples came to him privately. "Tell us," they said, "when will this happen, and what will be the sign of your coming and of the end of the age?" MAT-THEW 24:1–3

■

IT WAS FIVE HUNDRED years earlier that Jeremiah pronounced with much anguish that the people had forsaken God and that Jerusalem with its temple would become "a heap of ruins, a haunt of jackals" (Jeremiah 9:11). The temple itself was restored in Jesus' time, but the leaders and the people were as far away from God as ever. Instead of putting their trust in God, they put their confidence in the temple structure itself. Jesus was saying that when the people do not honor God as the centerpiece of their lives and faith, then the temple becomes a showcase of pretense and hypocrisy. And Jesus said even the temple will not stand but will be thrown down because the children of God have abandoned God just as their forbearers had forsaken him so many times before.

Jesus answered: "Watch out that no one deceives you. For many will come in my name, claiming, 'I am the Messiah,' and will deceive many. You will hear of wars and rumors of wars, but see to it that you are not alarmed. Such things must happen, but the end is still to come. Nation will rise against nation, and kingdom against kingdom. There will be famines and earthquakes in various places. All these are the beginning of birth pains." MATTHEW 24:4–8

■

JESUS TELLS US THAT there will be a period of time before he comes again when chaos and confusion will seem to reign. And he warns us not to waste our time trying to discern the exact moment when the "the end of the age" will occur. He promises he will come again, but as for the exact time and place, that is for only the Father to know (Acts 1:7). In times of wars and rumors of wars, Jesus tells us to focus on the opportunities at hand as they serve the Lord. In the Sermon on the Mount he says, "But seek first his kingdom and his righteousness, and all these things will be given to you as well. Therefore do not worry about tomorrow, for tomorrow will worry about itself. Each day has enough trouble of its own" (Matthew 6:33–34).

Then will appear the sign of the Son of Man in heaven. And then all the peoples of the earth will mourn when they see the Son of Man coming on the clouds of heaven, with power and great glory. And he will send his angels with a loud trumpet call, and they will gather his elect from the four winds, from one end of the heavens to the other. MATTHEW 24:30–31

■

As PAUL PREPARED TO depart for Jerusalem from Ephesus, he declared to the elders in a final farewell that he had "not hesitated to proclaim to you the whole will of God" (Acts 20:27). Why is this important for each of us? It is very easy, and not uncommon, to take a part of the Gospel narrative and expand it into the whole thing. Paul was obedient to the will of God through the Holy Spirit by focusing on every dimension of Jesus, from his miraculous birth to his arrest, trial, crucifixion, death, resurrection, and ascension. This is not Paul's story; it is God's story, carrying all the way back to the first words of Genesis. It can be tempting to simplify the narrative by transforming it into something other than what it is, but Paul refused to adjust the story for his own convenience. And Jesus does exactly the same thing in his prophetic teachings. While his followers wanted to know more about when "the Son of Man" would return, Jesus gave the general sweep of what will take place while keeping in place the mystery of God's timing. If we focus just on the question of when Jesus will return, we lose focus on the Jesus of the Gospels, the Jesus of Nazareth and Capernaum, of Jerusalem, and of all of the world.

But about that day or hour no one knows, not even the angels in heaven, nor the Son, but only the Father. As it was in the days of Noah, so it will be at the coming of the Son of Man. For in the days before the flood, people were eating and drinking, marrying and giving in marriage, up to the day Noah entered the ark; and they knew nothing about what would happen until the flood came and took them all away. That is how it will be at the coming of the Son of Man. MATTHEW 24:36–39

■

GOD'S KNOWLEDGE IS INFINITE; our knowledge is incomplete and often wrong. But still many of us spend hours and days looking for signs of what is to come while missing the opportunities of the moment to serve God's purpose in important ways. Jesus warns us away from this unproductive inactivity by telling us, "No one knows about that day or hour, not even the angels of heaven, nor the Son, but only the Father . . . Therefore keep watch, because you do not know on what day your Lord will come." In contrast, the religious leaders claimed a special knowledge of God's providence, but their intellectual pride was their sin. Paul looked at this foolishness from the perspective of God: "For the foolishness of God is wiser than man's wisdom, and the weakness of God is stronger than man's strength" (1 Corinthians 1:25).

When the Son of Man comes in his glory, and all the angels with him, he will sit on his glorious throne. All the nations will be gathered before him, and he will separate the people one from another as a shepherd separates the sheep from the goats. He will put the sheep on his right and the goats on his left. MATTHEW 25:31–33

■

WHEN WE PRAY THE Lord's Prayer, we say, Lord, "thy will be done." But do we walk in the way of God's will or do we turn down the "my will be done" path? God's will for each one of us is to transform the "my will" into "thy will," but for the rebellious heart, this change of direction can prove to be so hard that we give up, or, worse, fall back into the world of "my will be done." When Jesus refers to the day of final judgment, he is not necessarily looking for an accounting of all the things we have done wrong. No one will stand before the throne of God and say that they lived a life without sin. But have we chosen to live outside of the opportunities and blessings that God gifts to each one of us? Are we like the servant who doubled the value of the coins given to him by the master or are we like the servant who buried the coin out of fear rather than use it well in the service of his master? God calls each one of us to be his sheep—to follow him—not only for this life, but for all eternity.

Then the King will say to those on his right, 'Come, you who are
blessed by my Father; take your inheritance, the kingdom prepared for you since the creation of the world. For I was hungry
and you gave me something to eat, I was thirsty and you gave
me something to drink, I was a stranger and you invited me in, I
needed clothes and you clothed me, I was sick and you looked after
me, I was in prison and you came to visit me.' Then the righteous
will answer him, 'Lord, when did we see you hungry and feed you,
or thirsty and give you something to drink? When did we see you
a stranger and invite you in, or needing clothes and clothe you?
When did we see you sick or in prison and go to visit you?' The
King will reply, 'Truly I tell you, whatever you did for one of the
least of these brothers and sisters of mine, you did for me.' MAT-
THEW 25:34–40

■

JESUS CONTINUES TO TEACH what it means to do God's will in
this world. He sums it up this way: "Truly I tell you, whatever you
did for one of the least of these brothers and sisters of mine, you did
for me." To do the will of God requires us to see the image of God
in every person—young and old, rich and poor, male and female.
Our human categories deceive us and separate us artificially from
God's will. In his first letter, John reinforces this connection between God, his children, and each one of us: "Anyone who claims
to be in the light but hates his brother is still in the darkness. Whoever loves his brother lives in the light, and there is nothing in him
to make him stumble. But whoever hates his brother is in the darkness and walks around in the darkness; he does not know where he
is going, because the darkness has blinded him" (1 John 2:9–11).

Then he will say to those on his left, 'Depart from me, you who are cursed, into the eternal fire prepared for the devil and his angels. For I was hungry and you gave me nothing to eat, I was thirsty and you gave me nothing to drink, I was a stranger and you did not invite me in, I needed clothes and you did not clothe me, I was sick and in prison and you did not look after me.' They also will answer, 'Lord, when did we see you hungry or thirsty or a stranger or needing clothes or sick or in prison, and did not help you?' He will reply, 'Truly I tell you, whatever you did not do for one of the least of these, you did not do for me.' Then they will go away to eternal punishment, but the righteous to eternal life. MATTHEW 25:41–46

∎

WHY DOES JESUS SAY to some, "Depart from me, you who are cursed, into eternal fire prepared for the devil and his angels"? He is saying that for those who claim to worship and follow God, there is a cost to discipleship. We are called to the hard tasks of feeding the hungry, providing drink to the thirsty, giving shelter to the stranger, clothing the naked, and offering hope to the hopeless. All these people bear the image of God, even if they are the most marginalized members of society. Jesus says that even the most seemingly worthless people who live wrecked and broken lives are worthy in the eyes of God because each person was created in the image of God. The Good Samaritan was good because he crossed the road to help a man who had been robbed and left for dead. He could have passed by as others had done, but then he would have been just a Samaritan, because as Jesus puts it, "whatever you did not do for one of the least of these, you did not do for me."

Now the Passover and the Festival of Unleavened Bread were only two days away, and the chief priests and the teachers of the law were scheming to arrest Jesus secretly and kill him. "But not during the festival," they said, "or the people may riot." **MARK 14:1–2**

■

TRY TO IMAGINE JERUSALEM at the moment described by Mark. The city with its closely compacted buildings separated by narrow streets was beginning to teem with people as Passover approached. The streets were noisy with crowds that had come long distances to celebrate the Festival of Unleavened Bread, which commemorated the time when Moses, responding to God's command, prepared the people to begin the journey from bondage to freedom. But hidden unseen behind closed doors, the religious leaders were scheming to arrest and execute Jesus. In a way, they had, ironically, substituted their role as descendants of Moses for the role of descendants of the tyrant Pharaoh. Jesus had come to Jerusalem on a mission from God; the religious leaders were on their own mission to subvert God's purpose, even though they had convinced themselves that they were doing God's handiwork.

Then one of the Twelve—the one called Judas Iscariot—went to the chief priests and asked, "What are you willing to give me if I deliver him over to you?" So they counted out for him thirty pieces of silver. From then on Judas watched for an opportunity to hand him over. MATTHEW 26:14–16

■

WHY DID JUDAS DECIDE to betray Jesus? Judas was a disciple, one of the original Twelve, a man who followed Jesus from Galilee to Jerusalem and showed no signs of turning on the one who had called him to follow. But Matthew tells us that at some point he went to the chief priests and asked for money to deliver Jesus into their hands. Then Matthew says, "Judas watched for an opportunity to hand him over." The word "opportunity" provides a hint to the spiritual source of this betrayal. Luke makes it clear that at the very conclusion of the time that Satan tempted Jesus in the wilderness, Satan had not given up. Instead, we are told, "When the devil had finished all this tempting, he left him until an opportune time." The prince of the kingdom of darkness found his instrument of opportunity in the person of Judas. Even though Judas was a dedicated disciple of Jesus, he was subject to the same desires and appetites that all people experience. It might even be said that the closer one is to Jesus, the more intense the temptations become. At a moment of weakness, Judas tragically gave into Satan's whisperings and turned on the Son of God. Satan found his opportune time and entered Judas' heart to capitalize on what appeared to be his final road to victory.

Then came the day of Unleavened Bread on which the Passover lamb had to be sacrificed. Jesus sent Peter and John, saying, "Go and make preparations for us to eat the Passover." "Where do you want us to prepare for it?" they asked. He replied, "As you enter the city, a man carrying a jar of water will meet you. Follow him to the house that he enters, and say to the owner of the house, 'The Teacher asks: Where is the guest room, where I may eat the Passover with my disciples?' He will show you a large room upstairs, all furnished. Make preparations there." They left and found things just as Jesus had told them. So they prepared the Passover.

LUKE 22:7–13

■

LUKE TELLS US THAT the day of Unleavened Bread is the day the Passover lamb had to be sacrificed. This is an historical fact, but behind the historical is God's supernatural intention. The angel of the Lord told Mary that she would give birth to a son and would "give him the name Jesus because he will save his people from their sins" (Matthew 1:21). Upon seeing Jesus, John the Baptist said, "Look, the Lamb of God, who takes away the sin of the world" (John 1:29). Jesus came into the world for this very reason. Isaiah describes him as a Suffering Servant who will be "led like a lamb to the slaughter . . . for the transgression of my people he was stricken" (Isaiah 53:7,8). Just as Jesus knew in advance that a man carrying water would take Peter and John to the Upper Room, so he understood how this moment was a turning point in history. God was about to open the door to redemption. He was about to provide the Lamb (Genesis 22:8).

THE LAST SUPPER

When evening came, Jesus arrived with the Twelve. While they were reclining at the table eating, he said, "Truly I tell you, one of you will betray me—one who is eating with me." They were saddened, and one by one they said to him, "Surely you don't mean me?" "It is one of the Twelve," he replied, "one who dips bread into the bowl with me. The Son of Man will go just as it is written about him. But woe to that man who betrays the Son of Man! It would be better for him if he had not been born." While they were eating, Jesus took bread, and when he had given thanks, he broke it and gave it to his disciples, saying, "Take it; this is my body." Then he took a cup, and when he had given thanks, he gave it to them, and they all drank from it. "This is my blood of the covenant, which is poured out for many," he said to them. "Truly I tell you, I will not drink again from the fruit of the vine until that day when I drink it new in the kingdom of God." When they had sung a hymn, they went out to the Mount of Olives. MARK 14:17–26

■

THE DISCIPLES GATHERED TO share the Passover meal with Jesus. They were not thinking that this was the Last Supper. When they heard that one among them would betray the Lord, they were "saddened." What a strange response. Betrayal usually evokes anger, even a desire for revenge, but the followers were only concerned about their own innocence. They said, "Surely you do not mean me?" But Jesus simply said, "It is one of the Twelve . . . one who dips bread into the bowl with me." Jesus was not necessarily singling out Judas here, because Jesus already knew that each one of the Twelve would betray him within hours, and he would be left alone to face the foot soldiers of his enemy in the Garden of Gethsemane. Perhaps Judas' sin was the greatest, but none of the Twelve were exempt, and this put each one of them in a place that would require forgiveness and restoration.

. . . so he got up from the meal, took off his outer clothing, and wrapped a towel around his waist. After that, he poured water into a basin and began to wash his disciples' feet, drying them with the towel that was wrapped around him. He came to Simon Peter, who said to him, "Lord, are you going to wash my feet?" Jesus replied, "You do not realize now what I am doing, but later you will understand." "No," said Peter, "you shall never wash my feet." Jesus answered, "Unless I wash you, you have no part with me." "Then, Lord," Simon Peter replied, "not just my feet but my hands and my head as well!" JOHN 13:4–9

■

JESUS DISCOMFORTED HIS DISCIPLES by taking on a role usually delegated to servants. Peter objected because to him (and perhaps the others) the master should never assume the role of the servant. But just as he is King, Jesus is also servant, serving the will of the Father. In the Garden of Gethsemane, Jesus struggled between his own human will and God's will. In the end he finally said, "My Father, if it is not possible for this cup to be taken away unless I drink it, may your will be done" (Matthew 26:42). Jesus modeled what it means to be a genuine servant of God. Jesus came to serve, and ultimately, he came to die so that many might live: ". . . he humbled himself and became obedient to death—even death on a cross" (Philippians 2:8).

Then Jesus told them, "This very night you will all fall away on account of me, for it is written: 'I will strike the shepherd, and the sheep of the flock will be scattered.' But after I have risen, I will go ahead of you into Galilee." Peter replied, "Even if all fall away on account of you, I never will." "Truly I tell you," Jesus answered, "this very night, before the rooster crows, you will disown me three times." But Peter declared, "Even if I have to die with you, I will never disown you." And all the other disciples said the same.
MATTHEW 26:31–35

■

THIS IS A SAD moment. The disciples all declared that they would not fall away. Peter went so far as to say, "Even if I have to die with you, I will never disown you," but Jesus knew better and declared that Peter would betray him three times before the rooster crowed at sunrise. The disciples simply misjudged the level of courage it took to stand with Jesus in his moment of greatest crisis. The kingdom of God was being established, but strong opposition was rising up to stop it. Yes, the disciples abandoned Jesus to his enemies, but this would not be the end of the story.

"Do not let your hearts be troubled. You believe in God; believe also in me. My Father's house has many rooms; if that were not so, would I have told you that I am going there to prepare a place for you? And if I go and prepare a place for you, I will come back and take you to be with me that you also may be where I am. You know the way to the place where I am going." Thomas said to him, "Lord, we don't know where you are going, so how can we know the way?" Jesus answered, "I am the way and the truth and the life. No one comes to the Father except through me. If you really know me, you will know my Father as well. From now on, you do know him and have seen him." JOHN 14:1–7

■

JESUS MADE A DECLARATIVE statement to his disciples as they partook in the Passover supper. He said, "You believe in God." This was not conditional; he was not saying, "If you believe in God." He was affirming that they were believers. But then he said something that was more difficult for them to accept: "Believe in me also." Later he would make the same statement, but in reverse: "If you really know me, you will know my Father as well." To know the Son is to know the Father. To believe in the Father sets the foundation for believing in the Son. The two are indivisible. Based on his own claim, Jesus is not a way or a truth or a life. This might apply to a prophet or a king or a great man, but Jesus is saying something very different. Because the Son is the exact human representation of the Father, he can say with complete certainty that "I am the way and the truth and the life."

ASK ME FOR ANYTHING IN MY NAME, AND I WILL DO IT

Very truly I tell you, whoever believes in me will do the works I have been doing, and they will do even greater things than these, because I am going to the Father. And I will do whatever you ask in my name, so that the Father may be glorified in the Son. You may ask me for anything in my name, and I will do it. JOHN 14:12–14

■

JESUS' STATEMENT, "YOU MAY ask me for anything in my name, and I will do it" is not an invitation to profligacy or bad behavior. The key to understanding what Jesus is driving at is the phrase "in my name." He is saying: Ask for the power to do the things I have been doing. Ask to advance God's kingdom here on earth. Ask that you may use the authority Christ has given you to work through God in this life. Ask for the power to heal, to deliver the broken into new life, and to do God's work with boldness and compassion. Jesus is affirming Scripture, not contradicting it. He is saying, Pray boldly, trust broadly, and in everything you do, work to advance the kingdom in the unique way God has granted that work to you.

If you love me, keep my commands. And I will ask the Father, and he will give you another advocate to help you and be with you forever—the Spirit of truth. The world cannot accept him, because it neither sees him nor knows him. But you know him, for he lives with you and will be in you. I will not leave you as orphans; I will come to you. JOHN 14:15–18

■

WHAT IS THIS "SPIRIT of truth" offered by Jesus? It is the same Spirit that hovered over the waters as the heavens and earth were being created (Genesis 1:1–2). It is the same Spirit that David, in his confessional psalm begged God not to take from him (Psalm 51:11). Jesus told the Samaritan woman, "A time is coming and has now come when true worshippers will worship the Father in spirit and in truth, for they are the kind of worshippers the Father seeks. God is spirit, and his worshippers must worship in spirit and in truth" (John 4:23–24). Jesus knows the Father and the Father knows him, but the Holy Spirit was not released to the disciples until Jesus opened the way on the cross of Calvary. It was on Pentecost after the crucifixion, resurrection, and ascension of Christ that the Holy Spirit came to the disciples in Jerusalem, and then in miraculous ways spread into Judea and Samaria, and to the very ends of the earth (Acts 1:8).

THE PRINCE OF THIS WORLD IS COMING

I will not say much more to you, for the prince of this world is coming. He has no hold over me, but he comes so that the world may learn that I love the Father and do exactly what my Father has commanded me. Come now; let us leave. JOHN 14:30–31

■

JESUS CALLS HIM "THE prince of this world" not because he is worthy, but because he is an imposter who has drawn people away from the Father. He uses deception and lies to trade upon our gullible inclination to believe anything. Jesus says of himself that he is "the way, the truth and the life," but we are just as apt to fix on fables as believe Jesus' own declaration of who he is. God designed us to be free; he gave all men and women the power to choose, including the ability to worship false gods. From the beginning, Satan has attempted to undermine our freedom by presenting us with a continuum of choices that would detach us from our relationship with God. Satan always presents these choices as attractive alternatives, always withholding a clear picture of the consequences until it is too late. "It is for freedom that Christ has set us free. Stand firm, then, and do not let yourselves be burdened again by a yoke of slavery" (Galatians 5:1).

I AM THE TRUE VINE

I am the true vine, and my Father is the gardener. He cuts off every branch in me that bears no fruit, while every branch that does bear fruit he prunes so that it will be even more fruitful. You are already clean because of the word I have spoken to you. Remain in me, as I also remain in you. No branch can bear fruit by itself; it must remain in the vine. Neither can you bear fruit unless you remain in me. I am the vine; you are the branches. If you remain in me and I in you, you will bear much fruit; apart from me you can do nothing. JOHN 15:1–5

■

JESUS USES THE VINE as a metaphor to help us understand how God, through the Holy Spirit, infuses divine purpose into our lives. Jesus says, "I am the vine; you are the branches. If you remain in me and I in you, you will bear much fruit; apart from me you can do nothing." From the beginning God has called us to be fruitful within his design (Genesis 1:18). Each one of us has been gifted in a particular way to advance God's purpose in this world. But as branches separated from the vine, we will wither and die, producing nothing, if we don't remain in Jesus. "No branch can bear fruit by itself; it must remain in the vine." Jesus is telling his disciples and us that we must remain connected to him through the Holy Spirit to be fully fruitful in the challenges that lie ahead. His words were true then and are just as true today.

My command is this: Love each other as I have loved you. Greater love has no one than this: to lay down one's life for one's friends. You are my friends if you do what I command. I no longer call you servants, because a servant does not know his master's business. Instead, I have called you friends, for everything that I learned from my Father I have made known to you. You did not choose me, but I chose you and appointed you so that you might go and bear fruit—fruit that will last—and so that whatever you ask in my name the Father will give you. This is my command: Love each other. JOHN 15:12–17

■

As Jesus commanded his followers to "love each other as I have loved you," so we need to connect several dots to understand his meaning. The Great Commandment is to love God and to love our neighbor. Without the first commandment, though, living the second is not possible. Jesus says two things that open the door to living the first commandment. First, he says, "You are my friends." To be a friend of Christ is to be a friend of God. To be a friend of the Son is to be a friend of the Father. Then, Jesus defines friendship as a willingness to sacrifice for a friend: "Greater love has no one than this: to lay down one's life for one's friends." The price of loving one's friend can be costly, but not nearly as costly as the Father permitting his Son to lay down his own life for the sake of you and me. When Jesus tells his friends, "Love each other," he is telling them to conform to the very nature of the Father and the Son and to model that nature through everything they do and say.

THE WORLD HATED ME FIRST

If the world hates you, keep in mind that it hated me first. If you belonged to the world, it would love you as its own. As it is, you do not belong to the world, but I have chosen you out of the world. That is why the world hates you. Remember what I told you: 'A servant is not greater than his master.' If they persecuted me, they will persecute you also. If they obeyed my teaching, they will obey yours also. They will treat you this way because of my name, for they do not know the one who sent me. If I had not come and spoken to them, they would not be guilty of sin; but now they have no excuse for their sin. Whoever hates me hates my Father as well. **JOHN 15:18–23**

■

AS IF HIS DISCIPLES didn't already know the nature of the world they were confronting, Jesus repeated the warning that the path ahead would be filled with challenges, struggles, and even persecutions. He said, "If the world hates you, keep in mind that it hated me first." As we ponder the time Jesus spent here on earth, we remember that from his earliest years Jesus was threatened by the political and religious elites. Herod sent his soldiers to seek and kill the child born to be king. Throughout his three years of ministry, Jesus was challenged time and again, to the point where he asked the religious leaders, "Why are you trying to kill me?" (John 7:19) The answer is as true now as it was then: The world's system of belief and activity, permeated by the spirit of the prince of darkness, will always rise up in opposition to the threat of God's way encroaching on its way. Just as rulers of the worldly system opposed Jesus, they oppose those who follow him as well. And the opposition continues unabated even up to this very hour. So Peter in his first letter counsels, "do not be surprised at the painful trial you are suffering, as though something strange were happening to you. But rejoice that you participate in the sufferings of Christ, so that you may be overjoyed when his glory is revealed" (1 Peter 4:12–13).

THEY HATED ME WITHOUT REASON

If I had not done among them the works no one else did, they would not be guilty of sin. As it is, they have seen, and yet they have hated both me and my Father. But this is to fulfill what is written in their Law: 'They hated me without reason.' **JOHN 15:24–25**

■

THE WORLD JESUS MENTIONS here is a world that had so abandoned God that its only response was to turn on Him with an unreasoned hatred. This is a hatred that is without reason because it is unreasonable to deny God. "The fool says in his heart there is no God. They are corrupt, their deeds are vile; there is no one who does good" (Psalm 14:1). But even though men have abandoned God, God's response is not to abandon the creatures he made in his own image. Rather, he did the unexpected by sending his own Son to stand in our place and take on the punishment we deserve as payment for our own sinfulness and rebellion. God cannot just wink at our crimes of omission and commission. A price must be paid, for he is the God of both love and justice. By sending his own Son into this darkened world, God accomplished his objective by having his Son become a substitute for us—to pay the price that washes us of our unrighteousness.

When the Advocate comes, whom I will send to you from the Father—the Spirit of truth who goes out from the Father—he will testify about me. And you also must testify, for you have been with me from the beginning. All this I have told you so that you will not fall away. They will put you out of the synagogue; in fact, the time is coming when anyone who kills you will think they are offering a service to God. They will do such things because they have not known the Father or me. I have told you this, so that when their time comes you will remember that I warned you about them. I did not tell you this from the beginning because I was with you . . ." JOHN 15:26–16:4

■

JESUS SAYS THE HOLY Spirit is the Spirit of truth. He also calls the Spirit "the Advocate," and the image this conjures is of a trial setting, with the world as a prosecutor that has built a powerful case against you. Without a Defender you will be convicted and punished, even put to death. Jesus spoke to his disciples in this way because he was warning them that the world would come after them to defeat them, so they needed to be vigilant and prepared. Then comes the promise, for the disciples and for us: He will send the Advocate from the Father, the Spirit of truth, who will strengthen and embolden us, even as the opposition tries to defeat us. In his letter to the Ephesians, Paul reinforces the truth of Jesus' words: "Finally, be strong in the Lord and in his mighty power. Put on the full armor of God so that you can take your stand against the devil's schemes. For our struggle is not against flesh and blood, but against the rulers, against the authorities, against the powers of this dark world and against the spiritual forces of evil in the heavenly realms" (Ephesians 6:10–12).

THE SPIRIT OF TRUTH WILL GUIDE YOU

I have much more to say to you, more than you can now bear. But when he, the Spirit of truth, comes, he will guide you into all the truth. He will not speak on his own; he will speak only what he hears, and he will tell you what is yet to come. He will glorify me because it is from me that he will receive what he will make known to you. All that belongs to the Father is mine. That is why I said the Spirit will receive from me what he will make known to you. JOHN 16:12–15

■

JESUS CONTINUED TO PREPARE his disciples for a time when he would no longer be physically with them. He told them he would provide the Spirit of truth who would flood into their hearts and strengthen them to continue on. And he told them how this would happen: This Spirit would not speak on his own, but would speak only what he hears, and what he hears comes directly from Jesus and from the Father, because all that belongs to the Father belongs to Jesus. Jesus makes it clear that the will of the Father, the Son, and the Holy Spirit are one. The relationship of the Trinity to the disciples and followers of Jesus is what fueled the extraordinary growth of the young church in the first century.

"Though I have been speaking figuratively, a time is coming when I will no longer use this kind of language but will tell you plainly about my Father. In that day you will ask in my name. I am not saying that I will ask the Father on your behalf. No, the Father himself loves you because you have loved me and have believed that I came from God. I came from the Father and entered the world; now I am leaving the world and going back to the Father." Then Jesus' disciples said, "Now you are speaking clearly and without figures of speech. Now we can see that you know all things and that you do not even need to have anyone ask you questions. This makes us believe that you came from God." JOHN 16:25–30

■

THIS MOMENT IS A foretaste of what happened to the disciples after the ascension of the Lord, when the Holy Spirit came upon them and they "began to speak in other tongues as the Spirit enabled them" (Acts 2:4). Throughout all of the Gospels, Jesus uses poetic and figurative language to communicate with others. This is especially true in the Gospel of John, where he uses words and phrases like "light" and "streams of living water" to convey spiritual dimensions of everyday realities of life. Here his disciples finally seemed to understand what Jesus has been saying all along, but it was not that the language had changed; rather, it was a new understanding of what they heard that had changed. The Holy Spirit pierced through their earthbound understanding, even if only for a brief moment, to open the "eyes of their heart(s)" (Ephesians 1:18) to the realization that Jesus "came from God." It is not language that separates us from God. It is a heart dwelling on the daily and future desires of this life that creates a wall of separation between us and the Lord.

"Do you now believe?" Jesus replied. "A time is coming and in fact has come when you will be scattered, each to your own home. You will leave me all alone. Yet I am not alone, for my Father is with me. I have told you these things, so that in me you may have peace. In this world you will have trouble. But take heart! I have overcome the world." JOHN 16:31–33

■

IMMEDIATELY BEFORE JESUS SAID, "You will leave me alone," the disciples finally began to understand Jesus' true identity. But their understanding was limited to the idea that Jesus was sent by God to expel the Roman occupiers from Israel and restore David's kingdom. Jesus knew that he needed to push ahead toward the cross because that was the purpose of God's mission for him. His followers did not understand the true purpose of Jesus's earthly sojourn until after his crucifixion and resurrection. "After he was raised from the dead, his disciples recalled what he had said. Then they believed the Scripture and the words that Jesus had spoken" (John 2:22).

After Jesus said this, he looked toward heaven and prayed: "Father, the hour has come. Glorify your Son, that your Son may glorify you. For you granted him authority over all people that he might give eternal life to all those you have given him. Now this is eternal life: that they know you, the only true God, and Jesus Christ, whom you have sent." JOHN 17:1–3

■

IN THE FIRST PART of what is sometimes called his High Priestly Prayer, Jesus prayed, "Father, the hour has come. Glorify your Son, that your Son may glorify you." There is subtle irony in this request because the instrument of his glorification was the cross that was used to punish criminals. His death on a cross opened the way to his glorification, not only in his being lifted up on the cross, but also in his rising up on the third day from death to life—for himself and also for all who believe.

I pray for them. I am not praying for the world, but for those you have given me, for they are yours. All I have is yours, and all you have is mine. And glory has come to me through them. I will remain in the world no longer, but they are still in the world, and I am coming to you. Holy Father, protect them by the power of your name, the name you gave me, so that they may be one as we are one. JOHN 17:9–11

■

IN THE SECOND PART of the High Priestly Prayer, Jesus turned his concern to his disciples. While he returned to the Father, his disciples remained in the same world that has been in opposition to God since Satan prevailed over Adam and Eve. The disciples could not battle on alone; they needed protection if they were to prevail against the worldly forces lined up against them. For the disciples and for us, Jesus stands before the throne of God ceaselessly interceding on behalf of the children of God: "Holy Father, protect them by the power of your name, the name you gave me, so they may be one as we are one."

I PRAY ALSO FOR THOSE WHO
WILL BELIEVE IN ME

My prayer is not for them alone. I pray also for those who will believe in me through their message, that all of them may be one, Father, just as you are in me and I am in you. May they also be in us so that the world may believe that you have sent me. JOHN 17:20–21

■

JESUS CONCLUDED BY PRAYING for all who would come to believe through the ministry of the apostles and disciples. Jesus sees beyond the boundaries of time. He came from God and he returned to the Father, but for those who remained behind, he gave his authority to go out and spread the Good News of Jesus Christ to those who have never been with him. This prayer is perpetual; it is passed down through generations from believer to non-believer. It is as if this prayer passes through time like the concentric waves created by the action of one simple stone. But for us it is not only about the current urgencies; it is also about all those who will follow. There is great mystery in the power of this prayer for all believers; we cannot predict where it will land or even how or when it will act to transform a former enemy of God into a servant of the Lord.

Jesus went out as usual to the Mount of Olives, and his disciples followed him. On reaching the place, he said to them, "Pray that you will not fall into temptation." He withdrew about a stone's throw beyond them, knelt down and prayed, "Father, if you are willing, take this cup from me; yet not my will, but yours be done." An angel from heaven appeared to him and strengthened him. And being in anguish, he prayed more earnestly, and his sweat was like drops of blood falling to the ground. When he rose from prayer and went back to the disciples, he found them asleep, exhausted from sorrow. "Why are you sleeping?" he asked them. "Get up and pray so that you will not fall into temptation." LUKE 22:39–46

■

AS JESUS ENTERED THE Garden of Gethsemane (which means *olive press*), he felt the intense weight of the moment pressing down to the point of crushing him. He turned to his disciples twice to say, "Pray that you will not fall into temptation." He was right to be concerned about the steadfastness of his followers, but his far greater concern was his own temptation to not face the moment that was descending upon him. Luke tells us that God had not left Jesus alone at this moment, because his Father sent an angel to attend him and strengthen him. Even so, his human nature was in revolt and was directing him to flee from this trial that God had placed before him. It was here in a garden that Jesus confronted temptation head on and began to reverse the consequences that had flowed down through time from the first temptation in the first garden. He prayed, "Father, if you are willing, take this cup from me; yet not my will, but yours be done."

While he was still speaking a crowd came up, and the man who was called Judas, one of the Twelve, was leading them. He approached Jesus to kiss him, but Jesus asked him, "Judas, are you betraying the Son of Man with a kiss?" When Jesus' followers saw what was going to happen, they said, "Lord, should we strike with our swords?" And one of them struck the servant of the high priest, cutting off his right ear. But Jesus answered, "No more of this!" And he touched the man's ear and healed him. LUKE 22:47–51

■

INTO THE GARDEN CAME a posse of armed men to find and arrest Jesus. The immediate response of some of his disciples was to strike back, but Jesus knew this local fight must play out on a much larger scale. He said in prayer, "Father, your will be done." He accepted the role that he was given to play. He knew this was a drama that transcended the moment. He did not condemn Judas' betrayal but merely said, "Are you betraying the Son of Man with a kiss?" And as for fighting the crowd of men who came to take him prisoner, he said, "No more of this!" because he had already accepted the will of his Father in heaven. The battle he was actually waging was far more important than fighting the servants of the high priest. They were mere pawns in a spiritual battle that was being fought both here on earth and in the heavenly realms (Ephesians 6:12).

AM I LEADING A REBELLION?

Then Jesus said to the chief priests, the officers of the temple guard, and the elders, who had come for him, "Am I leading a rebellion, that you have come with swords and clubs? Every day I was with you in the temple courts, and you did not lay a hand on me. But this is your hour—when darkness reigns." LUKE 22:52–53

■

IT WAS DARK IN the Garden of Gethsemane, and that darkness represented the condition of a world that had come against the Son of Man. Of course, the chief priests and their henchmen did not see Jesus as the true Messiah. They saw him as a political figure who was a threat to their own position, and so under cover of night, they came to eliminate the threat. Jesus cut through their pretense by asking, "Am I leading a rebellion . . .?" In order to carry out their scheme, the chief priests needed to brand Jesus as a political zealot and troublemaker. They believed this would convince the Roman authorities that Jesus needed to be executed. What the opponents of Jesus did not understand was that they had become tools of Satan's plan to undermine Jesus' mission here on earth. Satan's moment of victory seemed to be at hand, but here in the garden, we witness only a skirmish in a much larger cosmic field of battle.

JESUS ARRESTED

Then the detachment of soldiers with its commander and the Jewish officials arrested Jesus. They bound him and brought him first to Annas, who was the father-in-law of Caiaphas, the high priest that year. Caiaphas was the one who had advised the Jewish leaders that it would be good if one man died for the people . . . Meanwhile, the high priest questioned Jesus about his disciples and his teaching. "If I said something wrong," Jesus replied, "testify as to what is wrong. But if I spoke the truth, why did you strike me?" Then Annas sent him bound to Caiaphas the high priest. JOHN 18:12–14, 19, 23–24

■

AFTER HIS ARREST, JESUS was bound and led to Annas, the father-in-law of Caiaphas, the high priest. Ironically, Caiaphas, very much a political figure, had disclosed the divine plan of having one die so that many might live. Caiaphas was not thinking of God; his only concern was preserving the power base he was part of. God's plan employs the same concept of one for all, but it has an entirely different application. Jesus, the Son of God, came to die so that God's original plan could be restored. When Adam sinned, he set in motion a course of events that would propel all of mankind away from the God who loves them. "Therefore, just as sin entered the world through one man, and death through sin, and in this way death came to all men, because all sinned . . . But the gift (from God) is not like the trespass. For if the many died by the trespass of the one man, how much more did God's grace and the gift that came by the grace of one man, Jesus Christ, overflow to the many . . . For just as through the disobedience of the one man the many were made sinners, so also through the obedience of the one man the many will be made righteous" (Romans 5:12, 15, 19).

PETER FOLLOWED AT A DISTANCE

Those who had arrested Jesus took him to Caiaphas the high priest, where the teachers of the law and the elders had assembled. But Peter followed him at a distance, right up to the courtyard of the high priest. He entered and sat down with the guards to see the outcome. MATTHEW 26:57–58

■

A SHORT TIME BEFORE this moment, Peter was bold. He may have been the one in Gethsemane who shouted, "Lord, should we strike with our swords?" Now Jesus had been arrested and led away to Jerusalem to stand before Annas and Caiaphas to be interrogated. Peter followed behind, and when he arrived at Caiaphas' courtyard, he sat and waited to see what would happen. Peter's world had collapsed; the triumphant entry into Jerusalem just a few days earlier must have seemed like a cruel joke. His hopes had evaporated and fear had filled the void where great expectations once resided. The disciples had scattered, and now he was alone. Little did he know that he was about to undergo the greatest trial of his life. But before that moment came, he waited.

HE HAS SPOKEN BLASPHEMY!

But Jesus remained silent. The high priest said to him, "I charge you under oath by the living God: Tell us if you are the Messiah, the Son of God." "You have said so," Jesus replied. "But I say to all of you: From now on you will see the Son of Man sitting at the right hand of the Mighty One and coming on the clouds of heaven." Then the high priest tore his clothes and said, "He has spoken blasphemy! Why do we need any more witnesses? Look, now you have heard the blasphemy. What do you think?" "He is worthy of death," they answered. Then they spit in his face and struck him with their fists. Others slapped him and said, "Prophesy to us, Messiah. Who hit you?" MATTHEW 26:63–68

■

CAIAPHAS, THE HIGH PRIEST, asked Jesus a direct question: "Tell us if you are the Messiah, the Son of God." A trap was being set because if Jesus said yes, then the religious leaders could accuse him of blasphemy. Jesus answered by quoting from the prophet Daniel, who spoke of the coming Messiah: "In a vision at night I looked, and there before me was one like a son of man, coming with the clouds of heaven . . . His dominion is an everlasting dominion that will not pass away, and his kingdom is one that will never be destroyed" (Daniel 7:13–14). The chief priest and his cohorts were infuriated when they heard Jesus reference the coming Messiah and his new dominion. They preferred to rule over the rotten kingdom that was rather than allow Jesus to establish the one willed by God. In the name of God they had chosen to war against the Son of God who came to establish a kingdom of God "that will never be destroyed."

I DON'T KNOW THIS MAN

While Peter was below in the courtyard, one of the servant girls of the high priest came by. When she saw Peter warming himself, she looked closely at him. "You also were with that Nazarene, Jesus," she said. But he denied it. "I don't know or understand what you're talking about," he said, and went out into the entryway. When the servant girl saw him there, she said again to those standing around, "This fellow is one of them." Again he denied it. After a little while, those standing near said to Peter, "Surely you are one of them, for you are a Galilean." He began to call down curses, and he swore to them, "I don't know this man you're talking about." Immediately the rooster crowed the second time. Then Peter remembered the word Jesus had spoken to him: "Before the rooster crows twice you will disown me three times." And he broke down and wept. MARK 14:66–72

■

THE CRISIS IN THE Garden of Gethsemane followed the guards and their captive to the courtyard before the house of Caiaphas. Peter hoped to hang onto his own anonymity by blending into the group of people milling about, but soon enough a simple servant girl identified him as a follower of Jesus. The moment of crisis had arrived for Peter. He had a choice: he could affirm that he was a follower of the "Nazarene," or he could deny it. Whatever his motivation, whether it was fear, confusion, or sorrow, Peter fell terribly short. His denials contradicted his claims of steadfast loyalty and love for the one he had once called "the Christ, the Son of the living God" (Matthew 16:16). Jesus had predicted that his followers would scatter in the moment of crisis, but the shock of realizing that even he, Peter, the most outspoken follower of the Lord, had betrayed the one he loved, must have been overwhelming. "And he broke down and wept."

When day came, the assembly of the elders of the people, both chief priests and scribes, gathered together, and they brought him to their council. They said, "If you are the Messiah, tell us." He replied, "If I tell you, you will not believe; and if I question you, you will not answer. But from now on the Son of Man will be seated at the right hand of the power of God." All of them asked, "Are you, then, the Son of God?" He said to them, "You say that I am." Then they said, "What further testimony do we need? We have heard it ourselves from his own lips!" LUKE 22:66–71

■

HUMAN JUSTICE IS MEANT to reflect the form and substance of divine justice, but in the early hours of the new day, a hastily convened quorum of the Sanhedrin met to place a veneer of justice on their plan to rid Jerusalem of the man they identified as a threat to their power and authority. Their assembly was nothing more than a travesty of justice. The leaders had predetermined the verdict of "guilty as charged!" Jesus said it all: "If I tell you, you will not believe; if I question you, you will not answer." The Pharisees and their partners in crime could not see that in their obsession to rid the world of this man, they had joined forces with Satan, the enemy of God.

Then they took Jesus from Caiaphas to Pilate's headquarters. It was early in the morning. They themselves did not enter the headquarters, so as to avoid ritual defilement and to be able to eat the Passover. So Pilate went out to them and said, "What accusation do you bring against this man?" They answered, "If this man were not a criminal, we would not have handed him over to you." Pilate said to them, "Take him yourselves and judge him according to your law." The Jews replied, "We are not permitted to put anyone to death." (This was to fulfill what Jesus had said when he indicated the kind of death he was to die.) JOHN 18:28–32

■

THE JEWISH LEADERS UNJUSTLY determined that Jesus was guilty of a capital offense, but they needed to shift the responsibility for his execution to the Roman authorities. So they transferred Jesus to Pontius Pilate's headquarters. Pilate was the consummate politician; he shifted the responsibility for handling this matter right back to the Jews. This was not their plan—they wanted Jesus dead before Passover, and Pilate was not playing the role they wanted him to play. As the day began, it looked like their plan might not work after all.

JESUS TAKEN TO HEROD

When Herod saw Jesus, he was very glad, for he had been wanting to see him for a long time, because he had heard about him and was hoping to see him perform some sign. He questioned him at some length, but Jesus gave him no answer. The chief priests and the scribes stood by, vehemently accusing him. Even Herod with his soldiers treated him with contempt and mocked him; then he put an elegant robe on him, and sent him back to Pilate. That same day Herod and Pilate became friends with each other; before this they had been enemies. LUKE 23:8–12

■

HEROD ANTIPAS AND JESUS are a study in contrasts. Herod's entire identity was built on maintaining rule over the territory the Romans had permitted him to control. He was corrupt, cruel, dissipated, and the ruler who had ordered John the Baptist's execution. But, at first, Herod appeared to be intrigued by the prisoner standing before him. Herod had heard reports of his ministry in Galilee and wanted to know more. But Jesus was non-responsive. He stood silently before the king, and soon enough the vehement accusations of the chief priests and the scribes influenced Herod to turn on Jesus and mock him. The entire legal, religious, and political establishment had risen up to crush Jesus, as if their entire world order depended on the death of this one man. They, of course, were right. It did.

WHAT IS TRUTH?

Then Pilate entered the headquarters again, summoned Jesus, and asked him, "Are you the King of the Jews?" Jesus answered, "Do you ask this on your own, or did others tell you about me?" Pilate replied, "I am not a Jew, am I? Your own nation and the chief priests have handed you over to me. What have you done?" Jesus answered, "My kingdom is not from this world. If my kingdom were from this world, my followers would be fighting to keep me from being handed over to the Jews. But as it is, my kingdom is not from here." Pilate asked him, "So you are a king?" Jesus answered, "You say that I am a king. For this I was born, and for this I came into the world, to testify to the truth. Everyone who belongs to the truth listens to my voice." Pilate asked him, "What is truth?" After he had said this, he went out to the Jews again and told them, "I find no case against him. But you have a custom that I release someone for you at the Passover. Do you want me to release for you the King of the Jews?" They shouted in reply, "Not this man, but Barabbas!" Now Barabbas was a bandit. JOHN 18:33–40

■

PILATE SPOKE FOR MUCH of modernity when he asked Jesus, "What is truth?" In more recent times, truth has been fragmented into tiny, incoherent particles that at most might be *a* truth, but not *the* truth. Pilate was a worldly man; he dealt with the realities of the push and pull of political forces, and he knew all factions claimed that their own cause or grievance had the banner of truth behind it. But earlier, before he was taken prisoner, Jesus declared, "I am the way, and the truth and the life. No one comes to the Father except through me" (John 14:6). Pilate saw only a man standing before him, no different from the bandit Barabbas. But Pilate inadvertently touched on the central question of the New Testament: Is Jesus "the Christ" (Mark 8:35) or is he someone else? Is it really true that if you know Jesus you will know God the Father as well? (John 14:7) Or is he merely a revolutionary troublemaker who had deeply annoyed the authorities? Pilate seemed indifferent to discovering the right answer. But we shouldn't have been because the answer to these questions makes all the difference.

But the chief priests stirred up the crowd to have him release Barabbas for them instead. Pilate spoke to them again, "Then what do you wish me to do with the man you call the King of the Jews?" They shouted back, "Crucify him!" Pilate asked them, "Why, what evil has he done?" But they shouted all the more, "Crucify him!" So Pilate, wishing to satisfy the crowd, released Barabbas for them; and after flogging Jesus, he handed him over to be crucified. MARK 15:11–15

■

IT IS IMPORTANT TO keep historic proportionality in mind here. This moment in time cannot be described in terms of hostile armies clashing in epic battles to win some territory. This was a single man standing before his accusers, waiting for his death sentence to be handed down. And yet it was at this very moment that all of human history changed course radically. Here God's divine purpose intersected with endlessly flawed world systems. Even though the world was paying little notice to the events unfolding during that Passover in Jerusalem, the greatest epic battle ever fought was being waged with supernatural intensity in the streets of the city of David.

Then the governor's soldiers took Jesus into the Praetorium and gathered the whole company of soldiers around him. They stripped him and put a scarlet robe on him, and then twisted together a crown of thorns and set it on his head. They put a staff in his right hand. Then they knelt in front of him and mocked him. "Hail, King of the Jews!" they said. They spit on him, and took the staff and struck him on the head again and again. After they had mocked him, they took off the robe and put his own clothes on him. Then they led him away to crucify him. MAT-THEW 27:27–31

■

WHAT HAPPENS TO HUMAN nature when it is uncoupled from love and justice and is replaced by unrestrained power? We see it here in the Praetorium, where the powerless prisoner was turned over to a company of soldiers. The soldiers stripped him, mocked him, and tortured him. They spit on him and struck him when he could not protect himself. The soldiers descended into the kind of cruel and depraved behavior that is often the default when raw political power is the sole touchstone. But the source of depravity was not the state, but the human heart: "For from within, and out of men's hearts come evil thoughts . . . murder, adultery, greed, malice, deceit, lewdness, envy, slander, arrogance and folly" (Mark 7:21–23). Those are Jesus' words. He knew that all men and women are subject to dark inclinations, but he also knew that he had come to die for people just like these Roman soldiers.

A certain man from Cyrene, Simon, the father of Alexander and Rufus, was passing by on his way in from the country, and they forced him to carry the cross. **MARK 15:21**

■

JESUS WAS CARRYING THE deadly instrument of his execution. The wood beams of the cross were heavy, and he had to drag them through the streets of Jerusalem to a small mound outside the gates of the city. Jesus had been scourged and had bled profusely. He was too weak to carry the cross, and so he faltered. It was at this moment that the Roman soldiers grabbed Simon of Cyrene to take the cross and carry it for Jesus to Golgotha. As Jesus has taken up the cross for each one of us, so Simon took it up for him. Though he did not know it, Simon became an example for the followers of Jesus. It cost Jesus everything to follow the will of the Father, and for his disciples it was costly too. Much earlier, before coming to Jerusalem, Jesus warned his disciples that the way ahead would not be easy: "If anyone would come after me, he must deny himself and take up his cross daily and follow me" (Luke 9:23). Simon of Cyrene did just that, literally.

AND THEY CRUCIFIED HIM

They brought Jesus to the place called Golgotha (which means "the place of the skull"). Then they offered him wine mixed with myrrh, but he did not take it. And they crucified him. Dividing up his clothes, they cast lots to see what each would get. It was nine in the morning when they crucified him. The written notice of the charge against him read: THE KING OF THE JEWS.
MARK 15:22–26

∎

MARK SIMPLY SAYS, "AND they crucified him." Four words that contain a world of meaning. It has been said before that Jesus was born to die. His life began in Bethlehem, and after a short exile in Egypt, he grew up in Nazareth. His ministry began in Galilee, but inexorably he was drawn to Jerusalem, and not just Jerusalem but Golgotha, "the place of the skull." He descended from heaven to live among us and then to be raised on a cross to die for us. "He himself bore our sins in his body on the tree, so that we might die to sins and live for righteousness; by his wounds you have been healed" (1 Peter 2:24). Even though he was in his very nature God, "he humbled himself and became obedient to death—even death on a cross" (Philippians 2:6–8).

Two other men, both criminals, were also led out with him to be executed. When they came to the place called the Skull, they crucified him there, along with the criminals—one on his right, the other on his left. Jesus said, "Father, forgive them, for they do not know what they are doing." And they divided up his clothes by casting lots. The people stood watching, and the rulers even sneered at him. They said, "He saved others; let him save himself if he is God's Messiah, the Chosen One." The soldiers also came up and mocked him. They offered him wine vinegar and said, "If you are the king of the Jews, save yourself." There was a written notice above him, which read: THIS IS THE KING OF THE JEWS. One of the criminals who hung there hurled insults at him: "Aren't you the Messiah? Save yourself and us!" But the other criminal rebuked him. "Don't you fear God," he said, "since you are under the same sentence? We are punished justly, for we are getting what our deeds deserve. But this man has done nothing wrong." Then he said, "Jesus, remember me when you come into your kingdom." Jesus answered him, "Truly I tell you, today you will be with me in paradise." LUKE 23:32–43

■

TWO CRIMINALS WERE CRUCIFIED with Jesus, one to the right of him and one to the left. One criminal joined the crowds and mockingly said, "Aren't you the Messiah? Save yourself and us!" But the other criminal saw things differently: "We are punished justly, for we are getting what our deeds deserve. But this man has done nothing wrong." It is not possible to know how this criminal came to understand that the man beside him was innocent; we have no information that he had known or followed Jesus before this fateful day. Perhaps he heard Jesus call out to God, "Father, forgive them, for they do not know what they are doing." Perhaps the Holy Spirit invaded his heart and opened his eyes to a reality that was imperceptible to all others. Whatever the case may be, this criminal received the forgiveness that Jesus granted him. His belief set him free, and so Jesus could say, "Truly I tell you, today you will be with me in paradise."

Near the cross of Jesus stood his mother, his mother's sister, Mary the wife of Clopas, and Mary Magdalene. When Jesus saw his mother there, and the disciple whom he loved standing nearby, he said to her, "Woman, here is your son," and to the disciple, "Here is your mother." From that time on, this disciple took her into his home. JOHN 19:25–27

■

JESUS WAS DYING, AND yet he spoke seven times. This was his third utterance, and it is tremendously poignant. He was looking down from the cross and saw his mother standing back from the hostile crowd. He also saw the apostle John, who the night before had fled Gethsemane. Here was Mary experiencing the unfolding of Simeon's prophetic words: "And a sword will pierce your own soul too" (Luke 2:35). Even in his moment of humiliation and suffering, Jesus remained steadfast to the great commandments of God. Of all the women in the world, God had chosen Mary to give birth to Jesus. Now Jesus turned to his disciple and said to him: This is my mother; take care of her, for the Father's love has flowed through her to me, and now it must flow from me to you and from you to her. And so it happened as Jesus commanded: "From that time on, this disciple took her into his home."

"ELI, ELI, LAMA SABACHTHANI?"

From noon until three in the afternoon darkness came over all the land. About three in the afternoon Jesus cried out in a loud voice, "Eli, Eli, lama sabachthani?" (which means "My God, my God, why have you forsaken me?"). When some of those standing there heard this, they said, "He's calling Elijah." Immediately one of them ran and got a sponge. He filled it with wine vinegar, put it on a staff, and offered it to Jesus to drink. The rest said, "Now leave him alone. Let's see if Elijah comes to save him." **MATTHEW** 27:45–49

■

"MY GOD, MY GOD, why have you forsaken me?" It is not just the fact that Jesus was dying on a cross; this cry to the Father was so shattering because Jesus now was carrying the entire weight of all the sin in the world. And the weight of sin is so great that it separated Jesus from the Father. Sin, of course, does that. After Cain murdered his brother Abel, God came to him and asked, "Where is your brother Abel?" Cain replied, "I don't know. Am I my brother's keeper?" (Genesis 4:9). The sin of murder alienated Cain, driving him from the land and separating him from God. He became "a restless wanderer of the earth . . ." (Genesis 4:14). Sin not only alienated men and women from one another, but it alienates us from God. Jesus took on all the sin of the world by taking our place on the cross. His pain was unbearable. He was utterly alone and experienced the deepest despair possible.

I AM THIRSTY

Later, knowing that everything had now been finished, and so that Scripture would be fulfilled, Jesus said, "I am thirsty." A jar of wine vinegar was there, so they soaked a sponge in it, put the sponge on a stalk of the hyssop plant, and lifted it to Jesus' lips. When he had received the drink, Jesus said, "It is finished." With that, he bowed his head and gave up his spirit. JOHN 19:28–30

■

JESUS SAID, "I AM thirsty," a statement describing the state of his physical condition. Then, shortly after he made this declaration, he said, "It is finished." This could be read as another statement of his acceptance of the onslaught of death, but given the sweep of the entire narrative, it is clear that Jesus was talking about the mission that began here on earth with an angel visiting a young virgin in the town of Nazareth. Matthew says that an angel came to Joseph in a dream and said, ". . . what is conceived in her is from the Holy Spirit. She will give birth to a son, and you are to give him the name Jesus, because he will save the people from their sins" (Matthew 1:20–21). The mission was nearing its earthly end, and Jesus had not faltered or turned aside. He had taken unto himself the sin of the entire world at unimaginable cost. That price had been paid once and for all. "It is finished."

THE CURTAIN OF THE TEMPLE
WAS TORN IN TWO

It was now about noon, and darkness came over the whole land until three in the afternoon, for the sun stopped shining. And the curtain of the temple was torn in two. Jesus called out with a loud voice, "Father, into your hands I commit my spirit." When he had said this, he breathed his last. The centurion, seeing what had happened, praised God and said, "Surely this was a righteous man." When all the people who had gathered to witness this sight saw what took place, they beat their breasts and went away. But all those who knew him, including the women who had followed him from Galilee, stood at a distance, watching these things. LUKE 23:44–49

■

THE CULMINATING MOMENT HAD arrived. Darkness came upon the land, and Luke reports that the curtain of the temple was torn in two. This was the curtain that separated the Holy Place from the Most Holy Place. It was the Inner Sanctum, where only a designated priest could go. It was a symbol of the separation that exists between a Holy God and a sinful people, but at the moment when Jesus called out, "Father, into your hands I commit my spirit," that division was ripped apart. Jesus had established himself as the mediator between the Father and the people. It was the moment when the prophecy of Joel began to become an actuality: "And afterward, I will pour out my Spirit on all people . . . And everyone who calls on the name of the Lord will be saved; for on Mount Zion and in Jerusalem there will be deliverance, as the Lord has said, among the survivors whom the Lord calls" (Joel 2:28, 32).

JOSEPH OF ARIMATHEA

As evening approached, there came a rich man from Arimathea, named Joseph, who had himself become a disciple of Jesus. Going to Pilate, he asked for Jesus' body, and Pilate ordered that it be given to him. Joseph took the body, wrapped it in a clean linen cloth, and placed it in his own new tomb that he had cut out of the rock. He rolled a big stone in front of the entrance to the tomb and went away. Mary Magdalene and the other Mary were sitting there opposite the tomb. MATTHEW 27:57–61

■

IN THIS MOMENT OF darkness it is possible to discern tiny seeds of hope. Yes, the disciples had abandoned him, and yes, Jesus' enemies seemed to have utterly triumphed, but some light was forcing itself through. Simon of Cyrene had lifted the burden of taking the cross off the shoulder of Jesus. John, the Apostle, had returned to the foot of the cross after having fled from the Garden of Gethsemane the night Jesus was taken prisoner. Then there was the soldier, who at the moment of Jesus' death, said, "Surely this was a righteous man." And there were the women, Mary the mother of Jesus and Mary Magdalene, among others, who stood vigil as the events surrounding the crucifixion unfolded. Finally, when it appeared there would be no place to bury Jesus, Joseph of Arimathea bravely stepped forward to claim the body so that it could be buried in his own tomb. The light had not gone out completely. Darkness reigns, but light flickers on the horizon.

The next day, the one after Preparation Day, the chief priests and the Pharisees went to Pilate. "Sir," they said, "we remember that while he was still alive that deceiver said, 'After three days I will rise again.' So give the order for the tomb to be made secure until the third day. Otherwise, his disciples may come and steal the body and tell the people that he has been raised from the dead. This last deception will be worse than the first." "Take a guard," Pilate answered. "Go, make the tomb as secure as you know how." MATTHEW 27:62–65

■

THE CHIEF PRIESTS AND Pharisees had had their way. Jesus was dead and had been laid in a tomb. It would seem that they had won, but they did not show the confidence that comes with victory. They remembered that Jesus said he would be raised from the dead in three days, and so they were concerned that somehow a deception would be perpetuated. They asked Pilate to seal the tomb and place a guard in front of its entrance so no one could gain access. The chief priests knew that Jesus was dead, but now they were driven by an irrational fear, as if their consciences were still alive to the enormous injustice they had engaged in.

THE STONE HAD BEEN ROLLED AWAY!

When the Sabbath was over, Mary Magdalene, Mary the mother of James, and Salome bought spices so that they might go to anoint Jesus' body. Very early on the first day of the week, just after sunrise, they were on their way to the tomb and they asked each other, "Who will roll the stone away from the entrance of the tomb?" But when they looked up, they saw that the stone, which was very large, had been rolled away. **MARK 16: 1–4**

■

LUKE TELLS US THAT at the ninth hour, just before Jesus died on the cross, the "sun stopped shining." The cold spirit of death spread across the land and everything was cast into darkness. But on the third day a new spirit revealed itself. The women, who had followed Jesus even to the cross, rose in darkness to go to the tomb to anoint the body of the Lord. Mark describes their journey to the tomb this way: "Very early on the first day of the week, just after sunrise, they were on their way to the tomb . . ." The spirit of darkness had had its moment. Now the Spirit of the Lord—the spirit of light and life— was revealing itself through the natural cycle of the sun. The women thought they were heading to a place filled with the darkness of death; instead they were about to encounter a tomb emptied of death because the tomb could not possibly contain the Son of the God.

As they entered the tomb, they saw a young man dressed in a white robe sitting on the right side, and they were alarmed. "Don't be alarmed," he said. "You are looking for Jesus the Nazarene, who was crucified. He has risen! He is not here. See the place where they laid him. But go, tell his disciples and Peter, 'He is going ahead of you into Galilee. There you will see him, just as he told you.'" Trembling and bewildered, the women went out and fled from the tomb. They said nothing to anyone, because they were afraid. **MARK** 16: 5–8

■

"HE HAS RISEN!" JUST three words, but they will become the triumphant words of the faith that will sweep across the Mediterranean world and beyond. Confronted with this strange and unexpected turn of events, the women who had come to anoint the Lord's body lying in the tomb were told to "go, tell the disciples and Peter" that Jesus is alive, not dead, and he had gone back to Galilee where the disciples would find him. The women were instructed to act: "Go," do not stand still and do not pause, but go and tell the others what you have seen and heard. These simple words, "go and tell" become the springboard for action that will spread so quickly from person to person throughout the world. The women at the tomb were transformed from mourners into witnesses in the flash of an instant. With this encounter at the tomb of Jesus, the seeds of the faith were planted.

Peter, however, got up and ran to the tomb. Bending over, he saw the strips of linen lying by themselves, and he went away, wondering to himself what had happened. LUKE 24:12

■

PETER WAS IN DESPAIR. His world had disintegrated. He had betrayed the one he loved, the one he called "the Christ of God" (Luke 9:20). Now Jesus was dead and the women had gone back to the tomb to anoint his body. This was how the world felt to Peter immediately before Mary Magdalene, Joanna, and Mary, mother of James, as well as others, brought the news that the tomb was empty. Peter did not walk; he ran to find the tomb indeed empty. While he was known for his impetuous nature, Peter did not jump to any conclusions. We are only told that he went away wondering what this meant. To fully appreciate the dilemma Peter faced here, we must put ourselves in his place. Everything that happened to Jesus had now apparently been reversed. The tomb was empty, and there were no easy explanations, leaving Peter genuinely perplexed.

THEY DID NOT BELIEVE

When Jesus rose early on the first day of the week, he appeared first to Mary Magdalene, out of whom he had driven seven demons. She went and told those who had been with him and who were mourning and weeping. When they heard that Jesus was alive and that she had seen him, they did not believe it. **Mark 16:9–11**

■

WHAT WE CALL HISTORY are events in time that are witnessed or recorded through direct observation, documents, and physical evidence. Here we have an account of the empty tomb that is credible, ironically enough, because of the person who testified. To those living in the first century, Mary Magdalene was anything but an ideal witness. If the account were made up, then the last person to choose as a witness was a woman with a questionable past. And yet Mark forges ahead and reports that Mary Magdalene was the first person to encounter the risen Lord. If Mark was trying to convince people that a supernatural event had occurred when it really hadn't, he might have used a different witness. The fact that Mark does not lends credibility to the story of the risen Lord; it does not detract from it.

COVER UP

While the women were on their way, some of the guards went into the city and reported to the chief priests everything that had happened. When the chief priests had met with the elders and devised a plan, they gave the soldiers a large sum of money, telling them, "You are to say, 'His disciples came during the night and stole him away while we were asleep.' If this report gets to the governor, we will satisfy him and keep you out of trouble." So the soldiers took the money and did as they were instructed. And this story has been widely circulated among the Jews to this very day.
MATTHEW 28:11–15

■

APPARENTLY PLAN A WAS declared inoperable, and so the chief priests and other leaders hastily devised another plan to discredit any rumors that Christ was not contained by the tomb in which he was buried. The leaders enlisted the soldiers in a cover-up to protect their own political interests. The lie was necessary because the chief priests were engaged in an evil enterprise. They had conspired to convict and execute an innocent man, and they were afraid the population would rise up against them and side with the followers of the leader they had martyred. They completely missed the supernatural implications behind the fact that Jesus was no longer in the tomb.

Now that same day two of them were going to a village called Emmaus, about seven miles from Jerusalem. They were talking with each other about everything that had happened. As they talked and discussed these things with each other, Jesus himself came up and walked along with them; but they were kept from recognizing him. He asked them, "What are you discussing together as you walk along?" They stood still, their faces downcast. One of them, named Cleopas, asked him, "Are you the only one visiting Jerusalem who does not know the things that have happened there in these days?" "What things?" he asked. "About Jesus of Nazareth," they replied. "He was a prophet, powerful in word and deed before God and all the people. The chief priests and our rulers handed him over to be sentenced to death, and they crucified him; but we had hoped that he was the one who was going to redeem Israel. And what is more, it is the third day since all this took place. In addition, some of our women amazed us. They went to the tomb early this morning but didn't find his body. They came and told us that they had seen a vision of angels, who said he was alive. Then some of our companions went to the tomb and found it just as the women had said, but they did not see Jesus." LUKE 24:13–24

■

THE PASSOVER HAD ENDED and people were streaming out of Jerusalem to return to their own towns and cities. Two of the travelers were heading back to the village of Emmaus when another traveler joined them. It was Jesus, but they did not recognize him. Instead they told him about the events that had ended in apparent disaster on the previous Friday: The two travelers were despondent because they had rested their hope on a political Messiah. As Moses liberated the Jewish people from the Egyptians, so Jesus, they had hoped, would liberate them from the Romans. What they did not see was that Jesus had been sent by God to liberate all people from the more insidious and intractable slavery of sin.

BEGINNING WITH MOSES AND ALL THE PROPHETS

He said to them, "How foolish you are, and how slow to believe all that the prophets have spoken! Did not the Messiah have to suffer these things and then enter his glory?" And beginning with Moses and all the Prophets, he explained to them what was said in all the Scriptures concerning himself. As they approached the village to which they were going, Jesus continued on as if he were going farther. But they urged him strongly, "Stay with us, for it is nearly evening; the day is almost over." So he went in to stay with them. LUKE 24:25–29

■

THE TWO TRAVELERS DEFINED the role of the Messiah narrowly by placing their hopes on Jesus freeing the people of Israel from the iron yoke of Roman rule. Jesus turned to the authority of Scripture to define the purpose of the Messiah as conceived by God Himself: "And beginning with Moses and all the Prophets, he explained to them what was said in all the Scriptures concerning himself." Jesus may have referred to sections of Exodus, many of the Psalms, and certain passages written by the prophet Isaiah. As Jesus taught his companions, he began to change the atmosphere of their minds and hearts. They did not want Jesus to leave, so they said, "Stay with us, for it is nearly evening; the day is almost over." As the sun declined behind the horizon and dusk began to turn to darkness, the light of understanding began to shine in their hearts. They made it clear that they did not want to let go of that light.

When he was at the table with them, he took bread, gave thanks, broke it and began to give it to them. Then their eyes were opened and they recognized him, and he disappeared from their sight. They asked each other, "Were not our hearts burning within us while he talked with us on the road and opened the Scriptures to us?" They got up and returned at once to Jerusalem. There they found the Eleven and those with them, assembled together and saying, "It is true! The Lord has risen and has appeared to Simon."

LUKE 24:30–34

■

A PERSON WHO LACKS compassion is often described as a person with a heart of stone. But this is not completely accurate. The unredeemed heart is more like an ember; it appears to have no life or heat, but buried deep inside, it still has the potential to ignite into flame. It just needs access to the pure oxygen of the truth of God. Walking to Emmaus, Jesus revealed the truth about himself as found in Scripture, but it was not until he was preparing to share a meal with his followers that "their eyes were opened and they recognized him . . ." Their hearts burst forth with joy, and they said, "Were not our hearts burning within us while he talked with us on the road and opened the Scriptures to us?" They left Emmaus immediately to return to Jerusalem to tell the other followers the good news: "It is true! The Lord has risen . . ."

JESUS APPEARED TO THE ELEVEN

Later Jesus appeared to the Eleven as they were eating; he rebuked them for their lack of faith and their stubborn refusal to believe those who had seen him after he had risen. MARK 16:14

■

THE FOLLOWERS HAD EXPECTED Jesus to transform the political landscape; they were believers in a movement that was circumscribed by the political forces of the moment. Jesus, they believed, would liberate Israel and return it to the glorious days of the kingdom of David. But now their leader had been captured and killed, and they had gone into hiding. It is not difficult to identify with their plight. By their own definition, they had lost everything and were threatened with capture and possible death. When Jesus appeared and rebuked them, he reminded them that the normal patterns did not apply, for his mission came from God and not from men. His mission was not to foment a political revolution, but to restore all mankind's relationship with God. At this moment of turmoil and apparent defeat, God's divine mission was almost impossible for them to grasp.

Now Thomas (also known as Didymus), one of the Twelve, was not with the disciples when Jesus came. So the other disciples told him, "We have seen the Lord!" But he said to them, "Unless I see the nail marks in his hands and put my finger where the nails were, and put my hand into his side, I will not believe." A week later his disciples were in the house again, and Thomas was with them. Though the doors were locked, Jesus came and stood among them and said, "Peace be with you!" Then he said to Thomas, "Put your finger here; see my hands. Reach out your hand and put it into my side. Stop doubting and believe." Thomas said to him, "My Lord and my God!" Then Jesus told him, "Because you have seen me, you have believed; blessed are those who have not seen and yet have believed." JOHN 20:24–29

■

MANY CAN IDENTIFY WITH Thomas' skepticism. Their perspective is grounded in the truism that to see is to believe. Furthermore, the followers of Jesus were in shock. Everything they hoped for seemed to have gone up in smoke. So, when Thomas heard that Jesus had risen and had been with the disciples, he must have concluded that they were blinded by grief and wishful thinking. When Jesus came to Thomas, however, he did not rebuke him. Instead, he said: Touch my hands and feel the wound in my side. Thomas responded instantly, moving from doubt to belief, and saying, "My Lord and my God!" Jesus then reminded Thomas and the disciples that they would soon face a doubting world and that their mission was to overcome that doubt by being steadfast in their own belief: "Because you have seen me you have believed; blessed are those who have not seen and yet have believed."

DO YOU LOVE ME?

When they had finished eating, Jesus said to Simon Peter, "Simon son of John, do you love me more than these?" "Yes, Lord," he said, "you know that I love you." Jesus said, "Feed my lambs." Again Jesus said, "Simon son of John, do you love me?" He answered, "Yes, Lord, you know that I love you." Jesus said, "Take care of my sheep." The third time he said to him, "Simon son of John, do you love me?" Peter was hurt because Jesus asked him the third time, "Do you love me?" He said, "Lord, you know all things; you know that I love you." Jesus said, "Feed my sheep. Very truly I tell you, when you were younger you dressed yourself and went where you wanted; but when you are old you will stretch out your hands, and someone else will dress you and lead you where you do not want to go." Jesus said this to indicate the kind of death by which Peter would glorify God. Then he said to him, "Follow me!" JOHN 21:15–19

■

AT ONE TIME PETER loudly proclaimed his undying loyalty to Jesus: "Even if all fall away on account of you, I never will . . . Even if I have to die with you, I will never disown you" (Matthew 26:13,15). Just a few hours later, Peter disowned Jesus not once but three times: "Then he began to call down curses on himself and he swore to them, 'I don't know the man!'" (Matthew 26:74). Peter had failed the Lord, and he had failed himself. He was overcome with sorrow, shame, and self-loathing, and he wept bitterly. Now Jesus had returned, and he stood before the one of whom he had said, " you are Peter, and upon this rock I will build my church . . ." (Matthew 16:18). Jesus tested Peter to prepare him for the mission ahead. Jesus asked Peter the same question three separate times: "Do you love me?" And with each affirmative answer, Jesus gave a command: "Feed my lambs." "Take care of my sheep." "Feed my sheep." Peter had been forgiven and commissioned at the same time. Now he could go out into the world to become the rock upon which the church would be built.

He said to them, "This is what I told you while I was still with you: Everything must be fulfilled that is written about me in the Law of Moses, the Prophets and the Psalms." Then he opened their minds so they could understand the Scriptures. He told them, "This is what is written: The Messiah will suffer and rise from the dead on the third day, and repentance for the forgiveness of sins will be preached in his name to all nations, beginning at Jerusalem. You are witnesses of these things." LUKE 24:44–48

■

JESUS RETURNED TO THE disciples; he ate with them, showed his wounded hands, and reminded them that everything that had happened had been foretold in the "Law of Moses, the Prophets and the Psalms." He summarized the message so that they would understand: "The Messiah will suffer and rise from the dead on the third day, and repentance for the forgiveness of sins will be preached in his name to all nations, beginning in Jerusalem." This is the Gospel message in a nutshell, and Jesus told his followers that they would be his witnesses throughout the world. This is the one reason for church: To lift up the name of Jesus through proclaiming, preaching, and declaring his Lordship to a world that has wandered onto a crooked and dangerous path. Growing the church is a vital cornerstone of God's restoration project; building the church is as simple as inviting people into that project.

GO AND MAKE DISCIPLES OF ALL NATIONS

Then Jesus came to them and said, "All authority in heaven and on earth has been given to me. Therefore go and make disciples of all nations, baptizing them in the name of the Father and of the Son and of the Holy Spirit, and teaching them to obey everything I have commanded you. And surely I am with you always, to the very end of the age." MATTHEW 28:18–20

■

WHEN JESUS SAYS, "ALL authority in heaven and on earth has been given to me," he means it. There are no qualifiers here. He is the risen Christ of God; obedience to the law as prescribed by the religious authorities is not the way back to God. Jesus says that following him only requires a willing desire to walk the path he walks. The message is this: Repent, believe, and be baptized "in the name of the Father and the Son and the Holy Spirit." The imperative is this: Make disciples who will become the foundation, walls, windows, and roof of the church itself. "As you come to him, the living stone—rejected by men but chosen by God and precious to him—you also, the living stones, are being built into a spiritual house to be a holy priesthood, offering spiritual sacrifices acceptable to God through Jesus Christ" (1 Peter 2:4–6).

STAY IN THE CITY

I am going to send you what my Father has promised; but stay in the city until you have been clothed with power from on high.
LUKE 24:49

■

WE HAVE BEEN HEARING the command to "go," but now Jesus seems to reverse course and says to stay in the city and wait. Immediately before he was taken prisoner in the Garden of Gethsemane, Jesus promised his disciples that they would receive the Holy Spirit at an opportune time, but even now after the resurrection and appearances, the time had not yet come. His promise was this: "But the Counselor, the Holy Spirit, whom the Father will send in my name, will teach you all things and will remind you of everything I have said to you" (John 14:26). He also said the Counselor, the Spirit of truth, will be with them forever. Jesus would not leave his disciples as orphans (John 14:16–18). The time was coming but had not yet come when the disciples would be "clothed with power from on high." That power comes directly from the Holy Spirit of God.

TAKEN UP INTO HEAVEN

When he had led them out to the vicinity of Bethany, he lifted up his hands and blessed them. While he was blessing them, he left them and was taken up into heaven. Then they worshiped him and returned to Jerusalem with great joy. And they stayed continually at the temple, praising God. LUKE 24:50–53

■

THIS DESCRIPTION OF THE Ascension of Jesus Christ is one of two accounts provided by Luke. Here he understates what happened by only saying, "he left them and was taken up into heaven." In Acts, Luke tells of two men dressed in white who suddenly appeared after Jesus had ascended and who asked the disciples why they were staring up into the sky. Then the men in white said, "This same Jesus who has been taken from you into heaven, will come back in the same way you have seen him go into heaven" (Acts 1:11). Jesus had promised his followers that he would not leave them as orphans; now they were told he would return in the same way he left. With his departure into heaven, his followers were left with this: On the previous Friday, Jesus had died on the cross at Calvary. On the third day, the day after Jewish Sabbath, he had risen from the tomb. With his ascension into heaven, they were told that he would come back again, just as he had left. And so, with all of these extraordinary events and promises to ponder, they returned together to Jerusalem to wait for what would come next.

After the Lord Jesus had spoken to them, he was taken up into heaven and he sat at the right hand of God. Then the disciples went out and preached everywhere, and the Lord worked with them and confirmed his word by the signs that accompanied it. MARK 16:19–20

■

THE SIMPLICITY OF MARK'S final words should not deflect our attention away from what actually happened. Usually, when the leader of a movement is killed, the movement begins to lose power. The followers, confused and afraid, scatter, and within a short time, little is left except the memory of what might have been. But with Jesus, an extraordinary reversal of ordinary expectations took place. After Jesus was taken up to heaven to sit at the right hand of God, the disciples were emboldened. They began to preach and build the church. Mark says, "the Lord worked with them and confirmed his word by the signs that accompanied it." The new kingdom began to form, and by the power of the Holy Spirit, the kingdom builders began to spread throughout Jerusalem and "in all of Judea and Samaria, and to the ends of the earth" (Acts 1:8).

WE KNOW THAT HIS TESTIMONY IS TRUE

This is the disciple who testifies to these things and who wrote them down. We know that his testimony is true. Jesus did many other things as well. If every one of them were written down, I suppose that even the whole world would not have room for the books that would be written. JOHN 21:24–25

■

JOHN ENDS HIS GOSPEL by stating that everything he has written is true, but then he says, even so, what has been written is but a small part of a huge story that could never be contained in books, even if those books filled up the whole world. John is saying that Jesus cannot be limited by the usual human limitations and boundaries. The Pharisees and the Sadducees and the powerful religious and political leaders in Jerusalem could not contain him. He could not be contained by King Herod or by Caiaphas or by Pontius Pilate. Even the tomb of Joseph of Arimathea could not contain him. For Jesus has risen and is seated at the right hand of God, and he has given his disciples in Jerusalem, and us, the authority through the power of the Holy Spirit to go and tell the rest of the world the good news that Jesus is the Christ.

SUGGESTED TOPICAL STUDIES

BEGINNINGS

Luke's Prologue
JANUARY 3

John's Prologue
JANUARY 4-9

Matthew Genealogy
JANUARY 10

Mary is Chosen
JANUARY 14-17, 19-21

The Shepherds as Witnesses
JANUARY 22-23

Jesus Named
JANUARY 24

Two Prophecies
JANUARY 25-26

The Magi
JANUARY 27-30

Escape into Egypt
JANUARY 31

Herod's Response
FEBRUARY 1

Jesus' Childhood
FEBRUARY 2-3

LIFE OF JOHN THE BAPTIST

John's Mission
JANUARY 8

John's Birth
JANUARY 10-14, JAN 18

John's Ministry
FEBRUARY 4-8, MARCH 12-18, MAY 14-15

John's Death
JULY 5-7

John's Importance
OCTOBER 19

SERMON ON THE MOUNT

The Full Sermon
MARCH 24-MAY 11

The Beatitudes
MARCH 25-APRIL 2

The Lord's Prayer
APRIL 17-22

STUDY OF SELECTED PARABLES

Introduction
MAY 24

Parable of the Sower
MAY 30-JUNE 5

Parable of the Weeds
JUNE 8-10

JESUS' IDENTITY

I Am the Way, and the Truth and the Life

Study of the Raising of Lazarus & The Aftermath

THE CRUCIFIXION AND RESURRECTION OF JESUS CHRIST

Jesus' Arrest & Peter's Denial

The Trial

The Crucifixion & Burial

The 7 Words on the Cross

Resurrection & Ascension